DOCTORS IN GRAY

DOCTORS IN GRAY

The Confederate Medical Service

by H. H. Cunningham

LOUISIANA STATE UNIVERSITY PRESS

Baton Rouge

Published by Louisiana State University Press
Copyright © 1958, 1986 by Louisiana State University Press
Second edition, 1960
All rights reserved
Manufactured in the United States of America

Library of Congress Catalog Card Number: 57-11544
ISBN 978-0-8071-1856-6 (paper)

The paper in this book meets the guidelines for permanence and durability of
the Committee on Production Guidelines for Book Longevity of the Council on
Library Resources. ∞

Title page illustration from *Battles and Leaders of the Civil War* (New York, 1888)

Louisiana Paperback Edition, 1993
Tenth printing, 2010

To
my
Mother
and
Father

For almost ten years now I have enjoyed the association of a generally earnest group of medical officers, hospital stewards, matrons, nurses, ward masters, and other persons connected in some way with the work of the Confederate Medical Department during the Civil War. It is my feeling that these individuals, some of whom were surprisingly competent and determined, have too long been slighted. This unhappy circumstance would appear to be a result, in part at least, of the long-standing emphasis on military and political aspects of the conflict.

Consequently, this work represents an attempt to present the story of the Confederate medical service in such a way that the contributions, praiseworthy and otherwise, of its members to the military effort and subsequent medical development may be clearly seen and understood. I have read and reflected on all I could locate of the records these individuals kept, what they wrote, and what others wrote about them both during and after the war. Many of the medical records in Richmond were destroyed by fire near the end of the struggle, but my bibliography attests the fact that numerous source materials are yet available. It is sincerely hoped that some light has been cast upon an important and hitherto neglected aspect of our Civil War.

My indebtedness to the many who have helped make this work possible is beyond calculation. The influence, counsel, and constant encouragement of Professor Fletcher M. Green, who suggested and supervised the study during the time I was one of his many graduate students at the University of North Carolina, is deeply appreciated. I am also grateful to certain other members of the History Department there. The late Professor Albert Ray Newsome was a source of inspiration throughout my graduate training, and his many splendid qualities will not be forgotten. Professors J. Carlyle Sitterson and Hugh T. Lefler read the manuscript at an early stage, and my work as a part-time instructor on the social science staff was ably directed by Professor Carl H. Pegg.

Several members of the medical profession, including Dr. William G. Morgan of the University of North Carolina Health Service and Dr. Donald M. Ross, surgeon of Burlington, North Carolina, are due my sincere thanks. Dr. Morgan read the entire manuscript, and Dr. Ross read the portion relating to his speciality; each made valuable suggestions. Dr. Hunter Holmes McGuire of Richmond, Virginia, was generous in supplying me with interesting information concerning his grandfather of the same name, one of the most famous Confederate surgeons. The use of certain data on Confederate dental history was graciously extended by Dr. William N. Hodgkin, Chairman of the Virginia State Dental Association's History Committee. And Mr. J. C. Fox, Jr., Chapel Hill pharmacist, lent assistance in regard to questions concerning his field.

It is a very real pleasure to acknowledge the substantial grant-in-aid to assist in the publication of this work voted in 1954 by the United Daughters of the Confederacy during their annual convention. I am especially indebted to Miss Désirée L. Franklin, former Chairman of the Mrs. Simon Baruch University Award Committee, for her role in making the grant possible.

Some of the most enthusiastic and encouraging support of all has come from my students, and they have not hesitated to comment freely on various parts of the manuscript. Members of library staffs everywhere have given indispensable assistance. Most important of all has been the aid rendered by my wife, Mary Shaw Cunningham, who, in addition to participating actively in the life of the college community and performing regular household duties, has spent untold hours in the dual capacity of research assistant and typist.

H. H. CUNNINGHAM

November, 1957

CONTENTS

ILLUSTRATIONS

DOCTORS IN GRAY

CHAPTER I

The Confederate Medical Problem

*T*he medical problem that confronted the doctors in uniform of the Confederate States Army and Navy was one of considerable magnitude throughout the war years. With little or no training and experience in military medicine or surgery and aside from the problem of preventive medicine the medical staff was faced with the grave responsibility of caring for more than three million cases of disease and wounds in an invaded and blockaded country. Joseph Jones, one of the most outstanding Confederate medical officers, estimated that the Confederate States mobilized more than 600,000 fighting men and believed that on the average each one of these fell victim to disease and wounds approximately six times during the war. Jones figured that 200,000 Southern soldiers were either killed outright or died as a result of illness or wounds.[1] In addition to the responsibility of administering to the sick and wounded of its own military establishment, the medical staff was required to care for thousands of sick and wounded among Union prisoners that fell into the hands of Confederate military and naval forces.

A brief survey of Confederate sick and wounded statistics throws much light on the task that confronted medical personnel. Over a nine-month period from July, 1861, to March, 1862, the Confederate Army of the Potomac, with an average

[1] Joseph Jones, a native of Georgia, obtained the A.B. and M.D. degrees from the College of New Jersey and the University of Pennsylvania, respectively. He accepted an appointment as professor of chemistry on the staff of the Savannah Medical College in 1858. Other teaching assignments prior to the outbreak of war took him to the University of Georgia and the Medical College of Georgia. His first military service was in the cavalry, but after six months he was transferred to the Medical Department and became one of its most indefatigable surgeons. Jones was a prolific writer. Samuel Cooper, Adjutant and Inspector General of the Confederacy, considered the figures of Jones correct.

3

strength of 49,394 troops, reported 151,237 sick and wounded. During a fifteen-month interval from January, 1862, to March, 1863, 113,914 cases of diseases and wounds were treated in the Virginia general hospitals, exclusive of those in and near Richmond; and for the period of twenty-three months between September, 1862, and August, 1864, a grand total of 412,958 sick and wounded were admitted to the Department of Virginia's general hospitals. In July, 1863, 8,390 patients were treated in the Staunton, Virginia general hospitals, and the Gordonsville, Virginia Receiving Hospital alone admitted 23,642 patients from June 1, 1863, to May 5, 1864—6,278 in June. Richmond's Chimborazo Hospital, the largest and most famous in the Confederacy, had 77,889 admissions during the war, while the Winder Hospital, a neighboring institution, followed close behind with 76,213 patients. It is not difficult to understand where these numbers were coming from when overall unit losses during the war are examined. A member of the First Tennessee Regiment, for example, reported that at the war's end only 65 men remained of some 3,200 who had been associated with the regiment throughout the conflict.

"We have lost 4 men dide in the year 1863, and the year 1862 we lost 12 men all of each year dide of disease." So wrote a lieutenant of Company I, Fifty-third North Carolina Regiment in reflecting on his company's losses. The observations of this officer were not unique, and the medical officer learned in this war, as had his counterparts in all previous military struggles, that the most formidable enemy of the man in uniform was disease. Throughout the war years the soldier was stalked relentlessly by this bitter foe. As raw recruits ripened into seasoned veterans the prevalence of sickness declined, but deaths from disease continued to exceed those resulting from battle. Early in April, 1862, an inspection revealed "about 2,000 effective men and about 1,557 on the sick report at Island No. 10 and Madrid Bend." On June 26, 1862, a South Carolina surgeon, writing from a camp near Richmond, declared that the sick men in the hospitals were "dying by the thousands." And in April, 1864, the surgeon of an Alabama regiment as-

4

serted that his daily ministrations "if done in civil practice, would amount to over two hundred dollars, in good times."

During the years 1861 and 1862, 1,219,251 cases of disease were reported to the Confederate Surgeon General from field and general hospitals east of the Mississippi River; the number of deaths from disease totaled 31,338. For an eighteen-month period beginning in April, 1862, and ending September 30, 1863, the medical record of one North Carolina regiment alone showed a total of 2,180 men suffering from sickness.

The naval forces of the Confederate States also encountered a great amount of illness. An abstract from quarterly reports of sick from January 1 to October 1, 1863, revealed 6,122 cases treated and 59 deaths. In November, 1864, the Secretary of War was advised that "there has been much sickness of a severe character, particularly at Savannah and Charleston." Some idea as to the crippling effect of disease may be had from the report of Flag Officer John K. Mitchell on August 22, 1864, that 226 men from the James River Squadron's seven vessels were on the sick list. The *Fredericksburg* alone reported that it had 61 incapacitated by illness.

Joseph Jones believed that only one-fourth of the deaths in the Confederate military forces—some 50,000—were properly attributable to the results of battle; it was disease, concluded Jones, that was the chief killer—taking the lives of 150,000 Southern soldiers. If Jones was correct the tragic aspect of the war is seen even more clearly. There is reason to believe, however, that the picture is even darker than that painted by Jones, inasmuch as Thomas Livermore, a student of Civil War losses, concluded that Jones underestimated the number of Confederate losses from disease. Computations of losses in the Union Army, for purposes of comparison, attribute 224,586 deaths to disease and 110,070 to the battlefield.

Whatever doubt there may be as to the accuracy of Confederate statistics there can be little mystery as to the misery felt by the sick soldier. His feelings were perhaps aptly stated by a dejected private at Camp Moore, Louisiana, who wrote: "How I wish this war was over, there ain't a bit of fun in it. I

5

wouldn't object to being at home again in the least, to set in clean chairs on a nice floor and to have my seat again at [the] table with the good things on it to eat is what I would like to have, though I can stand all this as well as any body else when I am well." "I put my trust in God," wrote another, "and in him alone I trust and pray . . . that I may be spared to get up and return home again in peace and plesure [sic] once more."

Although disease was the deadliest enemy of the Confederate soldier, gunfire took its toll as the war progressed, and the Southern surgeon became increasingly familiar with gunshot wounds. During the years 1861 and 1862, east of the Mississippi River, 8,087 men were reported as killed in battle and 77,293 more were treated for battle wounds; of the latter number 4,241 subsequently died and 1,235 more were discharged. Virginia's general hospitals, not including those in and near Richmond, treated 9,796 cases of gunshot wounds from January, 1862, to April, 1863; of this number there were 516 deaths. Between July, 1861, and February, 1865, the Charlottesville General Hospital in Virginia admitted 5,391 soldiers suffering from gunshot wounds, and the number of resultant deaths was 270.

The most cursory examination of casualty lists for various campaigns and battles is sufficient to indicate that surgeons were kept extremely busy. The Maryland campaign, for example, resulted in 8,724 wounded, and the Chancellorsville engagement alone saw the wounding of 8,700. A glance at regimental losses reveals that forty-two Confederate regiments suffered casualties of fifty per cent or more in single engagements. It was a Confederate regiment, the Twenty-sixth North Carolina, that at Gettysburg experienced "the severest regimental loss during the war." Although the official statistics for this regiment show a loss in killed and wounded of 71.7 per cent the actual losses were much greater and appear to have exceeded even the 85.5 per cent casualties of the First Minnesota in the same engagement and the 82.3 per cent losses of the First Texas at Antietam. William E. Fox, the recognized authority on regimental losses, expressed the opinion that the Twenty-sixth North Carolina would "become as well known in history as the Light Brigade at Balaklava." Actually, its losses were more than twice that of the Light Brigade.

The wounded list of only one regiment during a series of engagements is also informative. Such a list shows that the Fourteenth South Carolina Regiment had 45 men wounded at Fredericksburg, 56 at Manassas, 23 at Chantilly or Ox Hill, 40 at Shepherdstown, 189 at Gaines's Mill and Frasier's Farm, 126 at Chancellorsville, 154 at Gettysburg, 175 in the Wilderness, 45 at Fussel's Mill, 31 on the Darbytown Road, and 26 near Petersburg. Throughout the entire course of the war, the Second Virginia Cavalry—totaling altogether some 700 men— had 158 of its number killed and 394 wounded; 89 others died in service and 75 were captured. It is quite understandable then how a North Carolina soldier could write late in 1864 that "Our Co. has just about played out for both officers & men. We havent had an officer with the Co. since the last fight & only about 10 or 15 men." Hoke's Division, Army of Northern Virginia, from the time it was organized in May, 1864, until the end of the war, reported 4,045 men wounded and 694 killed in battle.

In addition to caring for their own sick and wounded, the Confederate surgeon was faced with the problem of treating the diseases and wounds of thousands of Union prisoners in Andersonville, Libby, Belle Isle, Salisbury, and other lesser known Southern prisons. The admissions into the Andersonville prison hospital numbered 17,875. Of this total no diagnosis was indicated for 1,430 of these patients, and only 458 were admitted for the treatment of wounds and injuries. This leaves 15,987 known cases of illness that were received there, and there were 11,086 deaths that occurred among these sick. Thus the mortality rate was almost unbelievably high. It might also be noted that at times the deaths in the stockaded prison exceeded those in the hospital. An outstanding authority on Civil War prisons asserts that from March 1 to August 31, 1864, there were 42,686 cases of diseases and wounds reported there.

The Danville, Virginia, prison hospital records, kept from November 23, 1863, to March 27, 1865, show that a total of 4,332 cases were received. Only 157 of the admissions were wound and injury cases, and no diagnosis was made in 7 cases. Thus the number of sick alone was 4,168; of this total there were 1,074 fatalities—almost thirty per cent. Accurate statistical information is lacking as to other prison hospitals, but thousands of prisoners were confined under circumstances that all too often contributed to a very high mortality rate. The Quartermaster General of the United States, for example, reported finding the graves of 12,112 Union prisoners at Salisbury after the war.

Such statistical data as that set forth above is perhaps sufficient to illustrate the gravity of the medical problem that confronted the doctors serving under the Stars and Bars. The high incidence of disease was especially distressing to doctors and fighting men alike due to the very close relationship between the health and well-being of the troops and the achievement of Southern independence. General Lee himself was struck down by disease at a crucial stage of the Wilderness Campaign (May, 1864), and Lee "in his tent was not Lee at the front." A sick soldier was of little military value, and the overall history of disease in the army constitutes such an important part of the war's medical story that it has been accorded extended treatment in subsequent chapters.

CHAPTER II

Confederate Doctors:
The Medical Background

Importance of the Medical Background

*A*n understanding of the Confederate practitioner's medical background is necessary before those who are interested in the medical history of the war can fully apprehend the way in which he performed his assigned duties or evaluate fairly the overall work of the medical corps. It must be remembered that the discoveries of Louis Pasteur, Joseph Lister, and their associates—which completely revolutionized medical and surgical procedure by creating a new theory and practice of medicine—were not known in America until later. Subsequent advances in medical science on up to the present time have, of course, made the theories and practices of Civil War medical men obsolescent, but perhaps it may be seen that the latter made important contributions to the more recent developments. First, however, it is relevant to inquire whether or not Southern doctors had received during the course of their education—formal or informal—sufficient scientific training to keep them abreast of such medical progress as had been made in America before 1860 and to note briefly the medical situation that existed on the eve of conflict.

Increase in the Number of Medical Schools

The rise of American nationalism during the second and third decades of the nineteenth century undoubtedly contributed to the increasing number of native medical schools. Most students still continued to get their training in the offices of old practitioners who served as preceptors, but an increasing number were seeking enrollment in medical schools that were usually connected to some college. Most of the early ones were established in the Northern states, although a medical department was established by the trustees of Transylvania University in 1799 and Maryland had a college of medicine by 1807. Harvard's medical school was highly regarded, and, at Philadelphia, the University of Pennsylvania, oldest medical institution in the United States, and Jefferson Medical College, established in 1825, attracted many Southern students. Although there were still some who studied in Edinburgh, Paris, and Vienna, most medical students were receiving their education in the North by 1830. Medical dependence on the North was as marked as economic dependence. A result of this reliance may be seen in the fact that 193 of 233 members of the North Carolina Medical Society in 1860 had obtained their professional training in the North. The University of Pennsylvania, the University of New York, and Jefferson Medical College had trained 107, 42, and 33, respectively.

Medical dependence, however, was not to continue so markedly throughout the ante-bellum era. For one thing, medical colleges sprang up in the South partially as a result of the general cultural advance being made throughout America at this time. For another, their establishment was urged in the South as one phase of the movement for Southern nationalism that got underway following the onset of the abolitionist agitation and sectional bickering. Furthermore, a constantly expanding population demanded more and more medical practitioners trained to combat diseases peculiar to the section.

Leadership in the establishment of Southern medical schools was usually assumed by urban medical organizations. It was perhaps proper that the first to be founded, the Medical College of South Carolina in 1824, was located in Charleston, the oldest center of Southern scientific knowledge. Four years later a medical department was created at the University of Virginia, and in the 1830's medical institutions were established at Augusta, New Orleans, and Richmond. Soon there were flourishing medical colleges at Mobile and Nashville. These colleges generally obtained financial support from state or local governmental bodies. For example, Georgia's state legislature donated $10,000 to its medical school in 1833, and the Augusta City Council added $5,000 more. In 1839 the City Council of Lexington, Kentucky, bestowed the sum of $45,000 on the medical department of Transylvania University. By 1861 there were twenty-one medical schools in the Southern states.[1]

Quality of Southern Medical Schools

Southern medical institutions compared favorably with their Northern counterparts in every respect. The better schools in the North gave a four- or five-month course of lectures to doctoral candidates, and this standard was adopted in the South. Virginia, however, required a nine-month term, and in 1837 the dean and trustees of the Medical College of Georgia went on record as favoring continuation of their sessions of six months, begun in 1832 for the purpose of allowing more time for anatomical demonstrations and study. This forward step was blocked by the unwillingness of "other Schools of Medicine" to co-operate. The public was assured, however, that the faculty would "make all the amends they can for the shortening of the course, by rendering their Lectures as demonstrative as possible, addressing the eye as well as the ear."

The medical faculties of Southern colleges also compared favorably with those in the North from both a quantitative and qualitative standpoint. Only two schools of medicine in America had as many as eight professors on their faculties in 1837, and one of these was the Medical College of Georgia. Teaching at the Medical College of South Carolina in 1833, to take an-

[1] Medical schools seem not to have been established recklessly at this time. A committee appointed by the Medical Society of North Carolina in 1850 to consider the propriety of establishing a medical college in that state reported in 1852 that such a school was "neither expedient nor desirable."

other school at random, were such men as Drs. John Edwards
Holbrook, Samuel Henry Dickson, and John Wagner. The distinguished Holbrook was the most outstanding American zo-
ologist of his time. Dickson, although still quite young, "was
widely noted as a brilliant public speaker and a prolific, pol-
ished writer." Wagner had been a student of Baron Guillaume
Dupuytren, the great French surgeon. At New Orleans was the
incomparable Warren Stone. "Old Stone," wrote one of his
students, "is a fine surgeon as good as any in America. The old
chap gets on a 'tight' sometimes and he can lecture then more
in an hour than most men can in four. . . . I like him very
much, his lectures being altogether practical and not theoreti-
cal and he always uses the plainest and simplest plan to explain
and teach the students." [2]

Southern medical college enrollments showed steady growth
until 1861. The increase in the number of graduates of the University of Louisiana from 35 in 1850 to 133 in 1861 reflects the
general trend, but this promising development was arrested
by the wartime course of events. [3]

Relatively high standards, noted professors, and growing
enrollments in most Southern institutions did not necessarily
mean that these schools, any more than those in other sections
of the nation, were turning out men entirely capable of meeting the medical needs of those who would soon be knocking on
their office doors. Students themselves were at times critical of
the training they received. One of these referred to the Medical
College of Virginia in 1861 as a "miserable concern" and expressed the desire not to attend lectures there. Two months
later the same student was writing of his disappointment in
finding the University of Louisiana's Medical School "not as
good as I had been led to expect but still a very superior school

[2] Stone has been credited with being one of the first, if not the first,
to advise "resection of the rib to facilitate drainage in suppurative pleuritis." He was also first perhaps "to introduce the silver ligature, which
he used successfully in the ligation of the common iliac artery."

[3] The year by year number of graduates was as follows: 1850—35,
1851—40, 1852—44, 1853—70, 1854—52, 1855—54, 1856—65, 1857—64,
1858—68, 1859—96, 1860—112, 1861—133, 1862—32. During this same
period there were twelve graduates in pharmacy.

the best in the Confederacy I doubt not." It was his opinion, despite considerable admiration for Warren Stone, that the seven professors "were inferior to those in Philadelphia as teachers." Others were not so quick to disparage, but the average doctoral graduate was ill-prepared by present standards to begin his practice. Many young doctors, North and South, began their medical careers without having had the opportunity to observe an operation closely. The early operations of South Carolina's James Marion Sims, an outstanding graduate of Jefferson Medical College, were "carried out largely by instinct" and based on descriptions of operative surgery in medical journals. Sims's entire physical equipment, when he began his practice, consisted of a set of surgical instruments, a seven-volume set of medical books, and a supply of medicine. Some young practitioners themselves undoubtedly felt that the sick "would be better off if they trusted entirely to nature rather than to the haphazard empiricism of the doctors, with their blistering, bleeding, and monumental dosing."

Appearance of Professional Journals and Societies

The increase in the number of Southern medical schools was accompanied by the appearance of medical journals and the growth of medical societies. In 1836 the *Southern Medical and Surgical Journal,* the first such periodical to be printed south of the border states, was established at Augusta, Georgia, by Dr. Milton Antony. Its publication ceased temporarily with Dr. Antony's death in 1839, but it was re-established in 1845. Other well-edited and stimulating journals also appeared which did not suffer from comparison with Northern medical publications. Occasionally the theses of medical students adjudged as outstanding by the faculty were published in these journals.[4]

Almost all Southern cities could boast of having medical societies by 1830, and state societies, promoted by the local or-

[4] Thesis topics of graduates from the Medical College of Georgia in 1839 included the following: Pleuritis, Delirium Tremens, Menstruation, Physiology of the Mind, Phthisis Pulmonalis, and the Liver and Bile.

ganizations, followed—albeit somewhat slowly. And in 1835, recognizing the need for a national medical society which might take the lead in improving the training program for medical students and in elevating generally the standards of the profession, Dean Paul Fitzsimons Eve and the faculty of the Medical College of Georgia made the first real effort to organize such a body. That the movement proved abortive was due, according to Eve, to the lack of interest manifested by the University of Pennsylvania in the matters of naming the meeting time and the number of delegates from the various medical colleges, honors which Eve believed the University of Pennsylvania should have by virtue of its seniority in medical training. "Posterity will judge of the liberality and wisdom of that act," predicted Eve, "which has deliberately rejected information at the present day, and in a country too, where from the grossest abuses in medicine, its practice has almost ceased to be honorable among men. Spirits of Shippen, Rush and Wistar, and thou time-honored Father of American Surgery, upon whom have your mantles fallen!" Although delayed, the creation of the American Medical Association did take place in 1847. This time the movement was led by the New York State Medical Society, but Southern leaders participated and also took part in the early administration of the national organization. Eve himself served as president of the association during the year 1857–1858.[5]

Professional Standards in the Late Ante-Bellum Era

One of the major objectives of the American Medical Association was to improve and standardize medical education, but little was accomplished along this line during the remainder of the ante-bellum period. Actually, the standards in medical

[5] Eve, then professor of surgery at the University of Nashville, was the first American surgeon to perform a successful hysterectomy, and he also worked out an operation for vesicle calculus. He wrote nearly six hundred articles for medical journals and has been called "the leading surgeon and the leading teacher of surgery of the South."

education, instead of being raised, were sinking throughout this era. Inferior schools were not altogether uncommon before 1848, but the number mushroomed in the 1850's. Most of the new institutions were private medical colleges, and their owners were eager for fees. Hence it came to be an easy matter for students to attend lectures at such schools for a few weeks and receive diplomas. Protests were made by graduates of the better schools, but there were not enough of the latter to meet the medical needs of an ever increasing population. Such licensing legislation as had been enacted during the latter part of the eighteenth and early part of the nineteenth centuries was repealed, and the restrictions against irregular practice were lifted.[6]

This new state of affairs was especially pronounced on the Southern and Western frontiers. Here were to be found in large numbers the individualistic apostles of Jacksonian democracy, and the frontier followers of Jackson were not the kind to concern themselves about strict standards of medical education. It was also true that even the more educated had become suspicious of doctors trained in the orthodox manner. Moreover, Americans everywhere embraced the laissez faire social philosophy, and if unrestricted competition in other phases of life was salutary, then why should there not be unrestricted competition in medicine? At the same time the disease rate was high, and practitioners were greatly needed.

The rise of the common man and the need for doctors generally lent encouragement to a considerable amount of quackery everywhere in America. Numerous systems of medicine appeared and flourished. Among the most popular sects were the allopathic, the homeopathic, and the hydropathic. There were also those who won a large following by preaching the curative powers of galvanic therapy and of electrochemical baths. To be found were "allopaths of every class of allopathy; homeopaths of high and low dilutions; hydropaths mild and

[6] In North Carolina at this time Drs. S. S. Satchwell and Edward Warren, members of the state medical society, were advocating the establishment of state medical examining boards.

heroic; chrono-thermalists, Thompsonians, mesmerists, herbalists, Indian doctors, clairvoyants, spiritualists with healing gifts, and I know not what besides," wrote one observant critic. Dr. S. S. Satchwell of North Carolina asserted in 1857 that the new fangled doctrines were confined mostly to the North, and the increasing intensity of the stormy sectional strife is perhaps reflected in Satchwell's charge that the North was "fast becoming a great laboratory for the manufacture of medical as well as political and religious heresies." At any rate, an outstanding medical historian sums up the situation in the South as follows: "Everyone was allowed to practice medicine by 1850, and it were only mild exaggeration to say that everyone did! Planter, housewives, overseers, pharmacists, sectarians, quacks—all had a hand in the game."

Everywhere the people had an unreasoning faith in extravagantly advertised patent medicines. The influx of German immigrants brought the trained prescription druggist, and a rather wholesome influence on the public was exerted by that individual, but still most people and their physicians, too, believed in heavy dosing. Dr. Oliver Wendell Holmes, in an address to the Massachusetts Medical Society in May, 1860, asserted that the community was "overdosed." Part of the blame, Holmes thought, rested on the profession, and part on the public itself, "which insists on being poisoned." "How," asked Holmes,

> could a people which has a revolution once in four years, which has contrived the Bowie-knife and the revolver, which has chewed the juice out of all the superlatives in the language in Fourth of July orations, and so used up its epithets in the rhetoric of abuse that it takes two great quarto dictionaries to supply the demand; which insists in sending out yachts and horses and boys to out-sail, out-run, out-fight, and checkmate all the rest of creation; how could such a people be content with any but "heroic" practice? What wonder that the stars and stripes wave over doses of ninety grains of sulphate of quinine, and that the American eagle screams with delight to see three drachms of calomel given at a single mouthful?

Concluding that, in general, more harm than good resulted from medication, Holmes astounded his listeners by declaring that with a few exceptions "if the whole *materia medica,* as now used, could sink to the bottom of the sea, it would be all the better for mankind,—and all the worse for the fishes."

The general mediocrity in American medicine was also reflected in other ways. Earlier scientific developments were largely ignored, and practitioners were wont to cite Hippocrates as authority for the contention that the only measurements that could be relied upon were the doctors' own perceptions. The lack of faith in measurements is illustrated by the rare use of clinical thermometers during the Civil War. One authority believes that the largest Union army probably used less than half a dozen such instruments throughout the entire conflict; yet they had been introduced over two centuries before the war's outbreak.

American medical literature was of an inferior quality and lacking in originality. Still noticeable, despite some efforts to prevent it, was the old dependence upon Great Britain. Instead of drawing from their own study and experience for the purpose of making original contributions, many Americans edited books written by British medical men. This uninspired practice, which involved the addition of a few lines to the text and another name on the title page, brought forth another protest from Dr. Oliver Wendell Holmes who asserted that most American medical writing was limited to "putting British portraits of disease in American frames."

Hopeful Signs

Such a discouraging picture of American medicine should not be allowed to obscure the fact that some noteworthy contributions to medical science were being made throughout the ante-bellum period. There were, for example, some remarkable developments in the field of surgery. Two factors, the

17

influence of French pathology and the independent outlook of those close to the frontier, appear to be chiefly responsible for the increased use of the lancet and scalpel by physicians all over the United States in the years before the war.

French skepticism about internal medication had increased as diseases came to be traced to lesions in various bodily organs. Logical thinking indicated removal of the diseased parts whenever practicable, and many doctors in the United States were not unwilling to act in accordance with such reasoning. Furthermore, practitioners in outlying sections of the country were far removed from the conservative influence of the older medical centers like Boston and Philadelphia and consequently much less fettered by tradition as to what surgery could or could not be attempted. It comes as no surprise then to find that much of the daring and dangerous surgery performed in the United States before the outbreak of war took place in states close to the frontier.

One of the most daring Southern surgeons of the antebellum era was Ephraim McDowell, a native of Virginia who settled in Danville, Kentucky. McDowell won the reputation of being the ablest surgeon west of Philadelphia, and in 1809 he made his greatest contribution to medical science by performing successfully an ovariotomy, an operation that he repeated a number of times without losing a single patient. Prior to McDowell's brilliant surgical achievement it was believed that such an operation meant certain death. Another dramatic triumph was celebrated in 1849 at which time James Marion Sims performed successfully his remarkable operation for vesico-vaginal fistula.[7] Still earlier in that same decade, Crawford Williamson Long, a practitioner in rural Georgia, first administered ether seriously in operative surgery. The successful application of surgical anesthesia increased the number of operations that could be attempted, but more surgical intervention also meant a greater mortality from postoperative infection. It was therefore fortunate that many Southern phy-

[7] Despite such operations as those performed by McDowell and Sims, the average doctor continued to depend on medication.

sicians had been students or were disciples of Benjamin Winslow Dudley, professor of anatomy and surgery at Transylvania University from 1817 until 1850. Dudley taught the virtue of boiled water and thorough cleansing of the entire surgical field during and after operations. He was fully aware that filth, dirt, and impure water somehow contained the seeds of disease.

In the field of dental surgery the United States enjoyed greater pre-eminence than Europe. This leadership was partly the results of efforts made by John Greenwood, George Washington's dentist, in New York City and Horace H. Hayden, a native of Connecticut, who served his apprenticeship under Greenwood. Anxious for dentistry to attain full professional status, Hayden, after receiving an honorary degree from the Jefferson Medical College, gave lectures on dental surgery at the University of Maryland. He then co-operated with others of similar interests in founding the Baltimore College of Dental Surgery in 1840 and became its first president. A regular course in dentistry was instituted at this school, the first of its kind established anywhere, and the D.D.S. degree was awarded to those who completed it successfully. That same year the American Society of Dental Surgeons was founded in New York, and Hayden was also chosen the first president of this group. Two years later, in 1842, Virginia dentists organized the first state dental society, and in 1845 this society became "the first incorporated dental society in the world." Elsewhere in the South state dental societies existed in North Carolina, Georgia, and Kentucky prior to 1861. It is also of some significance that Jefferson Davis, when Secretary of War during the Franklin Pierce administration (1853–1857), was an early advocate of army and navy dental corps. Following their success in gaining professional and social recognition in the United States, American dentists also won recognition in Europe where there was a considerable demand for their services. One leading dental surgeon, for example, Thomas W. Evans of Philadelphia, became the dentist of Louis Napoleon.

Some progress was in evidence, of course, in fields other than surgery. On the Southern scene, for example, the critical spirit manifested by Josiah Clark Nott, a South Carolinian practicing in Mobile, led him to advance a thesis far in advance of the doctrines accepted by most doctors before the Civil War with reference to the cause of yellow fever. Making use of his own observations and those of others, Nott reached the conclusion that this formidable disease must be caused by an insect or some lesser organism. Along with other flying insects he mentioned the mosquito as the possible culprit. Other doctors not infrequently recommended the drainage of swamps as a prophylactic measure, and communities that undertook land drainage noted a salutary effect.

A number of practitioners found time during the ante-bellum period to write for the general public. These men, aware of the shortage of doctors, wrote to instruct people in the application of home remedies. Some were also concerned over the growing lack of faith in the medical profession and hoped by a straightforward presentation of the facts to help counter-act this development and regain the public confidence.

It would appear from the foregoing that Southern medical development on the eve of the Civil War was at least as far advanced as that in the Northern states. The number of medical colleges had increased steadily, some of the most competent medical men in the nation were to be found serving on the faculties of the Southern schools, standards were relatively high, the enrollments showed an encouraging growth, medical journals circulated more widely, and professional societies were becoming somewhat commonplace. Unfortunately there were also certain depressing features manifesting themselves late in the ante-bellum period, such as the relaxing of licensing laws and the concomitant flourishing of quackery, which boded ill for many of the ensuing war's sick and wounded. Yet there were certain signs that seemed to portend a coming renaissance in American medicine which, given time to develop more fully, might well have prevented much of that war's tragic loss of life.

CHAPTER III

Organization and Administration of the Confederate Medical Department

The Beginning and Early Development

The medical department of the regular army of the newly born Confederate States of America was authorized by the Provisional Congress at Montgomery, Alabama, on February 26, 1861, in the "Act for the Establishment and Organization of a General Staff for the Army of the Confederate States of America." This measure, passed eight days after the inauguration of Jefferson Davis, provided for a medical department of one Surgeon General, four surgeons, and six assistant surgeons. Should additional personnel be required, the War Department was authorized to employ more assistant surgeons. The Surgeon General was to have the rank of colonel; surgeons and assistant surgeons were to rank as majors and captains respectively, but medical officers could exercise command only in their own department.

This modest beginning was followed by two important laws enacted on March 6, 1861, one of which authorized medical officers for the provisional army while the other established a pay scale for army medical officers. The former empowered the President to appoint one surgeon and one assistant surgeon for each regiment when volunteers or militia were called into the military service in such numbers that the medical officers of the regular army could not furnish them proper attention. Medical officers appointed under the authority of this act were "to continue in service only so long as their services may be required in connection with the militia or volunteers." According to the second measure, the Surgeon General would receive an annual salary of $3,000 whereas a surgeon's pay ranged from $162 to $200 a month and that of assistant surgeons from $110 to $150 for the same period—the exact amount paid to surgeons and assistant surgeons depending on their length of service in either grade. Certain allowances in addition to the base pay, such as fuel and quarters, were also granted by the act.

Large-scale epidemics of measles, malaria, typhoid fever, and other camp diseases early in the war were related to the growing military establishment. Consequently, on April 27, 1861, Secretary of War Leroy Pope Walker recommended to the President that the army medical staff be increased. As a result of such advice the Congress, on May 16, 1861, responded by authorizing the addition of six surgeons and fourteen assistant surgeons to the regular army's medical department. And, three months later, as it became apparent that a long war was in the making, the President was empowered "to appoint in the provisional army as many surgeons and assistant surgeons for the various hospitals of the Confederacy, as may be necessary."

Meantime, the medical needs of the Confederate States Navy, authorized by Congress on March 16, 1861, were receiving attention. The act of organization itself provided for the appointment of five surgeons and five assistant surgeons —such appointees becoming officers in the permanent naval program. It soon became evident, as in the case of the army, that many more officers would be needed, and before the year was out the President was authorized to appoint thirty additional assistant surgeons on a temporary basis. Such appointments were "to be made from the navy and from civil life . . . and to terminate at the end of the war." An increase of medical officers in the regular navy was also deemed necessary as the true nature of the war unfolded, and in April, 1862, new legislation expanded the permanent staff to twenty-two surgeons, fifteen passed assistant surgeons, and thirty assistant surgeons. The continuing need of the navy for medical officers is illustrated by a law of May 1, 1863, which gave the President power to appoint in the provisional navy as many additional medical officers as the public service required.

Naval officers were paid in accordance with a scale established by Congress in acts of March 16, 1861, and September 26, 1862. Fleet surgeons were to receive an annual stipend of $3,500 whereas a surgeon's remuneration for the first five years after the date of his commission was set at either $2,200 or $2,000 each year, depending on whether or not he was on sea duty. For service afloat passed assistant surgeons were to receive a yearly pay of $1,700; for shore or other duty they would be allowed $1,500, and, when on leave or awaiting orders, their annual pay would be $1,200. The yearly stipend of assistant surgeons ranged from $1,050 to $1,250.

Army regulations stipulated the proper uniform to be worn by the medical officer. The officer's tunic of gray cloth, known as cadet gray, was to have black facings with a stand up collar. His "trowsers" were to be made of dark blue cloth, and they were to have "a black velvet stripe, one inch and a quarter in width, with a gold cord on each edge of the stripe." A black cravat, ankle or Jefferson boots, white gloves, a star on the collar of the tunic, a sash of "green silk net," and a cap on which the letters "M. S." were embroidered in gold completed the prescribed dress. It is hardly necessary to add that few were ever able to clothe themselves in such regalia.

Efforts to Reorganize the Medical Department

Several unsuccessful efforts were made during the course of the war to alter the regulations concerning medical personnel as set forth above. On August 22, 1861, President Davis returned to Congress for reconsideration "An Act to authorize the appointment of an additional Assistant Surgeon to each regiment in the Army of the Confederate States." The President took the position that the expenditure which the proposal would require was unnecessary, inasmuch as existing enactments were adequate to meet the needs of the service. He wrote: "I am aware that there have been causes of complaint in relation to neglect of our sick and wounded soldiers; but this, it is believed, arises not so much from an insufficiency in the number of the surgeons and assistant surgeons as from inattention or want of qualification, and I am endeavoring to apply the proper remedy by organizing a board of examiners, so as to ascertain who are the officers really to blame, and replace them by others more competent and efficient. . . ."

Another proposal, "An Act to reorganize and promote the efficiency of the Medical Department of the Provisional Army," received the veto of the President on October 13, 1862. The bill was carelessly framed as evidenced by a provision "that the rank, pay, and allowances of a brigadier general in the Provisional Army of the Confederate States be . . . conferred on the Surgeon General of the same." As the President pointed out, however, there was no such officer as the Surgeon General of the provisional army and no medical department of the provisional army. There were other flaws in the bill, but the President found its fifth section particularly objectionable. The latter provided for an infirmary corps of fifty men in each brigade; it was contemplated that each such corps, officered by one first lieutenant, one second lieutenant, two sergeants, and two corporals, would aid in the care of brigade sick and wounded. Yet, as Davis indicated, "no provision whatever is made for any additional medical officers, nor does the act provide for any control by medical officers over these infirmary corps, nor assign to these corps any fixed duties."

In April, 1863, the House of Representative's Committee on the Medical Department reported favorably a bill which endeavored to meet the President's objections to the reorganization measure vetoed by him the previous fall.[1] Comprehensive

[1] The House of Representatives created a standing Committee on the Medical Department on August 29, 1862. The following men were subsequently appointed to this committee: Augustus R. Wright of Georgia, Caspar W. Bell of Missouri, John Goode, Jr. of Virginia, James Farrow of South Carolina, John P. Ralls and Grandison D. Royston of Alabama,

in scope, the bill proposed first that the Surgeon General be given the rank, pay, and allowances of a brigadier general in the provisional army. The second proposition called for the appointment in the provisional army of two assistant surgeons general, as many as ten medical inspectors charged with supervising hospitals and camp sanitary conditions, and as many surgeons as the President might direct. The assistant surgeons general and the medical inspectors were to enjoy the rank, pay, and allowances of a colonel of cavalry; and surgeons would receive the rank, pay, and allowances of either a lieutenant colonel or a major of cavalry, depending on their duty assignments. A third proposal provided for the establishment in the provisional army of an infirmary corps of medical officers "in number not to exceed one surgeon for each brigade and one assistant surgeon for each regiment, who shall not be attached to the organization of troops, but shall serve in the field, or in field hospitals, under such regulations as the Secretary of War shall prescribe." Finally, the bill stipulated that the appointment of regular army officers to positions created under the terms of the act would not affect the status of those officers in the regular army and that the bill conferred no command authority outside the medical department upon those who were appointed to the ranks provided for therein. This measure, although approved by the lower chamber by a vote of forty-four to twenty-seven, was blocked in the Senate where a separate reorganization bill had been framed. The Senate's bill, less comprehensive than the House measure, passed that body on April 11, 1863, but it was not concurred in by the House. Thus the proposals for reorganization of the army medical department expired.

A bill to reorganize the medical corps of the navy, introduced in the Senate on January 28, 1863, was referred to the committee on naval affairs. Approximately six weeks later, on March 13, it was reported out and laid on the table. No other

William N. H. Smith of North Carolina, James S. Chrisman of Kentucky, and Thomas Menees of Tennessee.

measure for this purpose was proposed during the life of the Confederate Congress.

The Surgeon General, according to available records, appears to have lent his support to the reorganization bill of April, 1863, and to have been disappointed upon the inability of the lawmakers to present a bill incorporating the propositions contained therein to the President. No serious criticism was registered, however, and the judgment of the medical officers themselves on the medical department's organization was stated succinctly in their journal early in 1864, as follows: "Although the organization of the medical department is not as complete as it is believed it could have been, had the ideas and suggestions of its experienced presiding officer met with more favorable consideration, still, in view of the exactness with which its varied duties have been defined and systematized, it may be confidently asserted that, in the full performance of these duties by its members, the objects for which it was instituted have been, if not perfectly, yet, to a very great extent, satisfactorily accomplished."

The Medical Service on Paper

A rather impressive medical organization gradually evolved from the enactments of Congress and the directives of the War Department as may be seen from a brief look at the overall structure in 1864. Six medical officers, including the Surgeon General, were on duty in the Surgeon General's office. Eighteen surgeons were serving as medical directors in the field and supervising the work of medical officers there. There were also eight medical directors of hospitals, six field medical inspectors, and seven medical inspectors of hospitals. Five army medical boards were engaged in the examination of applicants for appointment as assistant surgeons and of assistant surgeons for promotion. The number of principal hospitals which had been established in the various states was as follows: Virginia, 39, North Carolina, 21, South Carolina, 12, Georgia, 50,

Alabama, 23, Mississippi, 3, Florida, 4, and Tennessee, 2. Medical laboratories, with a surgeon in charge of each, were located at various points; and thirty-two medical purveyors, employed in the procurement and distribution of medical and hospital supplies, could be found throughout the Confederacy. The Navy's Bureau of Medicine and Surgery was located in Richmond with Surgeon William A. W. Spotswood of Virginia in charge, and there were naval hospitals at Richmond, Charleston, Wilmington, Savannah, and Mobile.

The Surgeon General

Administration of this extensive medical service was the responsibility of the Surgeon General. He was charged specifically "with the administrative details of the medical department, the government of hospitals, the regulation of the duties of surgeons and assistant surgeons, and the appointment of acting medical officers, when needed, for local or detached service." He was also responsible for the issuance of directives "relating to the professional duties" of his officers. Unfortunately, many important papers of the Medical Department were burned when the buildings in Richmond that housed the Surgeon General's office were destroyed by fire during the fall of the city. Historians interested in knowing how effectively he and his staff functioned have thus been deprived of much pertinent information.

The first Surgeon General was David C. DeLeon, a surgeon in the "old army." DeLeon, a resident of Mobile, Alabama, was ordered to assume the duties of "acting Surgeon General" on May 6, 1861, but his occupancy of the Surgeon General's office, consisting of only one room at that time, was of brief duration. On July 12, 1861, orders were issued relieving DeLeon and assigning Charles H. Smith of the office staff to take "temporary charge of the medical bureau." Then, a little over two weeks later, on July 30, 1861, Samuel Preston Moore, who was to preside over the Medical Department for the duration of the war, was ordered to duty as "acting Surgeon General." Entering upon his work immediately, Moore soon advised the Secretary of the Treasury, who was in charge of arrangements for establishing the public offices in Richmond, that it was "impossible to transact the business of this bureau (connected most intimately with the welfare of the Army in the field) in one single room, crowded to overflowing with employees, soldiers, and visitors on business." Moore weathered the storm of early confusion and performed his duties in an impressive manner. Consequently, his name was sent to the Senate for approval as Surgeon General late in November, 1861, and his nomination was speedily confirmed by that body.

Samuel Preston Moore's background, professional training, and army career qualified him for the high and responsible office to which he had been appointed. A native of Charleston, South Carolina, he was a direct descendant of Dr. Mordecai Moore, who had come to America in the seventeenth century as Lord Baltimore's physician. Educated in Charleston, Moore was graduated from the Medical College of South Carolina in 1834. The next year he was appointed an assistant surgeon in the regular army and began the first of many tours of duty which included assignments in Iowa, Kansas, Missouri, Florida, Mexico, Oregon, Texas, New York, and Louisiana. He saw service in the Mexican War and received his surgeoncy while at Jefferson Barracks, Missouri, immediately after that conflict. On duty in New Orleans as medical purveyor when South Carolina enacted its secession ordinance, Moore resigned his commission and practiced medicine in Little Rock, Arkansas, for a short time before he was called to take charge of the Confederate Medical Department.

Operation of the Medical Department under Samuel Preston Moore

Moore soon had the Medical Department operating efficiently. Examinations were prescribed to weed out incompetent personnel, the competent were assigned to key positions, and a reporting system intended to inform the Surgeon General of all pertinent medical facts and problems was instituted. Inasmuch as medical societies and the publication of professional journals and books were suspended early in the war, the Surgeon General took steps to provide needed discussion and publication on medical subjects. In the summer of 1863 he organized the Association of Army and Navy Surgeons of the Confederate States, "the oldest American military medical society," and was himself the association's first president. This group met regularly to hear reports on medical and surgical subjects proposed by its members.[2]

In the realm of publication, Moore encouraged the publication of the *Confederate States Medical and Surgical Journal* (January, 1864–February, 1865), ably edited by Surgeon James Brown McCaw. Well-written editorials, articles by Confederate surgeons on their medical and surgical experiences, and analyses of articles in foreign journals characterized this fine periodical. Despite numerous difficulties its editor reported in May, 1864, that the journal had "attained a larger circulation than was ever reached before by any Southern Medical periodical and promises . . . to surpass the most sanguine expectations of its friends." The Surgeon General also prompted the publication and distribution to his medical officers of two highly useful books: *Resources of the Southern Fields and Forests, Medical, Economical, and Agricultural,* written at Moore's request by Surgeon Francis Peyre Porcher of South Carolina, and *A Manual of Military Surgery,* prepared by a group of surgeons working under Moore's direction. Both were published in 1863. It was the hope of the Surgeon General that these volumes would 1) enable his medical officers to supply many of their drug needs through the preparation of medicines from plants indigenous to the Southern states and 2) improve surgical procedures.

One of the chief distinctions claimed for the Surgeon General is that he introduced the hut or one story pavilion hospital, the forerunner of the modern general hospital. In the pavilion

[2] The last meeting of the association was held on March 18, 1865.

type hospital arrangement the sick and wounded were not lumped together in large buildings, but received treatment in a number of huts. Each hut thus became an independent ward housing from twenty-five to fifty patients. A general hospital consisted of from forty-five to sixty huts.

The Surgeon General as an Administrator

Moore proved to be a capable administrator. He was intelligent, thorough, impartial, and industrious. One of his admirers praised "his great work as an organizer, his remarkable executive ability, fitness for the high position, and his official work." Another, the medical director of Virginia hospitals, reported that the Surgeon General "attends to all papers coming to his office in regular rotation, and neglects none." And still another of his associates asked "where, or under what government so complicated and extensive as this, was there ever a department of the public service characterized by such order and precision? Every paper emanating from that office," he asserted, "was a model of despatch and neatness."

It must be said, however, that the Confederate Surgeon General was extremely addicted to the formality of army discipline and that consequently his relationship with the officers of his department was not such as to make him an object of affectionate regard. According to a fellow officer "the Emperor of the Russians was not more autocratic. He commanded and it was done. He stood *in terrorem* over the surgeon, whatever his rank or wherever he might be—from Richmond to the trans-Mississippi, and to the extremest verge of the Confederate States." "I have been to see the Surg. Genl. but once," wrote a medical officer on temporary duty in Richmond, "& shall not go again unless I am compelled."

Moore's spit and polish attitude was reflected in his insistence that subordinates conform to the precise rules of military correspondence in their communications to his office. He complained of the many leaves of absence granted to medical officers and failed to apprehend why those serving in general hospitals even wanted them. A warning went out from his office that charges would be preferred against those who failed to comply with regulations, and on one occasion the Surgeon General instructed a medical director to arrest the entire membership of an examining board and institute court martial proceedings because it had committed a minor infraction of orders. Officers with tender sensibilities who incurred Moore's displeasure were often offended, but even most of these acknowledged his ability. "He was a man of great brusqueness of manner," recalled one who knew him, "and gave offense to many who called on him, whatever their business, and without any regard to their station or rank, though he was an able executive officer, and I believe an efficient and impartial one." Underneath his rough exterior, however, there was a more appealing and sympathetic side as is evidenced by his correspondence with the mothers of hospitalized soldiers. He is known to have written comforting letters to those who were concerned about their loved ones after making personal investigations at their requests.

Maintaining a Medical Corps

Few of the Surgeon General's responsibilities gave him more trouble than that of appointing and maintaining an efficient corps of medical officers. The nucleus of officer personnel for both the army and navy was formed by those who resigned from the medical staffs of the United States army and navy. When the year 1861 opened the medical corps of the United States Army consisted of one Surgeon General, thirty surgeons, and eighty-three assistant surgeons. Three surgeons and twenty-one assistant surgeons tendered their resignations and entered the Confederate service. The percentage of medical officers who left the Union navy to join the Confederacy was about the same: twenty-eight of a total complement of one hundred and forty-eight.[3] Among these twenty-eight was

[3] The number may have been somewhat larger. A register of Confederate naval officers published in 1931 indicates thirty-five resignations

William A. W. Spotswood of Virginia, the top-ranking naval surgeon of the Confederacy.

The need for many more medical officers coincident with the assembling of large armies and the extensive amount of disease early in the war led at first to the appointment of many incompetents. A number of these were weeded out by examining boards and even before the year 1861 came to a close Judah P. Benjamin, then Secretary of War, was able to advise the President that "Quite a number who had been appointed on the recommendation of the men themselves have proven unequal to the duties of their station; others were found incompetent from carelessness and neglect, while in some instances there was gross ignorance of the very elements of the profession. The efficiency of the corps has been greatly increased by the purgation it has undergone. . . ."

Throughout the war special orders issued by the Adjutant and Inspector General's Office continued to list the names of medical officers dropped from the rolls after their rejection by examining boards. And the problem of how to keep from engaging incompetent private or contract physicians at times when the regular staff could not provide adequate medical attention was also a difficult one.

Army Medical Boards

Army and medical regulations authorized the Secretary of War to appoint army medical boards composed of medical officers whose functions consisted of examining both applicants for appointment as assistant surgeons and assistant surgeons with sufficient tenure to be qualified for promotion. Such boards were to "scrutinize rigidly the moral habits, professional acquirements, and physical qualifications of the candidates, and

---

from the medical corps of the Union navy. Another register reportedly containing a list of all officers who had resigned from the United States Navy was found on a Confederate gunboat captured in North Carolina waters. On this list were the names of nine surgeons, ten passed assistant surgeons, and eleven assistant surgeons.

report favorably, either for appointment or promotion, in no case admitting of a reasonable doubt." These regulations were made for the purpose of providing the regular establishment with an able corps of medical officers, but the examining procedure for officers in the provisional army was the same. That previous favorable reports on officers did not ensure tenure may be seen in the Surgeon General's ruling that those who were "too delicate to perform all the duties required of them, must resign."

Disparaging comments were occasionally directed at the medical boards and the quality of their examinations. Mrs. Phoebe Y. Pember, a matron in Richmond's large Chimborazo Hospital, claimed that the examining board in that city "often rejected good practitioners, and gave appointments to apothecary boys." An assistant surgeon in South Carolina described the examination as "a perfect farce." And, according to Surgeon Aristides Monteiro—who seemed to have nothing but contempt for those in charge of the Medical Department— examining boards held theories quite foreign to those taught by medical college faculties. One member of the board which examined him, he declared, was a former classmate at the University of Virginia who had left that institution without a diploma. "Another member," he went on, "was eccentric," while another "owed his promotion to nepotism—a very common disease at that time. A fourth member was very drunk." Two members of this board, he related, held opposing views as to the proper treatment for gunshot wounds of the lung. When the question as to such treatment was asked during the course of his examination, Monteiro claimed to have satisfied his questioners by asserting that he would use both methods in his attendance upon such cases. Edward Warren, a noted North Carolina physician, served for a time on a medical board. His work on the board was exceedingly disagreeable, he remembered, because of the prejudice and irritability of the board chairman. "He only knew of the standard of attainment existing in the old army," wrote Warren, "and he voted generally against those who failed to come up to its requirements, especially if they chanced to be North Carolinians." Further west, Andrew J. Foard, the Army of Tennessee's medical director, complained of "a lazy set of med. Officers" on the examining board at Montgomery, Alabama, and warned them that unless they did better "the effect of Cavalry service would be tried on them."

Some criticism was undoubtedly deserved, but it would appear that in general the boards were held in high esteem, and successful candidates were regarded as possessing sufficient qualifications for appointment in the medical corps. Thomas Williams, the Army of the Potomac's medical director, expressed complete confidence in his medical officers' competence late in 1861, as all had "passed rigid examinations before the Army Medical Board." A young Confederate medical officer named Simon Baruch, the father of Bernard Baruch, testified to the rigidity of examinations although it is interesting to note that at the time he received his appointment he had yet to treat his first patient.

One of the most enlightening comments as to the thoroughness of examinations given by medical boards is that of George E. Waller, hospital steward in the Twenty-fourth Virginia Regiment. Waller was examined in Richmond and received an unfavorable report from the board. The following passages from his letter about the matter throw light on the nature of the examination he was given and on the proportion of failures:

. . . You can get some easy position on the medical staff by a little reading up on manutia but you must read closely, for if they give you a close examination like they did me it will require close reading on manutia. I will give you some idea of the examination I got—first Peticolas [A. E. Peticolas, Professor of Anatomy, Medical College of Virginia] examined me on the anatomical structure of the eye, its various coats and the inflammation of thim with their differantial diagnosis. Also the differant modes of treating their differant inflammations with the various results of said inflammations. When he was through with the eye he than took me on the Brain, its anatomical arrangement and microscopical apperance, with the various distrabution of the nerves; when done with this next came the artaries with their distrabutions and ramifications. Then dislocations of the hip. . . . Next came the Prof. of Practice. He took me on Dropsy of the differant regions, what causes produced it in one region and what in another. Next Pneumonia, and its various changes. The symptoms of the differant stages with the Physical signs. And a thousand other questions that I do not recolect. A Third man came whose examination was just as hard. And after all this, they gave me a sheet of Foolscap just as full of questions as it could be. . . . I was not at all disappointed when I was pitched for I had talked with Peticolas prior to my examination and he told me that four out of five wer thrown. . . .

The Medical College of Virginia

The Surgeon General's task of attempting to maintain an able complement of medical officers was made more difficult by the fact that all but one of the Southern medical schools were forced to close their doors early in the struggle between North and South. Only the Medical College of Virginia, located in the capital of the Confederacy, was able to withstand the impact of war. The valuable training in military medicine and surgery that could have been received by students in Southern medical colleges, staffed in part by medical officers and having numerous hospitals nearby in which students might observe practically every kind of wound and disease, can well be imagined. Since such was not available to most, however, those who might otherwise have been in school, and even some practitioners, sought glory on the field of battle.[4] "I would not be surprised if the session closed earlier this year than usual," wrote a student at the University of Louisiana Medical School in February, 1862, "as we have but few students and not enough to defray expenses of the college." This school closed its

[4] A good many Southern doctors, including such able practitioners as Joseph Jones and Hunter Holmes McGuire, began their army service in the ranks.

doors following the March graduation, and the story of other medical colleges was a similar one.[5]

Orienting itself to wartime conditions, the Medical College of Virginia shortened its sessions and graduated two classes each year. With a faculty of eight, including James Brown McCaw, head of Chimborazo Hospital, this institution trained approximately four hundred students during the war. Most of these were assigned to military hospitals in and near Richmond or saw service as medical officers in the Army of Northern Virginia, and hundreds of disabled soldiers received treatment in the college infirmary.

There was, therefore, a distinct relationship and area of co-operation between the Medical Department and the Medical College of Virginia. The Surgeon General, in an address delivered after the conflict, stated that in trying to meet the needs of the service for medical officers "a certain number of young gentlemen were annually appointed hospital stewards, with the privilege of attending the lectures of the Richmond Medical College, and on graduation, letters of invitation were issued them for examination for appointment in the corps." In other words, the Medical Department used the college as a training school for many of its future officers. A further tie between the medical service and the Virginia school existed after the Association of Army and Navy Surgeons, on the motion of Surgeon W. A. W. Spotswood, voted unanimously to grant honorary memberships in their organization to all members of the college faculty who were not already attached to the army or navy.

The Number of Medical Officers

Joseph Jones estimated that altogether something less than three thousand medical officers served in the Confederate army

[5] The entire faculty of the Medical College of South Carolina entered the Confederate service. Federal authorities used the buildings of the Missouri Medical College as a prison during the war.

and navy; only seventy-three, he thought, were naval officers. At the Nineteenth Annual Meeting of the Association of Medical Officers of the Army and Navy of the Confederacy in 1916, however, the "Committee on the Roster of the Medical Officers of the Confederate States" reported the following number of officers to have been nominated by the President and confirmed by the Senate for duty in the army medical service:

Surgeons General	1
Surgeons	1,242
Assistant Surgeons	1,994
	3,237

The same committee found the following number of medical officers to have been nominated and confirmed for service in the navy:

Surgeons	26
Passed Assistant Surgeons	13
Assistant Surgeons	63
Assistant Surgeons for the War	5
	107

Surgeon Samuel H. Stout, medical director of the army and the Department of Tennessee's general hospitals, listed the names of 329 medical officers who served under him from 1862 to 1865. All of these figures are exclusive of contract physicians. In view of such statistics it is interesting to note that one line officer who served throughout the war could remember having seen only one medical officer.

The Hospital Program

Both the Medical Department and Congress were compelled to give considerable attention to the establishment of an effective and efficient hospital program. Vast expenditures for the procurement of medical and hospital supplies were necessary, and these aspects of the Confederate medical service are so important that they must be developed more fully in subsequent chapters. Several basic statutes pertaining to hospitals should be noted, however, to illustrate the general approach toward these matters once the authorities realized that careful planning was imperative.

One illustration of the effort to effect improvement in the hospital program—and to recognize the predilection manifested by many for the state rights idea at the same time even in the midst of a bloody war—was the "Act to better provide for the Sick and Wounded of the Army in Hospitals," dated September 27, 1862. Prior to the passage of this measure the medical authorities had followed no definite system in assigning patients to the various hospitals. Representative James Farrow of South Carolina voiced the commonly shared opinion that "most of the hardships which beset the soldier whilst in hospitals, grew out of the practice of mixing up soldiers from all portions of the Confederacy, in the same hospital, and scattering men from the same neighbourhood and regiment" in many different institutions. The bill, as approved, provided that hospitals "be known and numbered as hospitals of a particular state"; and directed that, when feasible, the sick and wounded be assigned to hospitals representing their states.[6] There appears to have been general compliance with this act although it was pointed out by some that it resulted in greatly increased expenditures.[7]

Another significant measure enacted to improve the hospital service became law on May 1, 1863. This statute, an amendment to the legislation of September 27, 1862, directed the Surgeon General to establish, in addition to hospitals already existing, a number of "way hospitals." Such institutions

[6] The act of September 27, 1862, also authorized the employment of matrons, assistant matrons, ward masters, and additional nurses and cooks as needed.

[7] Considerable evidence could be presented to show that medical officials attempted to comply with this act. Early in 1863 Representative David Clopton of Alabama obtained support for a resolution which instructed the Committee on the Medical Department "to inquire into the expediency of establishing one or more hospitals in each State, and of providing for the transportation to such hospitals of the sick and wounded soldiers from such States respectively who may be unfit for service for thirty days."

were to be located along the routes of important railroads and were to furnish rations and quarters to sick and wounded furloughed and discharged soldiers during the course of their journeys home. They were to be administered in the same way as general hospitals. The law was a much needed one, and it was soon implemented by specific directives from the Surgeon General's office. Seventeen way hospitals were established in Virginia and North Carolina alone.[8]

Furlough and Discharge Procedures

It also took some time for the authorities to develop workable and sound procedure in the granting of furloughs and discharges to sick, wounded, and disabled troops. Numerous recommendations and bills were proposed, but no comprehensive measure was enacted until May 1, 1863. In the meantime furloughs and discharges were being conferred pursuant to army regulations, directives from the Surgeon General, and general orders issued by the Adjutant and Inspector General's Office. With so much confusion resulting from this state of affairs the Confederate soldier, notoriously unamenable to discipline, sometimes took matters in his own hands. One medical officer complained in the late spring of 1862 that "these Georgia Cols as well as privates, dont seem to have any just idea of the true character of the war. They all want furloughs to see their families, or if they get a cold, they must go home or never get well, and if there is a battle impending, they take diarrhea, Rheumatism or something of the kind and some dont wait to get sick, but run strait off. Out of 330 or so men sent from Camp McDonough [Atlanta] to Marietta Ga/20 miles distant from here towards Chattanooga/ I can only find 195. The ballence have deserted, or failed to come up."

In August of that same year Senator Benjamin H. Hill of

---

[8] In North Carolina way hospitals were established at Weldon, Raleigh, Greensboro, Salisbury, Charlotte, Goldsboro, Wilmington, and Tarboro.

Georgia asserted that he had "learned from the Secretary of War, that not one man in three, who were furloughed, ever returned to the army." It was also declared, with some exaggeration, that too much delay was encountered by those entitled to furloughs and discharges; applicants for discharges might die before their papers were processed, it was predicted. Representative Caleb C. Herbert of Texas claimed that some patients in the Richmond hospitals had been there for more than a year, and he thought that "hundreds" were hospitalized who were permanently disabled. Thus, he professed to believe, "the Government was subjected to millions of expense, with no possible good to anybody."

In May, 1863, "An Act regulating the granting of Furloughs and Discharges in Hospitals" was passed upon the heels of such assertions. Boards of examiners, comprised of hospital surgeons, were provided for by the enactment, and these were to examine applicants for furloughs and discharges in their hospitals twice each week. Applicants for furlough, found unfit for military duty and likely to remain so for at least thirty days, were to receive furloughs for such period of time as the board should deem them unfit for duty, but not to exceed sixty days. Discharges might be recommended by the board, but recommendations for discharge had to be approved by the Surgeon General or the commanding general of the army or department to which the soldier belonged. A further stipulation of this law was that which required surgeons in charge of hospitals to visit each patient under their care at least once daily.[9]

Provision was made later for the extension of furloughs when soldiers were unable to travel; yet Vice-President Alexander H. Stephens complained that many thousands had died in returning to the army before they were fully recovered. On February 17, 1864, Congress amended the act regulating

[9] Senator Louis T. Wigfall opposed the bill and termed it "a proposition to take this power [of granting furloughs] from the hands of the President and the line officers and give it to the surgeons." This, Wigfall felt, "would be a bouleversement of the whole army."

furlough and discharge procedure by extending the disability period which entitled the sick and wounded to furloughs to a minimum of sixty days.

A brief survey of furlough and discharge statistics suggests why the matter of sound administration was of so much importance. Hospital reports for the Department of Virginia, covering the period from September, 1862, to August, 1864, reveal that 60,506 men were furloughed and 4,667 discharged during this 23-month interval. Thus an average of 2,631 furloughs and 203 discharges were granted monthly in this one department alone. The largest number of furloughs allowed in one month was the 6,556 given in June, 1864, whereas the single month high for discharges was the 1,550 allowed in September, 1862. Medical Director Samuel H. Stout, noting that 1,882 of 6,889 soldiers treated in the Tennessee hospital district during June, 1863, were furloughed, brought this "startling fact" to the attention of his medical officers and asked if there was not some solution for "this evil." The furlough problem was a difficult one, however, and it was frequently necessary to furlough large numbers of the sick and wounded to provide beds for new battle casualties. Available records indicate that the number of discharges dropped sharply after the passage of the regulatory legislation, but the number of furloughs showed a noticeable increase and reached record highs in the summer of 1864.[10]

Perhaps the most valid criticism directed against the new policy for granting furloughs and discharges was set forth by Surgeon Lafayette Guild, the Army of Northern Virginia's medical director. It was Guild's opinion that "a very large number of soldiers" became permanently disabled for field service due to the fact that after being wounded they had

[10] Records kept in the Confederate Adjutant and Inspector General's Office list a total of 27,599 discharges conferred during the course of the war, but the list is probably not complete. It appears that mistakes were sometimes made. John Thomas Graves, a Missouri soldier discharged in 1863 for reasons of poor health, died in the Missouri State Confederate Home at the age of 108 in May, 1950. Graves was the oldest Confederate veteran at that time.

been sent home where their wounds were neglected "at a period during the process of healing when judicious surgical attention was required to prevent Anchylosis, Atrophy or contraction of the muscles and other deformities." To avoid this loss of manpower Guild was in favor of granting furloughs only to the permanently disabled. He also proposed the establishment of a hospital in which men who had developed deformities while on furlough could be treated. It is likely that Guild overstated his case, but undoubtedly many of the wounded who were sent home would have fared better in the hospitals under ordinary conditions. In general, the act worked reasonably well.

The Invalid Corps

The growing shortage of manpower gave increasing concern to the authorities, and this concern was manifested by President Davis in his message to Congress of December 7, 1863, which contained the recommendation that an invalid corps be organized. Such a corps, he believed, "could be made useful in various employments for which efficient officers and troops are now detached." Congress responded with "An Act to provide an Invalid Corps," and this measure became law on February 17, 1864. Provision was made by the enactment for a corps of officers and men who were retired or discharged as the result of wounds or disease contracted in the line of duty. As something of a reward for their service-incurred disabilities the rank, pay, and emoluments of officers and men assigned to the corps were to continue during the war or as long as they remained on the retired or discharged list. Each member of the invalid corps was required to undergo a physical examination at least once every six months in order that any change in his condition might be discerned. It was expected, of course, that many in the invalid corps might be able to perform limited service, and the Secretary of War was authorized to assign officers and to detail men "for such duty as they shall be qualified to perform." Men relieved from disability were to be ordered back to their commands. An amendment of January 27, 1865, reduced the compensation of retired officers to half pay.

A Register of Officers of the Invalid Corps, maintained in the Confederate Adjutant and Inspector General's Office, lists a total of 1,063 names. Of this number 231 were described as "totally disqualified," and almost all the remainder were assigned to some sort of duty. A Register of Enlisted Men of the Invalid Corps, kept in the same office, includes a total of 5,139 names, and those deemed "totally disqualified" numbered 2,061. The record is not complete as to what proportion of the others was assigned to light service.

Congressional Appropriations

Large sums of money were required by the Medical Department to purchase medical and hospital supplies, to establish and support military hospitals, and to meet unusual demands made upon it. Surgeon General Moore's estimates of his needs always received respectful attention from Congress, and that official, in a postwar address, adverted to the cooperation he had received from the legislative branch of the government. Congressional appropriations to the Army Medical Department increased steadily during the war, finally totaling almost $74,000,000. Appropriations to the navy's medical staff also increased year by year and totaled almost $2,000,000.[11] These figures do not include the salaries paid to army and navy medical officers.

The increasing medical expenditures, while partially the result of wartime inflation, reflect a constant increase of medical services. Not only did the appropriations for such items as medical and hospital supplies, the establishment and support

[11] The total expenditures of the United States Army Medical Department from June 30, 1861, to June 30, 1866, exclusive of salaries to medical officers, reached the sum of $47,351,982.24.

of military hospitals, and the pay of contract physicians mount steadily, but new items were added from time to time and old ones dropped or absorbed in the new. By 1863, following the passage of the act of September 27, 1862, one of the most comprehensive measures of the war, the objects of appropriation had become almost standardized. Experience and investigation enabled the Medical Department to perform its significant functions much more effectively.

CHAPTER IV

Confederate General Hospitals: Establishment and Organization

The Problem and Early Confusion

*T*he problem of the establishment of a sufficient number of "general" hospitals—so called because admission thereto was not restricted to troops from particular units—properly staffed and equipped, to care for the sick and wounded transported from the camps and battlefields had to await the painful realization that an all-out military effort to win Southern independence was necessary. Even after the authorities became fully cognizant of this fact it is no wonder that the tasks of mustering and outfitting a large military force, creating a fiscal system, and obtaining recognition from abroad took immediate precedence over almost all other concerns in the early months of the conflict. As a consequence the early hospital picture was confused and depressing.[1]

Confusion attendant upon the early epidemics and the extensive casualties that resulted from the battle of First Manassas (July 21, 1861) and the bloody engagements fought during the campaigns of 1862 was everywhere apparent. All sorts of buildings—private homes, hotels, barns, warehouses, stores, churches, courthouses, and others—were converted into temporary hospitals. Samuel P. Day, an English observer, found about fifteen hundred patients being cared for in twelve Richmond hospitals after the first clash at Manassas, and many were being treated elsewhere. According to Day, only "a fractional part of the sick and wounded" were in the hospitals, and there was hardly "a gentleman in or about Rich-

---

[1] Only $50,000 was appropriated by Congress for the establishment and support of military hospitals in 1861.

mond who had not from one to four patients in his house, upon whom the utmost attention was bestowed." [2] In Charlottesville, Virginia, Edward Warren, North Carolina surgeon, saw the disabled "scattered through hotels, private houses, public halls, and wherever it was possible to spread a blanket. In fact," wrote Warren, "from what I could gather, the whole country, from Manassas Junction to Richmond in one direction, and to Lynchburg in another, was one vast hospital, filled to repletion with the sick and wounded of Beauregard's victorious army." Warren also noticed a need for additional medical officers, and this need was cited on several later occasions by the Army of the Potomac's medical director.

Conditions in the West were no more satisfactory. When Samuel H. Stout took charge of Nashville's Gordon Hospital in October, 1861, for example, he found "no organization, no register, and no books of any kind"—nothing but 650 sick troops, many of whom were lying upon the floor. In the first winter of the war the disabled from General Braxton Bragg's army were brought to Nashville and housed in vacant homes and stores where medical officers were aided in their ministrations by numerous ladies and a few students from the local medical college. And, from Chattanooga's Foard Hospital, early in 1862, the surgeon in charge advised the post surgeon of "the distressed condition of this Hospital." He, the other doctors, and the nurses were sick, overworked, and despondent. Mrs. Ella King Newsom, noted hospital executive, began her work at Bowling Green, Kentucky, that same winter and

[2] Several claims have been made for the first Confederate hospital, one in behalf of that established at Williamsburg, Virginia, in May, 1861, by Mrs. Letitia Tyler Semple, daughter of former President John Tyler. Her hospital was organized in a female seminary that stood on the edge of the colonial capital and contained seventy-five cots. Claim has also been made that the Wayside Home in Kingston, Georgia, was the first of the Confederacy's hospitals, and the Division of State Parks, Historic Sites and Monuments, has erected a marker to that effect. General Hospital No. 1, which occupied the city almshouse, was the first to be organized in Richmond; it accommodated five hundred patients and was used to house the Union sick and wounded after the battle of First Manassas.

found there men suffering from inefficient organization, inadequate buildings, lack of supplies, and cold weather. Further south, from Mobile, Alabama, Dr. Josiah C. Nott wrote: "The whole affair now is horrible. . . . There is a great deal of *bad* sickness & if the whole thing is not changed, the whole command will be rendered worthless." Nott's uneasiness was not lessened by his belief that the prevailing disease, a strange mixture of malaria and typhoid, was actually "aided by the stupidity of Doctors or rather quacks." He also remarked on the absence of any recognized authority.

A special committee, appointed by the Provisional Congress to inquire into the organization and administration of the medical and certain other departments, made several significant observations when it made its report late in January, 1862. According to the committee those troops serving on the Potomac and in western Virginia were not within reach of hospital service. In general, concluded the committee, the armed forces were short on hospital accommodations, medical personnel, and medical stores.

The Picture in 1862

The hospital picture in the East had brightened somewhat by the spring of 1862, but crowded conditions continued to exist and the ensuing campaign was to cause considerable embarrassment. A special hospital investigating committee, created by the Confederate House of Representatives, made its report on April 21, 1862. This committee, headed by John P. Ralls of Alabama, found twenty Confederate and state hospitals in Richmond and believed these twenty to be capable of accommodating five or six thousand patients. It reported a shortage of medicines—pointing out that available transportation for medical stores was woefully inadequate—but otherwise found the men adequately attended. The food was well prepared, and sanitary conditions were such as to be "worthy of commendation." Reference was not made to the space deficiency by the committee but, on the same date that its report was tendered, Surgeon General Moore adverted to the problem and asserted that it "must occur until the buildings being fitted are completed."

More suitable buildings were being taken over for hospitals and some construction was under way, but facilities that existed by the spring of 1862 were not sufficient to care for the casualties of Seven Pines (May 31–June 1, 1862) and the Seven Days (June 25–July 1, 1862). Once again all available space was utilized as in "the heat of early summer a stream of wounded poured into the hospitals of Richmond in such numbers that there was soon no room for them in the congested wards." Volunteer workers, including children, came forward in large number as the wounded spilled into homes, hotels, warehouses, and other makeshift buildings. The Confederate capital, object of the Union army's spring and summer offensive, truly became, as described by a witness, "one vast hospital." Needless to say the mortality rate was high. "It is impossible to tell how many are dying here," wrote a Georgia surgeon, "but the number is tremendous—a grave yard of 50 acres nearly filled from one Hospital."

Much of the mortality was no doubt the result of crowded conditions. Under such circumstances, according to Joseph Jones, "the simplest diseases assumed malignant characters; the typhoid poison altered the course of mumps, and measles, and pneumonia, and was the cause of thousands of deaths; and the foul exhalations of the sick poisoned the wounds of the healthy men, and induced erysipelas, pyaemia, and gangrene." Part of Jones's statement would not hold up under the scrutiny of modern medicine, but he saw clearly the relationship between congestion and an increasing mortality rate.

Confusion in the West also continued well into 1862. After the bloody battle of Shiloh (April 6–7, 1862) the Confederate army fell back, and the disabled were removed to its new base at Corinth, Mississippi, a key railroad center in the northern part of the state. All available space was taken, but the suffering was intense. One of the large buildings used for a hospital was the Tishomingo Hotel. Here, according to Ella K. Newsom, "Every yard of space on the floors, as well as all the beds, bunks and cots were covered with the mangled forms of dying and dead soldiers." Kate Cumming, matron at this hospital, noted in commenting on the congestion there that "when we give the men any thing [we] kneel, in blood and water. . . . There seems to be no order," she added. "All do as they please. . . . We have a new set [of nurses] every few hours." For a time amputated limbs were scattered over the hospital yard. At the Buckner Hospital, Gainesville, Alabama, Fannie A. Beers, another matron, found a scarcity of hospital supplies and noticed "rooms crowded with uncomfortable-looking beds." Things were no better elsewhere. Kate Cumming was so distressed by the situation at Okolona, Mississippi, that she wrote: "If our government can not do better by the men who are suffering so much, I think we had better give up at once." She found some solace, however, in recalling "how much mismanagement of this kind there was in the British army at the commencement of the Crimean war," and she concluded that "it is not much to be wondered at if we, a people who have been living in peace so long, should commit errors at first." [3] In Chattanooga, rapidly becoming an important medical center of the Confederacy, "every spare building" was serving as a hospital.

In the summer of 1862 a special inspector gave official verification of the confused and disorganized state of the medical department in the West. He remarked on the lack of order or system in the hospitals behind the lines, spoke of the "almost utter hopelessness of adequate hospital arrangements," and advised "the distribution of the sick on plantations." The crowded conditions in the makeshift hospitals at Magnolia, Mississippi, and Ringgold, Georgia, in the late summer and early fall indicate that the situation had undergone no marked improvement.

[3] All of the Okolona churches were used as hospitals.

Improvement

Definite progress in the organization of a system of general hospitals was apparent, however, as 1862 neared its close. Hospital appropriations had been increased, adequate government facilities were now better able to care for the disabled, far-sighted legislation was being enacted by Congress, and the War Department was extending its control over all hospitals housing military personnel. Many of the small hospitals were shut down as the larger institutions favored by the Surgeon General were erected, thirty-five hospitals in Richmond alone being closed between September, 1862, and March, 1864.[4] The Robertson Hospital, managed by Sally L. Tompkins, avoided that fate only when Miss Tompkins gave convincing proof of her hospital's success in returning men to duty.

Hospital Center of the Confederacy and Chimborazo

General improvement continued during the year 1863 as significant general hospital arrangements were completed by the medical staff. In addition, numerous way hospitals had been established, and the medical service now appeared to be properly staffed for the trials ahead. From the standpoint of capacity and overall arrangement the most impressive hospitals in the South were located in Richmond. The Southern capital early became the chief medical center of the Confederacy, and the hospitals there were built under the watchful eye of the Surgeon General and with scrupulous regard for his convictions concerning hospital construction.[5]

[4] Hospitals with a capacity of less than one hundred patients were viewed with disfavor by the medical authorities.

[5] Charles S. Tripler, Medical Director of the Union Army of the Potomac, held the same preference for frame huts over large buildings as Moore. Declared Tripler: "They admit of more perfect ventilation, can be kept in better police, are more convenient for the sick and wounded and their attendants, admit of a ready distribution of patients into proper classes, and are cheaper."

Most famous of the Confederacy's hospitals was Chimborazo. This institution, erected on Chimborazo Heights overlooking the James River and opened on October 11, 1861, had a capacity of over eight thousand patients; it has been described as the largest military hospital in the history of this continent. Its site commanded an excellent view, an abundant supply of good water was readily available, and there was natural drainage on three sides. Chimborazo may properly be considered a hospital center, to use a modern term, inasmuch as it consisted of five separate hospitals or divisions; each hospital or division comprised thirty buildings or wards; and each building could accommodate from forty to sixty patients, whose bunks were arranged in several rows. Altogether, as additional construction took place, there were 150 buildings erected; each was 100 feet long, 30 feet wide, and one story high. Ventilation was afforded by doors and windows. A number of tents were pitched upon the surrounding slopes to which convalescent patients were assigned. Wide alleys or streets separated the various buildings, and the hospital had its own cemetery.

Five soup houses, five icehouses, Russian bathhouses, a bakery capable of making ten thousand loaves of bread daily, and a brewery in which four hundred kegs of beer were brewed at a time were also a part of the Chimborazo establishment. A large farm, "Tree Hill," owned by Franklin Stearns, was used by the hospital for the pasturage of some two hundred cows and from three hundred to five hundred goats. Hospital trading vessels operated between Richmond and Lynchburg and Lexington to obtain needed provisions.

The Secretary of War designated Chimborazo and its ground an independent army post, and James Brown McCaw was appointed its commandant and medical head.[6] Each di-

---

[6] James B. McCaw's grandfather, also a doctor, came to Virginia in 1771, received a captain's commission from Lord Dunmore, and was a Loyalist in the American Revolution. McCaw's father graduated from Edinburgh and served with American troops in the War of 1812. McCaw himself had three sons who became physicians; most famous was Walter Drew McCaw, the eldest, who became Chief Surgeon of the American

vision of the hospital had its surgeon in charge, directly responsible to McCaw, and the surgeons in charge supervised the work of some fifty assistant surgeons who were in charge of the various wards. The idea of arranging general hospitals into divisions managed independently by medical officers responsible only to the surgeon in charge appears to have been a distinctive feature of all the large hospitals in the Department of Virginia.

Other Richmond Hospitals

Another large institution located in the Confederate capital, whose organization and administration were similar to that of Chimborazo, was the Winder Hospital. Opened in April, 1862, the Winder extended over 125 acres of land, had a capacity of almost 5,000 patients, and consisted of six divisions, each headed by a medical officer. Its hospital facilities included "the most approved Russian, steam, plunge, and shower baths," water closets, a bakery, an icehouse, a sixteen-acre hospital garden worked by convalescents, and sixty-nine cows. Two canal boats were used to obtain additional food for the inmates. The youthful Alexander G. Lane, only twenty-seven years of age at the time of his appointment, directed the Winder establishment.

The Jackson Hospital, located about two miles above the city and opened in the summer of 1863, was a third large Richmond institution. Its wooden barracks were able to accommodate twenty-five hundred patients. Apparently well supplied with medicines and food, this hospital had water closets, two large icehouses, a large bakery, a hospital garden, and sixty cows. An official of the United States Sanitary Commission, reporting at the close of the war; gave the following favorable impression of the hospital: "Jackson Hospital, as established and conducted by the rebels, was excellent; in some respects,

Expeditionary Forces in World War I and attained the rank of brigadier general.

few military hospitals of our own surpass it. It was excellent in its general plan of organization; in its location and its arrangement of buildings; in its administration; in its thorough policing; in the exceeding cleanliness of its bedding, and in the very liberal provision made by the Rebel Government for the Hospital Fund."

Altogether there were twenty Confederate hospitals in Richmond after the medical situation there was brought under control. Forty-three surgeons, sixty-five assistant surgeons, and eighteen acting assistant surgeons were on duty in those hospitals early in 1864, and the patients, pursuant to provisions of the act of September 27, 1862, were assigned to hospitals containing other men from their native states. Chimborazo, for example, received the sick and wounded from Maryland, Virginia, Tennessee, Kentucky, and Missouri. Those from other states were apportioned among the Winder, Jackson, Howard's Grove, and Louisiana hospitals. Considerable progress had been made, and a Richmond visitor in the summer of 1863 observed that the hospital accommodations in and around the capital were "most perfect and ample for such of our sick and wounded soldiers as may be sent to this point." Echoing such praise was a Richmond newspaper's comment that the medical staff was "fast approaching perfection in the systematic arrangement of the various hospitals in and around the city."

Virginia Hospitals outside the Capital

There were several other large Virginia hospitals, notably the general hospitals at Danville and Charlottesville, but none was as carefully planned as the big Richmond institutions. Pavilion type hospitals were erected at Manassas, Petersburg, and a few other points; in general, however, the establishments consisted of both old buildings converted into hospital use and new structures especially built for such service. The Liberty General Hospital, for example, which had a capacity of about eight hundred patients and was the largest hospital on the Virginia and Tennessee Railroad, consisted in October, 1863, of four large tobacco factories, two big cabinet shops, one extensive brick building that formerly housed the Piedmont Institute, and two new buildings, one not quite completed, erected by Benjamin Blackford, the surgeon in charge. The older buildings were obtained for a monthly rental of $290, and their retention was recommended by Blackford partly on the basis that "it is much cheaper to rent the buildings . . . than to build new hospitals at the present prices of lumber." Construction costs no doubt acted as a deterrent to much new building. By January, 1864, there were twenty-nine Virginia hospitals located outside of Richmond, and these were staffed with fifty-six surgeons, fifty-seven assistant surgeons, and eight acting assistant surgeons.

Hospitals in the Carolinas and Florida

The hospitals established in North Carolina, South Carolina, and Florida, though usually not as large, appear to have resembled the Virginia institutions located outside the capital. In Raleigh, for example, the capacities of the three general hospitals located there, General Hospitals Nos. 7, 8, and 13, ranged from two hundred to four hundred patients. General Hospital No. 13, known as Pettigrew Hospital, was the only one especially built for hospital purposes, whereas General Hospitals Nos. 7 and 8 occupied structures at the fairgrounds and Peace Institute respectively. Pettigrew Hospital, directed by Surgeon Edmund Burke Haywood, was the largest. It was opened in the summer of 1864 and had a laundry, dispensary, bathhouse, guardhouse, and stable; the hospital was occupied, however, before its construction was completed. Some sixty medical officers were on duty in the general hospitals of the Carolinas and Florida at the beginning of 1864.[7]

[7] There were twelve important hospitals located in South Carolina in November, 1864; Florida had four.

The Georgia Hospitals and Samuel H. Stout

Outside of Virginia the greatest concentration of Confederate general hospitals was to be found in Georgia. Here were to be found after the Chattanooga-Chickamauga-Missionary Ridge campaign (June–November, 1863) fifty such institutions as compared to a total of twenty-six in Alabama and Mississippi. For the most part the Georgia hospitals, as well as some of those in the latter states, were under the direct supervision of Samuel Hollingsworth Stout of Tennessee, one of the most remarkable medical men of the Civil War; and the vast scope of his administration may perhaps be seen in the fact that early in 1864 he was in the process of increasing his hospital facilities to accommodate twelve thousand patients.

Stout received his medical degree from the University of Pennsylvania in 1848 and was practicing his profession in Giles County, Tennessee, at the beginning of the war. After entering the army he served successively as regimental surgeon, surgeon in charge of Nashville's Gordon Hospital, and post surgeon and medical director at Chattanooga before General Braxton Bragg, on March 28, 1863, assigned to him "the general superintendence of all hospitals which have been, or may hereafter be established in the District of the Tennessee, —which includes those at Chattanooga, Rome, Atlanta, and all intermediate points." Years after the war Stout recalled the general reaction to the news of his appointment: "When Genl. Bragg placed me in charge of all the hospitals of his department, I well remember the chagrin manifested by many medical men and professors of colleges from the cities, who unmistakably manifested their disappointment. Some I heard as saying 'Who in the hell is that fellow Stout?' Several personally asked me where I hailed from. I told them good humorously and with a gentle tone of sarcasm 'I had been living for more than a dozen years in a hollow beech tree in the backwoods of Giles County, Tenn.' . . ."

Stout was embarrassed somewhat after his appointment by

a subsequent order from Richmond which assigned him to duty as an inspector of general hospitals in General Bragg's army and by the Surgeon General's reference to him in that capacity. Complete official confirmation of his medical directorship was forthcoming, however, and the Surgeon General recognized that Stout was an exceptional administrator. Stout, perhaps more than any other medical officer of the Confederacy, recognized the importance of medical records and preserved material of his department to the time of his death.[8]

Stout's accomplishments at Chattanooga prior to the withdrawal of Confederate forces from that vital rail center were noteworthy. There he first made use of existing facilities: the Academy Hospital, for example, was established in the Masonic Female Institute of the city, and its initial capacity was increased from sixty-four to five hundred before the end of the summer of 1862. He also constructed a number of pavilion type buildings which he claimed were superior in arrangement to Chimborazo and described them as follows:

> The pavillion wards erected under my direction, were of such width that only two rows of bunks could be arranged or accommodated in them. The bunks were placed crosswise of the room, the head of each being from one and a half to two feet from the side wall. Thus, an aisle or vacant space of from eight to ten feet in width was left in the middle of the ward throughout its whole length. Sometimes the wards were built one above another. Near the floor, and just under the ceiling overhead, were longitudinal openings with sliding shutters one foot in width that could be closed or opened at the will of the surgeon in charge. Overhead, in the ceiling, were also openings with sliding shutters and latticed structures on the comb and in the gables, which were opened or closed as occasion required.

Stout prided himself on the mobility of his hospitals and criticized the deficiency of the Richmond hospitals in this respect. By the end of 1862 the hospitals under his control at Chatta-

[8] Stout wrote the Surgeon General of the United States twelve years after the war to ask whether or not funds had been appropriated "for the purpose of purchasing or collecting and collating valuable records, such as are in my possession. . . ."

nooga and Cleveland, Tennessee, and Tunnel Hill, Catoosa Springs, Dalton, Ringgold, Rome, and Atlanta, Georgia, could accommodate over 5,500 patients. Hospitals were not located in haphazard fashion. Medical officers were sent out to inspect various localities from the standpoints of health conditions, water supply, nearness to transportation facilities, agricultural productivity, and patriotic fervor on the part of the residents. As a result of the movements of Bragg's army, Stout had located all of his main hospitals in Georgia by the close of September, 1863—at Dalton, Kingston, Rome, Cassville, Marietta, Atlanta, Newnan, LaGrange, Griffin, and Forsyth. Stout calculated their aggregate capacity after the relocation to be about seven thousand. His emphasis on mobile hospitals had been well placed; when the Chattanooga hospitals—Academy, Foard, and Gilmer—were moved to Marietta, for example, their original organization remained unchanged.

Problems in the West

The casualties of the Army of Tennessee in the battles of Chickamauga and Missionary Ridge were so great that Stout was compelled to obtain additional hospital accommodations. Most of the buildings around the public square in Marietta were occupied, and nearly all of the large buildings, stores, and churches in Atlanta were utilized. At Americus a large brick structure, formerly used as a college, served as the Bragg Hospital's chief building. An entire square of stores, many of which were dilapidated, the courthouse, all of the churches except one, a women's college, and a number of tents provided hospitalization for the disabled at Newnan. The five-hundred-patient tent hospital at Cherokee Springs covered thirty acres of land on which there were numerous mineral springs and shady recesses; it had a fine bakery, plus ample kitchen and dining facilities. Covington's six hospitals made use of all the churches, "every little store," and a women's college. Fannie A. Beers described Fort Valley as "a pleasant and very hospitable town, where new and excellent hospital buildings had been erected."

As a consequence of the frequent necessary movement of the hospitals behind the Army of Tennessee, and the many bloody battles engaged in by that army, Medical Director Stout and his officers were compelled from time to time—as was seen above—to obtain buildings for the disabled at points where facilities were being established or extended, and to acquire them in a hurry. Many owners of buildings desired were understandably loath to give them up, however, and Stout felt that impressment of the property was the only alternative in such instances. "You have no idea what a time we have had getting possession of buildings which have been impressed for hospital purposes . . . ," wrote the surgeon in charge of the Marietta hospitals. "They are great people here to send up requisitions asking that their houses be spared," he added, "thereby losing much time in moving out." At LaGrange, another surgeon informed Stout that he was meeting "with a considerable opposition in procuring two of the buildings selected": the Methodist school and a hotel. Finding it mandatory to request six private buildings to replace those of the S. P. Moore Hospital destroyed by fire in Griffin, the surgeon in charge at that place reported that he had been unable to possess these buildings "peaceably" and asked for additional authority. Stout himself, in an endorsement of this letter, stated that "illiberality and opposition of occupants of buildings has forced me to take many inferior and inappropriate buildings." [9]

That considerable bitterness was generated by the government's requisition of private buildings may be illustrated by the case of Surgeon James Mercer Green, the medical officer in charge of the Macon hospitals. At that city Green was prevented by court action from taking possession of the Planter's

---

[9] Ministers sometimes opposed the use of churches as hospitals. Kate Cumming tells of an Atlanta minister who delivered a good sermon on the "glories of heaven, but spoiled it by saying, with bitterness, that there would be no taking churches there for hospitals."

Hotel, and according to his account of the matter, the judge "went out of his way to say that we could not take the Female College. . . ." Green's anger may be seen in the concluding passages of his report to Stout: "I want these people to have some little of the burdens of the war as well as all its profits. It is disgusting to see the contemptuous indifference & even hatred that many of these wealthy foreigners & Yankees & some disloyal men of Southern birth have to everything concerning the soldiers, Hospitals, etc. I desire most sincerely to learn some of these men their duties to the Govt. that protects them." It appears that "some of these men" failed to learn "their duties" inasmuch as Green, who was a native of Macon, faced court action after the war for impressing a private residence. On the other hand many examples of self-sacrificing patriotism could be cited. The same surgeon who complained of public opposition at Marietta, for example, was met with so much kindness at Forsyth when he moved his organization there that he was led to believe "there is life in the old land yet. I am much pleased with the spirit manifested by this community," he concluded, "& I have found a disposition on the part of the Post Officers & citizens to cooperate heartily in making arrangements to care for my sick & wounded."

Despite the opposition sometimes manifested by the people to the Medical Department's impressment of their buildings for hospital purposes, Stout himself advised Surgeon General Moore in October, 1863, that his chief problems in closing, moving, and reopening hospitals stemmed from "the want of prompt, active and zealous co-operation" on the part of the Commissary and Quartermaster Departments. "When hospitals are removed," Stout reported, "it is often the case that they are for weeks without aid from these departments. The ingenuity and resources of the surgeons are taxed largely in supplying their wants. Considering [the] amount of work done by them recently and the good condition of the hospitals," Stout concluded, "much credit is due to the indefatigable energy of the medical department, which with all its deficiencies can justly claim to be under better discipline and better

organized than any of the staff departments of this army."
The failure of the Confederate government to do something
toward resolving the problems pointed out by Stout was responsible to a considerable extent for his difficulties in the
summer of 1864, much more serious than those in 1863, and
the inability of the medical officers to provide proper accommodations and treatment for the Army of Tennessee's sick and
wounded. Failure of the Quartermaster Department to supply
hospital tents requested by the medical service, for example,
compelled Stout to house the disabled troops wherever shelter
could be found. "To state that the men have been jostled about
from place to place until their lives, in many instances, have
been dragged out of them," reported Medical Inspector Edward N. Covey in September, 1864, "that the hospitals have
been terribly crowded; that Gangrene is very much on the
increase; that a large amount of Hospital property has been
lost; that, at this moment, most of the sick and wounded of
this Department, are being treated in buildings entirely unfit
for the purpose is to state only a few pertinent facts. . . ."

Evidence indicates that at least in some instances the sick
and wounded in Stout's department were assigned to hospitals
or wards containing other men from their states, pursuant to
the act of September 27, 1862. In Atlanta, Fair Ground Hospital No. 1 received Tennessee troops, Fair Ground Hospital
No. 2 those from Mississippi, the Medical College Hospital
those from Alabama, the Gate City Hospital those from Kentucky and Florida, and the Empire Hospital those from
Georgia and the Carolinas. A later directive ordered that, if
able to bear transportation, the Texas disabled should be sent
to the Texas Hospital in Auburn, Alabama, and those from
Florida and Kentucky to Newnan, Georgia. Stout let it be
known, however, that the "nature of the case and the ability
of the patient to bear transportation are the chief considera-
tions in assigning men to particular hospitals." Georgia
militiamen apparently preferred their own state hospitals to
those of the Confederacy, whatever the arrangements made.

Praise of Stout's Hospitals

Stout's administrative problems were made more difficult of course by the need to move his hospitals from time to time, but the institutions under his control received frequent praise from inspecting officers and other contemporaries. A medical officer visiting Atlanta in the early fall of 1863 reported that he was highly gratified "to witness the general comfort afforded to the patients at the Hospitals, and the favorable progress of most of the cases. The percentages of mortality among the wounded," he stated, "have been surprising [sic] small, and there are not a large number that would indicate a fatal result." Atlanta was an important medical center, and the Fair Grounds Hospitals there were built and operated in a manner similar to that of Chimborazo, Winder, and Jackson in Richmond.[10] The general condition of the hospitals at Dalton, Kingston, and Rome late in 1863 was commended in a comprehensive inspection report after a tour of all the institutions located at those points.

A contemporary newspaper account of the four Macon hospitals, which registered over five thousand patients for a twelve-month period beginning in April, 1863, was also highly complimentary. "We are happy to be able to state from our own investigation," ran the account, "that the Hospitals established in this city . . . are all that the warmest friend of soldier and the most tender philanthropist could desire or expect. We visited each of the four Hospitals in the city and were shown the various departments, from the ward rooms and dispensaries, to the laundries and the kitchens, and found every provision made, and every effort exerted, to make the inmates comfortable and contented. . . . We can assure those who may have friends or relatives in the Hospitals of Macon, that they are as well cared for, and as attentively nursed, as could

[10] Stout was told by Tobias G. Richardson, medical inspector on General Bragg's staff, that none of the Richmond hospitals surpassed those at Marietta from "a domestic point of view" and "in feeding you are infinitely superior."

be desired. As for ourselves we would rather board in any of them than in nine-tenths of the first class Hotels in the country." A brief description of the Ocmulgee Hospital in Macon is perhaps illustrative of most in this area. This institution, located on the banks of the Ocmulgee River, was housed in four buildings which along with the lot rented for $2,700 per year. New construction made it possible by the summer of 1864 for Surgeon Stanford E. Chaillé, the medical officer in charge, to accommodate comfortably five hundred patients in what he pronounced "a No. 1 Hospl." There is no question but that Stout's hospitals compared very favorably with those elsewhere. "The management of your Department so far as I can at present judge," a high ranking medical inspector apprised Stout early in the spring of 1864, "is far superior to that of any other in the Confederacy."

Hospitals of the Gulf Area

Hospitals of the Gulf states appear generally to have been established in buildings used previously for other purposes. Montgomery with six Confederate hospitals, within Stout's jurisdiction, and Mobile with five, administered by Medical Director J. F. Heustis, together had almost half of the institutions in this area. That these establishments were not large ones is evidenced by the fact that the overall capacity of the Montgomery hospitals, which were under the immediate control of Surgeon W. M. Gentry, was only 1,350 patients. The general hospital at Eufaula had only thirty-six beds and was apparently in a disorganized state when Surgeon Paul De Lacy Baker took charge of it in February, 1864. As a matter of fact, Phoebe Pember of Richmond's Chimborazo Hospital visited a number of hospitals in the Gulf area and concluded that they "did not compare with those I had left in Virginia, either in arrangement, cleanliness or attendance." On the other hand, the Blind Asylum Hospital in Jackson, Mississippi, was described by a Confederate surgeon as "a neat and airy building, properly shaded and ventilated, and furnished with an abundance of good cistern water." [11]

Plans for Further Construction

Surgeon General Moore undoubtedly planned additional hospital construction and hoped to establish centers that would provide more effectively for the care of the sick and wounded. At the March 26, 1864, meeting of the Association of Army and Navy Surgeons he appointed James B. McCaw to prepare a report on the site and construction of military hospitals, and shortly afterwards he asked Stout for carefully executed drawings of all the hospitals in his department. The proper proportion of patients to cubic capacity; necessary hygienic measures to ensure rapid recovery; origin, communication, prevention, and cure of infectious maladies peculiar to military hospitals; and the employment of disinfectants were some of the hospital problem's aspects that particularly interested the Surgeon General. Needless to say, the nomadic character of the medical organization in Stout's area made the matter of hospital construction one of constant concern.

The Closing of Hospitals in the East

Actually, the early months of 1864 witnessed the closing of certain hospitals in the East. In Richmond, Chimborazo morning reports for January showed that only 578 sick and wounded were receiving treatment in that institution, and Mc-

[11] W. G. Stevenson, who later fled to the North, asserted that he had charge of a hospital in Selma, Alabama, which was housed in a large female seminary. There, he wrote, "Wines, jellies, strawberries, cakes, flowers, were always abundant, served by beautiful women, with the most bewitching smiles." In Vicksburg, according to an observer, "some of the most elegant residences" were converted into hospitals. Kate Cumming praised very highly the Medical College Hospital in Atlanta, the Blind School Hospital in Macon, and the Levert, Ross, and Cantey hospitals in Mobile.

Caw was directed to transfer those to one division and to discharge all matrons whose services were not essential. Simultaneously, the Surgeon General ordered the temporary closing of General Hospital No. 1 and the Winder and Howard's Grove institutions; their patients were to be transferred to the Chimborazo and Jackson establishments; matrons were to be retained and arrangements were to be made whereby Negro workers could be returned when required; in the meantime every alternate building was to be dismantled and rebuilt in a nearby pine grove to provide better ventilation and reduce the possibility of fire.[12] A request of General Lee in February that still more hospitals be closed so that detailed nurses might be released for field service brought forth a sharp protest from the Surgeon General to the Secretary of War.[13]

The Campaign of 1864 and Its Effects

The military campaign of 1864 opened, in the East, with the sanguinary battles of the Wilderness and Spotsylvania (May 5–12), and on May 18 Medical Director William A. Carrington notified the Secretary of War that the hospitals then open were "insufficient." Two days later Carrington advised Quartermaster General Alexander R. Lawton that he was "much pressed" for hospital space, stated his preference for using tent hospitals rather than reopening the factories, and informed Lawton that more were "imperatively required." On May 24 Carrington reported almost eighteen thousand sick and wounded in Virginia hospitals, and the situation was such, he explained, that he was operating with ninety fewer medical officers than allowed by Moore's orders. In a communication to the Quartermaster Department on May 27, Carrington asserted that lumber to increase the capacity of the

[12] A fire at Winder Hospital on January 21, 1864, destroyed seven wards, a loss estimated to be at least $50,000.

[13] In April, 1864, Phoebe Pember wrote that General Bragg, then serving in Richmond, had been closing hospitals and "dispersing all the corps just when the spring campaign is about to begin."

Jackson and Howard's Grove hospitals must be furnished "immediately."

After the battle of Cold Harbor (June 3) orders were issued to crowd hospitals beyond their usual capacity and to bivouac in appropriate areas around them those men who were not seriously sick or wounded. There was also some impressment of needed buildings on important railroad junctions. Extensive Federal cavalry operations throughout Virginia caused concern for hospitals lying in the path of these forays, but, in general, such hospitals seem to have been respected by the enemy. Medical officers in charge of hospitals located in areas threatened by occupation were instructed not to vacate them, but to send off those patients who were only slightly disabled and as many Negro attendants as could be spared. "Only in cases where Hospitals have been wholly or in part vacated," advised Carrington, "have they been plundered or burned." [14]

The battle of Cold Harbor was the last large-scale engagement between Lee and Grant, and the hospital emergency in Virginia caused by the heavy casualties of the entire Wilderness campaign seems to have passed by the latter part of July, 1864. By that time there was no longer any necessity for crowding Richmond hospitals beyond their normal capacities. In the meantime, Grant, unable to overcome Lee's forces north of the capital, moved his entire army below the James River (June 12–16) and laid siege to the Confederate positions at Petersburg. When Lee transferred his army there he requested that the Petersburg hospitals be closed and all their occupants removed. Three hospitals—the Confederate States, the West End Park, and the Central Pavilion—remained open, however, to care for the casualties that came in daily, but the Central Pavilion was closed after the battle of the Crater (July 30). Thereafter the hospital situation in this area remained

[14] Benjamin Blackford, Confederate surgeon, believed that the Wayside Hospital at Liberty, Virginia, destroyed during a raid, was deliberately fired by the enemy. One of the Chimborazo Hospital canal boats was captured by some of Sheridan's raiders, and its cargo, mostly food and clothing valued at $58,889, was burned.

relatively unchanged until the Confederate collapse in April, 1865.[15]

As Grant moved against Lee south of the Rapidan River in May, 1864, William Tecumseh Sherman led his Army of the Cumberland against the forces of Joseph E. Johnston, based at Dalton, Georgia. The Atlanta hospitals were moved downstate to Macon in view of Johnston's steady though skillful retreat toward the Georgia capital, and a serious emergency occurred as a result of the battles around the city (July 20–22) and its subsequent occupation by Sherman's troops. Heavy Confederate casualties and the movement of the Georgia hospitals south of a line running generally from Augusta to West Point led to "squatting them in little towns, where every available house from a common grocery to the town church," was utilized, most of them "entirely unfit for the treatment of the sick and wounded." Hundreds of the disabled were sent to Alabama hospitals, and the seriousness of the situation in the latter may be seen in the report of the surgeon in charge of the hospital at Eufaula that he had for the arriving patients "no pans, no tubs, no spittoons, no medicines, no nurses, no ward masters, no adequate medical assistance, no hospital clothing," and consequently was "simply unable properly to discharge the obligation imposed upon me." Worse confusion, however, lay ahead.

Near Disintegration of the Hospital System in the West

When General John B. Hood, who had taken over Johnston's command on July 17, launched his invasion of Tennessee in November, a number of the hospitals in Georgia and Alabama were transferred by Stout to northern Mississippi upon the request of Hood's medical director that hospitals be established at Iuka, Corinth, and suitable points on the Mobile and Ohio Railroad. Transportation breakdowns, however, and the

[15] Normal operations, it seems, continued to the end. Plans were under way to reduce the size of certain hospitals and enlarge others.

overall turmoil naturally associated with an army's retreat almost disrupted the hospital service. In less than thirty days Surgeon William P. Harden, in charge of the Empire Hospital at Macon, Georgia, was ordered to move his organization from Macon to Tuscumbia, Alabama, from Tuscumbia to Corinth, Mississippi, from Corinth to Meridian, and from Meridian to Opelika, Alabama. Among the incidents that befell Harden was that which occurred at Demopolis, Alabama, where "a car heavily laden with drugs, Hospital Stores, and a portion of the Laundry was precipitated from an embankment twenty feet high and crushed, killing the steward, and one of the attendants and injuring or destroying much of the Hospital property. . . ." Even Stout felt that his department could "be of but little service to the army," and Medical Director A. J. Foard of the Army of Tennessee wrote Stout that "Everything is as clear as mud." After criticizing the latter for the location of the hospitals, he summed up the turn of events: "The poor sick and wounded are calling on the doctors for help when there is no help—for they are rendered powerless—and the officials are abusing the doctors for not being omnipotent" and "omnipresent. . . ."

There was a certain resiliency about these doctors in gray, however, and a deep devotion to duty. Despite the near chaotic conditions, Surgeon William Lytle Nichol in Cuthbert, Georgia, was anxious to get his buildings up and bring his smallpox cases under control. Surgeon Dudley D. Saunders, at Auburn, Alabama, was still in a fighting mood in April, 1865, and thought that the legislators of that state "deserve to be hung" for not having done more to prevent the capture of Montgomery. The much-traveled William P. Harden was on the road with his hospital again that same month; he was directed to establish a "Way Side Home" in Atlanta. And from West Point, Georgia, on April 27, Surgeon John Wimbish Oslin, in charge of the Reid Hospital, reported as follows to his medical director: ". . . I am reorganizing as rapidly as possible, will soon be under full sail again. Have plenty of provision for several months to come. . . ."

Difficulties in the East

Joseph E. Johnston, back at the head of the Army of Tennessee, attempted to stop Sherman's drive across the Carolinas and in this region, as was the case further west, it became increasingly difficult to care for the army's disabled troops, many of whom were sent to general hospitals without proper arrangements having been made for their reception. Peter E. Hines, medical director of North Carolina's hospitals, attempted to make all necessary preparations for Johnston's men, but he was compelled to admit that he was not able to provide for them because of "the want of straw for beds and lumber for fitting up houses for hospital purposes." [16] Medical officers did the best they could in a situation made almost hopeless by the deteriorating military situation, and here as elsewhere considerable ingenuity was often displayed. The youthful Simon Baruch, for example, related the following account of his experience at Thomasville, North Carolina, where he had been sent to prepare hospital accommodations:

> . . . with the help of some half duty men I had built a bakeoven and cleaned out some factories and a hotel, when I received a telegram announcing that 280 wounded from the battle of Averysboro were on the way to Thomasville. I immediately sent out an armed guard to bring all the men and large boys to headquarters, impressed them with the fact that they must assist me in my necessarily hasty preparations. I commandeered two wagons, put two men on each, sent one to gather pine straw, the other to gather pine knots. I commandeered a large number cf girls from a female college to fill the straw sacks I had prepared. I went personally from house to house and obtained assistance from the women in baking bread and preparing rye coffee and bacon for the expected wounded. Next I had piles of pine knots placed in front of the buildings which, when lighted, illuminated the town so that when the train arrived the wounded could be

[16] The lack of adequate accommodations evidently was the cause of much suffering at Salisbury.

comfortably unloaded into the factories and two churches which I had also emptied of pews, etc. . . .[17]

Lee's surrender made any further improvisation unnecessary.

Conclusion

Thus, after an early period of confusion that was characterized by the lack of proper hospital facilities, a Confederacy-wide program of hospital organization spearheaded by Surgeon General Samuel P. Moore and such able medical directors as William A. Carrington and Samuel H. Stout was established that went far toward meeting the needs of the armed forces. The failing fortunes of the Confederacy in the closing months of the war reacted adversely upon the hospital system, but the Confederate surgeon, aided by the volunteer work of many men, women, and children, struggled against powerful odds to supply the sick and wounded with satisfactory hospital accommodations.

[17] Receiving and distributing hospitals were set up in Raleigh's churches and other available buildings to handle the incoming patients. Rations drawn for these men were for a time prepared by ladies in the city.

CHAPTER V

Administration of General Hospitals

Problems of Administration

*T*he confusion, so noticeable with respect to the establishment of hospitals in the early part of the Civil War, was also apparent in certain matters that affected their efficient operation. Particularly conspicuous was the confusion regarding hospital control and hospital attendants.

Authority over the Hospitals

General hospitals were located in centers such as Richmond, Atlanta, and Montgomery where there were local commanding officers. From the beginning the extent of the local commander's authority over hospitals within the limits of his post excited controversy, but it was not until October 28, 1862, that a directive which dealt with this problem was issued. This directive, a general order issued by the Adjutant and Inspector General's Office, placed general hospitals under the authority of the local commanders; it recommended, however, that the hospitals and their medical officers be left to the management of the surgeons in charge of such institutions. Soldiers in the hospitals were of course under sole authority of the medical officers in charge. Friction between the latter and the local commanders nevertheless continued to exist. Surgeon William Lytle Nichol, in charge of the Rome hospitals in Georgia, was actually placed under arrest for refusing to obey a special order of the post regarding civilian personnel. And Surgeon Dudley D. Saunders at Marietta was embarrassed because the commandant at that post, a native of Louisiana, manifested "a disposition to pander to the whims of the troops from his state." Saunders found this situation "detrimental to good order & Discipline in the hospitals" and "disagreeable. . . ."

There was at first also a very imperfect chain of command in the general hospital organization. Hospital surgeons received orders from the Surgeon General, medical directors of armies, and line officers in the field. Moreover, assignment orders issued by generals in the field sometimes conflicted with those issued from Richmond. Such a situation was hardly conducive to efficiency, and, according to Medical Director Samuel H. Stout, it was General Braxton Bragg who was responsible for inaugurating a more satisfactory system. In July, 1862, Bragg appointed Stout Superintendent of Hospitals in the Department of Tennessee, and A. J. Foard, Medical Director of the Army of Tennessee, was relieved thereby of that responsibility. According to Stout "The happy working of his [Bragg's] policy touching the hospitals suggested the appointment by the War Department of Medical Directors of Hospitals. . . . The Surgeon General had never thought of it before. In undertaking to control all the general hospitals . . . from his office in Richmond, he had . . . 'over-cropped himself.' " Stout's remarks cannot be discounted because it was on March 12, 1863, that the order was issued which placed general hospitals "under the supervision and control of medical directors" chosen especially for such purpose and forbade interference with such arrangement. As a result of this directive there were eight medical directors of hospitals serving the Confederacy in the fall of 1864, and the chain of command ran directly from the Surgeon General to those officers and from them to the surgeons in charge of general hospitals.

The Problem of Attendants

It was also necessary to revise the program undertaken early in the war for the purpose of obtaining hospital attendants. At first most of the attendants were enlisted men

71

or volunteers, many of whom were temporarily incapacitated for field service. Frequent changes naturally resulted as these were returned to regular duty, and on August 21, 1861, Congress authorized the employment, when necessary to care for the sick and wounded, "of nurses and cooks, other than enlisted men, or volunteers, the persons so employed being subject to military control, and in no case to receive pay above that allowed to enlisted men, or volunteers."

The hiring of hospital attendants, white and black, pursuant to the law of August 21, 1861, did not improve markedly the quality of such workers. Appropriations for their services were not large, and no provision had yet been made for hospital matrons. Kate Cumming contended that she had to spend more time supervising her new Negro attendants than she did in working with detailed soldiers, although Surgeon James B. McCaw asserted in May, 1862, that it would be "impossible to continue the Hospitals" without the 256 slaves employed at Chimborazo. Actually there is little reason to believe that Negro attendants were more inefficient than white workers, and their services were deemed necessary throughout the entire war. Medical Director William A. Carrington did assert, however, that Negro "wenches" were "one of the greatest pests and nuisances" about a hospital.[1] Competent nurses were simply hard to find. Most of those in general hospitals continued to be men on temporary duty, lacking previous experience, and their ministrations left much to be desired. A medical officer at Danville, Virginia, in July, 1862, described his nurses as "rough country crackers who have not enough sense to be kind." He returned one nurse to the field because he had cursed a patient. Two months later the same officer, then in Gordonsville, Virginia, asserted that he had "miserable nurses" who did not "know castor oil from a gun rod nor laudanum from a hole in the ground." Meantime, a special committee of the Provisional Congress, after investigating the Medical Department, recommended in its report of January 29, 1862, that a corps of nurses be established. "Good nurs-

---

[1] Many of the slaves in hospitals were hired by the year.

ing," the committee maintained, "is of equal value to medical attention."

The Act of September, 1862

Definite improvement finally came about after Congress in September, 1862, passed "An act to better provide for the sick and wounded of the army in hospitals." This law provided for the allotment to each hospital, "with rations and suitable places of lodging," two matrons, two assistant matrons, two matrons for each ward, such other nurses and cooks as might be needed, and a ward master for each ward, "giving preference in all cases to females where their services may best subserve the purpose." It was generally recognized by this time that women made better nurses than men and acted also as boosters of the morale of hospitalized troops. Skillful service was rendered by the Catholic sisterhoods—to whom belonged the only really trained nurses in the South—to the inmates of such hospitals as the St. Francis DeSailes and the Louisiana in Richmond, but their number was small.[2] Other patriotic women, though less well-trained, set up a number of hospitals, and the low mortality rates therein were rather convincing proof of feminine superiority in nursing. It was in cognizance of this fact, and with high hopes that many women would come forward, that the law stipulated a preference for women as hospital attendants. Quite a few did accept appointments, but the prevailing opinion that fulltime service in hospitals was not respectable work for women undoubtedly acted as a deterrent in keeping many from taking up this important work.[3]

[2] Unofficial Southern headquarters for the Sisters of Charity was Richmond. From here they were sent on various missions.

[3] When Kate Cumming was matron in a Chattanooga hospital during the fall of 1862, she wrote: "There is a good deal of trouble about the ladies in some of the hospitals of this department. Our friends here have advised us to go home, as they say it is not considered respectable to go into one."

Hospital Personnel

Following the passage of the above mentioned act, each hospital was staffed, in addition to medical officers, with stewards, matrons, assistant matrons, ward matrons, nurses, cooks, laundresses, and other miscellaneous workers. Their duties were many.

The medical officer in charge of each general hospital was responsible for the efficient administration of his institution. He was to receive patients, distribute them to the proper wards, visit them as often as necessary each day, and "enforce the proper hospital regulations to promote health and prevent contagion." Included among the records he was required to maintain was a register of patients, a prescription and diet book, a case book, copies of all requisitions, annual returns, and an order and letter book. Numerous reports had to be prepared for higher authority. A list set forth by a hospital steward at Lynchburg in 1863 gives some idea of what was expected. Two daily reports were demanded: a morning report and a transcript of all admissions and discharges. Weekly reports included a report of sick and wounded, a statement of the hospital fund, and a report concerning admissions and deaths in the hospital to the Army Intelligence Office, an agency set up to obtain such information for the benefit of friends and relatives. The monthly reports had to do with the sick and wounded, surgical cases, return of medical officers, return of hospital stewards, return of hospital attendants, detailed men examined and returned to duty, requisitions for hospital supplies, receipts for hospital supplies, and a statement of the hospital fund.

It was sometimes pointed out that surgeons in charge of general hospitals were so encumbered with executive duties that they were unable to administer in a professional way to the sick and wounded.[4] The personal testimony of John H. Claiborne, surgeon in charge of the Petersburg hospitals dur-

---

[4] Some believed that each hospital should have a responsible executive officer to administer the institution. Such positions, it was thought, should

ing the siege of that city, lends support to such assertions. According to Claiborne, "After the arrival of Lee's army my duties as senior or executive officer were greatly increased, and my position was neither safe nor a sinecure. From the first day of the occupation of the city to the last, I had no further opportunity of taking a knife in my hand or of administering a dose of physic. . . ." Usually, however, there was a lull in activity after the summer campaigning, and senior surgeons occasionally took that opportunity to visit other hospitals in their quest for improved methods of treatment and administrative efficiency.

Each general hospital was allowed, in addition to the surgeon in charge, one medical officer or contract physician to every seventy or eighty patients. These officers were under the jurisdiction of the surgeon in charge and aided in enforcing the hospital regulations. Illustrative of the difficulty in maintaining an exact ratio is the statement of John Grammar Brodnax, head of Petersburg's Second North Carolina Hospital, that he and an assistant were caring for four hundred patients in the summer of 1862.

Hospital stewards were authorized by Congress in an act of May 16, 1861. They received their appointments from the Secretary of War upon recommendation of the Surgeon General and held the rank of sergeant. Appointees were to be skilled in pharmacy and to possess such qualities as honesty, reliability, intelligence, and temperance.[5] Medical regulations made the steward "responsible for the cleanliness of the wards and kitchens, patients and attendants, and all articles in use." He was also the custodian of the hospital stores, and as such he prepared the provision returns and received and distributed the rations. "The Steward is the machine of a Hospital," wrote one who held this position. "All matters, all requisitions, orders, etc. come to me for approval or disapproval."

---

be accorded sufficient rank and salary to attract men possessed of administrative ability.

[5] Not all met these standards. John G. Brodnax reported that a steward in his institution treated the ladies with disrespect and encouraged insubordination among the Negro servants.

The two matrons allowed by the law of September 27, 1862, were "to exercise a superintendence over the entire domestic economy of the hospital, to take charge of such delicacies as may be provided for the sick, to apportion them out as required, to see that the food or diet is properly prepared," and to perform "all such other duties as may be necessary." Assistant matrons, also two in number, were charged with the supervision of the hospital laundry and the care of patients' clothing. The two ward matrons authorized for each ward of one hundred patients were responsible for the preparation and cleanliness of beds in the ward, for ascertaining that the food was prepared carefully and furnished to the sick, for seeing that medicines were administered, and for assuring that all patients received needed attention.[6] Ward masters, in addition to being responsible for the effects of the patients, received the furniture, bedding, cooking utensils, and other property from the steward and maintained all necessary records therefor. The duties of nurses, cooks, laundresses, and other such attendants are self-explanatory.

Return of Able-Bodied Nurses to the Field

Provision was made in the act of September 27, 1862 for the permanent detail of soldiers as nurses and ward masters in case a sufficient number of these attendants could not be obtained outside the military service.[7] Since the number of workers obtainable proved to be inadequate a large number of soldiers was serving continuously in the capacity of hospital attendants. There were, for example, 164 soldiers employed at Chimborazo early in 1863. It was widely believed, however, that such men should be in the field if they were able to bear arms,

[6] Matrons were sometimes subjected to unusual and embarrassing experiences. Phoebe Pember complained that a patient in her division at Chimborazo insisted upon "pulling off all his clothes" every time she entered his ward.
[7] Medical directives authorized hospital surgeons in Virginia to apply for the detail of enlisted men almost a year before the passage of this act.

and a general order issued by the Adjutant and Inspector General's Office, dated July 8, 1863, recommended that "as far as practicable," able-bodied soldiers fit for field service be relieved by men unfit for such duty. This order was implemented by directives from the Surgeon General's office, one of which required monthly examinations of all enlisted men detailed for hospital duty and the return to their commands of all "not positively disqualified for field service. Another stipulated that, except for hospital stewards, "no able-bodied white man between the ages of 17 and 45 or detailed soldiers fit for field duty, will be retained in any capacity in or about hospitals, but will be returned to their commands if soldiers, or turned over to Conscript Officers if liable to conscription."

Examining boards found quite a few potential nurses and ward masters among the disabled applicants for furloughs and discharges, but hospital surgeons were exceedingly loath to give up men who had become inured to some of the mysteries of nursing. Surgeon Edmund Burke Haywood, who had charge of General Hospital No. 7 in Raleigh, stated the case in a succinct protest to Surgeon General Moore. Wrote Haywood: "It will be impossible to keep a hospital in fine order and the patients well cared for with broken down disabled men. Nurses who are detailed on account of permanent disability know that they are not likely to be returned to the field, and therefore do not exert themselves to please. They are generally . . . discontented at being detailed . . . instead of being furloughed or discharged. . . . A nurse who is liable to be removed to duty in the field, for disobedience or neglect of duty, is much more easily managed and ten times as efficient. A disabled man cannot lift the sick, carry out the beds, scour the floor or sit up at night, or do many other things which are necessary in a well conducted hospital. . . ." Numerous other surgeons, such as Benjamin Miller Wible and Robert Battey, located at Tunnel Hill and Atlanta, Georgia, respectively, referred to the seriousness of this problem.

Meantime, charges continued to be made that the hospitals were filled with troops able to undergo service in the field, and, early in 1863, an inspector of hospitals in the Army of Tennessee reported that surgeons in charge of hospitals were being "insulted by officers coming with very sweeping orders . . . taking all detailed men, thereby virtually disorganizing the Hospitals." From Americus, Georgia, over a year later, Kate Cumming wrote that an examining board was returning to the field men who were laboring under serious physical handicaps. "If we can not do without such men," she opined, "I think the country is badly off indeed."

General Lee's need for manpower late in the war was so acute that, early in 1864, he requested authority from the Secretary of War to send an examining commission of surgeons to the hospitals. A commission was finally established on September 14 of that year and instructed to make an inspection of the Virginia and North Carolina hospitals "with authority to return to the field all detailed men and patients fit for duty." It is not known how many men the commission returned to the field, but soon after its tour of inspection hospital surgeons were being asked by the Surgeon General why they had retained certain men found physically fit by the commission. S. S. Satchwell, in charge of General Hospital No. 2 in Wilson, North Carolina, pointed out that one of the men pronounced fit by the inspectors was not even able to get to the depot. Hospital surgeons were understandably exasperated by intrusions of this kind, but it was hardly to be expected, at this critical time, that those who might be useful at the front would be allowed to remain in the hospitals.

Activities of Patients

Hospital patients, in addition to serving as attendants, were active in many other ways. Convalescents gathered medicinal plants, tended hospital gardens, worked on fortifications during emergencies, and were not infrequently assigned to temporary duty as guards for hospitals and medical depots. With respect to guard service, late in the war the Surgeon General advised medical directors that "Soldiers who have lost their left hand or arm, and otherwise healthy, but who are incompetent to perform clerical duty, can, in the use of a pistol, act as efficient guards for Hospitals and Purveying depots." He thought that the guard could be made up largely of such men.

Convalescents were also organized along with the hospital attendants into military companies and were expected to aid in the defense of the post if necessary. In May, 1863, three hundred such patients from Winder Hospital were armed and ordered to defensive positions along the James River; and a year later the Chimborazo head was advised that the convalescents there would be "subject to duty for local defence at the discretion of the military authorities." When an enemy force appeared before Wilson, North Carolina, Surgeon S. S. Satchwell asserted that "the citizens flew to their trunks and wardrobes, the militia flew to the woods, and the 'Hospital Defenders' . . . composed of the halt and the maimed and the blind, of those who had divers miseries in the bowels, in the back, and especially in the breast, flew to arms—to rally in defense of their bunks, their rations . . . and all they hold dear (and what is there not dear now?)" Fortunately perhaps this invincible band was not tested under fire due to the withdrawal of the enemy.[8]

Similar developments took place in the hospitals back of the Army of Tennessee. In Macon, two companies of attendants and convalescents were activated near the close of 1864, one from the two Fair Ground institutions and one from Polk Institute and Empire hospitals. Surgeon Dudley D. Saunders organized six companies on his post at Auburn, Alabama, but he was afraid the enemy might not respect hospitals in the future if he placed a fellow medical officer in command. Convalescents from the Buckner and Bragg hospitals in Newnan,

[8] In July, 1863, Satchwell also congratulated the surgeon in charge of the general hospital at nearby Goldsboro upon "the brilliant successes, achieved in behalf of Goldsboro and Southern Independence by the 'Hospital Invincibles' under your command."

Georgia, actually participated in a clash with Federals near that hospital center shortly after the fall of Atlanta.[9]

The Hospital Ration

One of the most important aspects of hospital administration was that of providing the sick and wounded troops with a sufficient amount of nourishing food. The act of September 27, 1862, passed by Congress to better provide for the occupants of army hospitals, fixed the commutation value of rations for these men at $1. A so-called hospital fund was thus established, and the Subsistence Department was charged with transferring the commuted portion of this fund to the surgeon in charge of the hospital. The surgeon in charge used the fund to purchase supplies that were not furnished by the Subsistence Department. When a hospital fund exceeded $5,000 the amount in excess of that figure was to be deposited in the Confederate Treasury or some other depository for government moneys. Surgeons were to keep careful records to show the use that had been made of the hospital fund.

Subsequent legislation increased the commutation value of rations for the sick and wounded. An act of May 1, 1863, fixed the amount at $1.25 and extended the law's application to include all disabled troops "whether in hospitals or other places, used in camp or in the field as hospitals." In a law approved on February 15, 1864, Congress raised the amount to $2.50, and on June 14, 1864, the lawmakers fixed the value at "the government cost of said rations, and one hundred per centum thereon: Provided, That said one hundred per centum on the government cost of each ration commuted shall constitute a hospital fund, and be drawn and appropriated as the Secretary of War

[9] Major A. H. Cole, Inspector-General, Field Transportation, made the interesting proposal to General A. C. Myers, the Quartermaster-General, on July 2, 1863, that a thousand convalescents be mounted and sent to Pennsylvania for the purpose of procuring horses in the rear of Lee's army. General Myers thought the plan might "succeed admirably."

shall deem necessary, to purchase supplies for the use of the sick and disabled of the army in hospitals."

It was intended that the hospital fund should be used for the purchase of such perishables as fruits, eggs, butter, chickens, milk, and vegetables. Cows were at times purchased with money from the hospital fund as evidenced by the fact that four were bought for Atlanta's Empire Hospital in the spring of 1863. The demand upon markets near the general hospitals was often extremely heavy. As a result, surgeons were instructed that when it was necessary to obtain more vegetables than were being produced in hospital gardens effort should be made to contract for produce which would bear rail transportation—thereby relieving the local demand and procuring the vegetables at a lower cost. Purchasing agents were authorized to travel beyond the boundaries of their hospital districts if supplies could not otherwise be found. Officers in charge of hospitals were also allowed, when the state of the hospital fund permitted, to buy whatever means of transportation might be necessary to haul their purchases from the country. At times, special agents were appointed for entire hospital districts to help medical officers obtain certain needed items.

Despite the steady increase in the commutation allowance of rations for the disabled in hospitals and a reasonable amount of diligence manifested by hospital agents, medical officers were not infrequently hard pressed in their efforts to obtain a sufficient supply of food. Phoebe Pember wrote early in 1864 that the allowance was "barely" adequate but, she added, "we do our best to prevent dissatisfaction." No serious problem was entirely separated from currency depreciation, and Surgeon Edmund Burke Haywood in Raleigh found that spiraling prices more than kept pace with the allowance increases. In February, 1862, Haywood bought chickens for 20¢, eggs for 15¢ a dozen, and beef for 12½¢ a pound, but three years later these same items sometimes cost him as much as $4.50, $4.05, and $3.33 respectively. And near Chattanooga, in the summer of 1863, a soldier learned that potatoes were selling for $15 a bushel, onions for $3 a dozen, and watermelons for $10 each. Surgeons were sometimes guilty of competing with each other in their search for supplies and thereby encouraging extortionate prices. As a result of such competition, Medical Director Carrington, in August, 1863, ordered the Richmond officers in charge of hospitals to meet and arrange a common price schedule for articles bought with the hospital fund.

Articles such as mutton, pork, bacon, wheat, flour, corn, meal, dried peas, rice, salt, vinegar, sugar, and molasses were supposed to be furnished by the Subsistence Department, and the hospital agents were not allowed to draw on the hospital fund for the purchase of these commodities. Occasional inability of the Subsistence Department to supply the hospitals adequately was a source of real trouble. There was, for example, no bacon, mutton, pork, wheat, beans, and rice issued to Raleigh's Pettigrew Hospital for more than six weeks early in 1865. As a matter of fact, late in the war subsistence stores were generally short when supplied at all, and there was much complaint from the hospitals.[10]

Diet in the Hospitals

Closely related to the food supply was the matter of a proper diet for the sick and wounded. Surgeon General Moore was anxious to establish a standard diet table for military hospitals, and, early in 1863, he issued a direct order that in all hospitals at least three kinds of diet—full, half, and low—be served.[11] Further regulations directed each hospital surgeon, during the morning call on his patients, to prescribe the proper diet on a "diet roll" for each individual in the ward. Matrons sometimes sent surgeons a list of foods that were

[10] Fannie Beers, a matron, reported the issuance of mule meat as part of the ration. Another, Emily Mason, wrote near the end of the war that a pint of corn meal and a gill of sorghum constituted the daily ration. Flour, bacon, and lard were issued to hospitals in the Army of Tennessee on a half-ration basis at times.

[11] It was reported that Robert Battey, surgeon in charge of Marietta's Polk Hospital, reduced the diet schedule "to a perfect system."

available, and ward matrons were responsible for seeing that patients received the articles of food that composed the different diets. The diet roll for each ward was subject to the inspection of the patients, and it was supposed to be hung in a conspicuous place.[12]

Kate Cumming declared that the "great trouble about hospitals is the sameness of the diet" and there does not appear to have been much variation in the offerings from day to day. One surgeon asserted that "the victualing range was so limited that there was more of a distinction than a difference" between the hospital diets. "Full diet," he explained, "was beef and cawn [sic] bread, and whatever else could be had, such as vegetables. Half diet was soup and toast, and such like; while low diet was rice and milk,—if you could get the milk." Surgeons in charge of hospitals generally attempted to vary the diet as much as possible and to provide special foods for those who required them.

General Hospital No. 9 in Richmond, a wayside and receiving hospital, seems to have served a more varied fare than most. In 1864 this institution offered two diets—one for "Specials" and one for "Regulars." A typical breakfast for "Specials" consisted of beef hash, boiled eggs, rolls, butter, and choice of beverage whereas "Regulars" were served beef hash, rolls or flour bread, and coffee. Items on the dinner menu for "Specials" often included fried chicken, baked duck, beef soup, baked beef, beets, corn, sweet potatoes, Irish potatoes, turnips, rice, snap beans, tomatoes, and flour bread. For the same meal "Regulars" received beef soup, peas, rice, sweet potatoes, Irish potatoes, turnip salad, and flour bread. Beef was served almost daily in various forms for both breakfast and dinner. Hash was the standby for breakfast, and the notation "beef for hash" occurs with monotonous regularity on the steward's accounts of supplies issued.[13]

[12] Of 132 diets prescribed at the Ross General Hospital in Mobile on October 3, 1863, exactly 100 were full, 27 were half, and only 5 were low.
[13] The hash made for breakfast on March 22, 1865, required ninety-five pounds of beef, sixty-five pounds of potatoes, and eighteen pounds of meal.

83

Certain medical officials were required to make frequent inspections of the diet served in general hospitals and to make full reports of their findings. At times even the surgeons in charge were directed by higher authority to make personal investigations. Writing from Tullahoma, Tennessee, in March, 1863, a medical inspector of hospitals expressed the opinion that "any efficient officer in charge of a hospital ought to be able to feed our sick better than can be done at our best hotels." And, he advised Medical Director Samuel H. Stout, "something ought to be done to improve the fare of the sick at *all* of the hospitals." Over a year and a half later, this same inspector reported to Stout that the meals at the Lumpkin Hospital in Cuthbert, Georgia, left something to be desired "for while the special diet was good in quality & mode of preperation [sic] there was nothing prepared for the dinner of the convalescents but corn-field peas boiled with a little lard, and bread baked of sour and musty meal." The removal of the surgeon in charge was recommended.

Inspection reports of the officers of the day in Richmond's large Jackson Hospital have been preserved, and these provide some insight as to the true state of dietary affairs. It was sometimes found that the prescribed diets were not served because of carelessness. "For some of Dr. Whistler's patients for whom he had prescribed Half diet & some particular articles named," reported one officer, "they sent some fat fried meat & gravy." Some confusion also resulted from the failure of matrons, in making food requisitions, to understand the diet table issued by the Surgeon General. It was further noted that food and beverages were not always sufficient or well prepared. One report stated that "The supper of the 2nd Division consisted only of bad imitation of coffee and one slice of bakers bread." On another occasion an officer of the day, inspecting conditions during breakfast, "found not more than 3 or 4 ounces [one pint was the usual allowance] of coffee in a cup, & this cold & badly made. When," he continued, "the coffee consists of an infusion of common grains . . . it does seem that each man might have at least a half pint & this might be moderately *warm* if not hot." [14] A scarcity of cooking utensils, another officer pointed out, "renders it necessary that the meals should be cooked in instalments." Reports were not always negative, however, and the diet was at times declared "to be very good indeed & sufficient in quantity."

The special committee appointed by the Provisional Congress to inspect the medical department reported in January, 1862, that the sick were provided with poorly cooked rations,[15] and it is not surprising to learn that the sick and wounded themselves often complained of both the quality and quantity of the diet which they received. A petition from 360 Chimborazo patients who complained of the poor fare in that institution was presented on the floor of Congress on September 16, 1862, and not quite a year later Medical Director William A. Carrington informed the medical officer in charge of that same hospital that the Alabama inmates had repeatedly criticized the diet served at convalescent tables. A Tar Heel in Winder Hospital wrote home that all he got to eat was "raw beef and sower loaf bread. . . . Turnips & colords," he declared in disgust, "are cooked without any meet." Miss Emily V. Mason, a matron at Winder, related after the war how the men in that hospital, tired of eating dried peas day after day, finally revolted and threw them all over the floor and walls. Soon after that crisis, according to Miss Mason, some two hundred men, avid for bread, tore down the bakery, and she quelled this uprising by reminding the men of her many acts of kindness to them—among which had been her willingness to stew their rats when the cook refused to do so. The Jackson, Howard's Grove, and Stuart hospitals in Richmond also housed patients who were unhappy over dietetic matters. A special committee of the Confederate House of Representatives planned an investigation of the diet at Stuart Hospital, but it

[14] Surgeon General Moore, on December 2, 1863, directed that coffee, in view of its scarcity, should "be used solely for its medicinal effects as a stimulant."

[15] A House committee reported on April 21, 1862, however, that the food furnished Richmond hospitals was "good in quality and well prepared."

is not known whether the committee found time to make the visitation.[16]

Men in the Chattanooga hospitals complained of the nature and insufficiency of the diet, and Kate Cumming herself sometimes made reference to the fact that many in the Army of Tennessee's hospitals suffered from the lack of nutritious food.[17] The bill of fare for supper in a Montgomery hospital late in the war was described by an inmate as "a thin slice of light bread and a plate of soup, already dished out and placed at every plate. I ate it," he related, "but it only made me hungry." Breakfast, however, he found more satisfactory. A soldier in a Port Hudson, Louisiana, hospital, unhappy over the diet, remarked that he "would just as soon lie on my back and let the moon shine in my mouth."

Hospital tables were almost certain to be filled with an abundant supply of appetizing food during the Christmas season, and, for a few days at least, the complaints were stilled. Matrons in particular were active in promoting Christmas and New Year's dinners, and the townspeople were very co-operative. At the hospital center of the Confederacy Emily Mason obtained, for her division's Christmas dinner in 1862, 15 turkeys, 130 chickens and ducks, a barrel of corned beef, 240 pies, a barrel of cider, and an undisclosed amount of rice custard, pudding, oysters, and eggnog. Phoebe Pember served 24 gallons of eggnog, among large quantities of other items appropriate to the season, at Chimborazo on Christmas Day in 1863, and bounteous repasts were provided at other Richmond hospitals throughout the holiday season. The hospitalized were not forgotten during the next Christmas season either, and although the hospital fund was too small from a relative

[16] On November 14, 1864, the House instructed its Committee on the Medical Department to report a bill "for the better organization of hospitals, so as to secure a proper preparation of the food for the patients therein."

[17] At Cherokee Springs, Georgia, however, in the summer of 1863, Miss Cumming wrote that there was "a profusion of all kinds of good things. . . ."

standpoint to allow much preparation, Mrs. Pember reported that ladies "drove out in carriages and ambulances laden with good things."

Rising prices and the failure of the Subsistence Department to furnish adequate stores to the hospitals naturally had a detrimental effect upon the hospital diet. Never altogether adequate as a general rule, with respect to either quality or quantity, the diet became even less so during the closing months of the war.

Hospital Sanitation

Another very important aspect of hospital administration was the maintenance of proper sanitary conditions. The Surgeon General insisted that the hospitals and the patients therein should be kept scrupulously clean. Beds, according to regulations, were to be arranged so that each patient would have eight hundred cubic feet, and the officer of the day was instructed to make a thorough examination of all matters affecting sanitation. Illustrative of directives issued to insure cleanliness was one sent out by Medical Director Carrington that made it "obligatory and not persuasive" for all men admitted to hospitals to be given baths as soon as their condition allowed. Another, issued by the same official, demanded a thorough and regular policing of hospital grounds, and one circulated by the Surgeon General called for the removal of infected padding from bed comforts. Congress naturally manifested an interest in the problem of sanitation, and early in 1863 the House of Representatives requested its Committee on the Medical Department to investigate the expediency of closing all Richmond hospitals until they were thoroughly cleaned and fumigated.[18] Apparently such action was not deemed necessary.

[18] Congress authorized the issuance of hospital clothing for the use of the sick and wounded during the time of hospitalization.

Officers engaged in the inspection of hospitals occasionally reported the grounds in need of policing, a lack of ventilation or general cleanliness, and a failure to wash the tableware properly. One investigation of St. Mary's Hospital, Dalton, Georgia, even revealed that plates were not being washed until they had been used by two sets of patients.[19] It was the nonuse or careless use of sinks, however, that seemed to cause most trouble and irritation. Individual hospital regulations forbade patients to use places other than sinks or latrines for the purpose of relieving themselves, but Confederate soldiers were, to say the least, notoriously nonchalant in regard to this matter. Patients at the Jackson Hospital in Richmond, for example, insisted upon using the tubs located at the end of the wards and intended for slops; this habit proved a source of much annoyance to the matrons and other feminine workers. Convalescents at Chattanooga's Lookout Hospital were "caught evacuating *the contents of their bowels* within a few paces of the sinks" and creating a sanitary problem thereby. At the Gordon Hospital in Nashville, the patients filled the drain pipes of the water closets with cloth, paper, and sticks; then, according to the officer in charge, the pipes overflowed and "underneath and upon the floors there accumulated fecal matter that caused the air of the whole building to be pervaded with mephitic gases, so intolerable as sometimes to overpower healthy men." The notation "unclean and offensive" was used by an inspecting officer to describe the sinks at General Hospital No. 1 in Savannah, and the floors and seats of sinks at Richmond's Jackson Hospital were on at least one occasion "smeared with excrement."

Despite some indifference on the part of a few medical officers and the careless toilet practices of numerous patients, the sanitary condition of most hospitals week in and week out seems to have been quite satisfactory. Surgeon Alexander G. Lane, head of Winder Hospital in Richmond, asserted that

[19] In early April, 1863, Robert Battey described the Atlanta hospitals as "less cleanly and in worse condition than any in the District of Tennessee."

his medical officers were "compelled to keep their divisions in perfect order," and sanitary precautions were also observed in the capital's other institutions. As early as September, 1861, a special Congressional committee, appointed to inquire into hospital arrangements, reported that the Richmond hospitals were in "a neat condition for the most part, some of them in excellent order" and well supplied. Another committee, appointed by the House of Representatives in March, 1862, to investigate the medical department, was generally pleased with the sanitary conditions found in hospitals.

Soldiers, inspectors, and others also testified to the cleanliness of the general hospitals. One Rebel, while complaining about the smell of a Montgomery institution, acknowledged that the hospital was nice and clean. After his inspection of hospitals used by the Army of Tennessee, Inspector S. P. Hunt reported as follows early in 1863: "My inspection has taken place at a very unfavorable time, the weather having been very rainy, and it being impossible to have the hospitals as clean as would be desired, but in every case there is an evident desire for the greatest possible clenliness [sic]. . . ." Late in 1864 inspection teams remarked on the excellent sanitary conditions that existed in two North Carolina hospitals—General Hospitals Nos. 3 and 13, located in Goldsboro and Raleigh respectively, and about this same time the Nott Hospital in Mobile was reported to be "cleanly, well administered, and well appointed" in all particulars. Similar words were used by inspectors to describe most hospitals in the Trans-Mississippi Department. One of the most glowing tributes to hospital cleanliness was that given by a visitor to the four Macon institutions, which were under the control of Surgeon James Mercer Green. "What most attracted our attention and approbation," he commented, "was the perfect cleanliness of each and every part of the establishments. The kitchens were as free from dirt or disorder as the offices of the surgeons in charge, and we confidently assert that no gentleman's residence in the whole South is cleaner or more tidy" than the Macon hospitals.

Hospital Discipline

Medical officers in charge of general hospitals were confronted with a number of disciplinary problems, and some of these were of a rather serious nature. Among the most troublesome offenses were desertion, absence without leave, theft, drunkenness, gambling, and general unruliness. As to desertion, hospital reports for the Department of Virginia alone, covering the period from September, 1862, to August, 1864, reveal that 5,895 patients deserted during this 23-month interval—an average of over 256 each month. Sometimes, it appears, the hospitals became centers from which men were seduced by army recruiting officers. General Lee, for example, became greatly perturbed early in 1864 because he believed that soldiers were being prevailed upon to leave the Virginia hospitals for the purpose of joining General John Hunt Morgan's command.

Desertion and absence without leave were not uncommon because hospital guard forces were as a rule neither large nor efficient. In citing the need for a guard for Chattanooga's Academy Hospital in September, 1862, Samuel H. Stout asserted his belief that there were at least a hundred men who should be returned to duty from that establishment "but who evade inspection by wandering from the Hospital without leave." [20] Richmond medical officials finally ordered that patients found in the city without proper authority would be returned to their commands if they were able to travel. Surgeon Randall M. Lytle, in charge of the Lookout Hospital at Chattanooga, asked for a guard after convalescents began "precipitating large stones from the mountain" in the direction of men working below. Others, he complained, who had been detailed as guards "have deserted their Posts & left the Mountain without permission." [21]

[20] One patient in Richmond's Howard's Grove Hospital appears to have engaged in business as an auctioneer and slave trader during his sojourn there.

[21] Two attendants killed the surgeon in charge of the Foard Hospital in Chattanooga.

Kate Cumming contended that her sick would carry off the tableware "no matter how closely" it was watched, and on occasions convalescents were guilty of plundering orchards and gardens near the hospitals. In calling Medical Director Stout's attention to the fact that patients in the Montgomery hospitals were allowed to cook potatoes, smoke, and eat nuts in the wards, a hospital inspector condemned the general "laxness of discipline" in the institutions of that city and recommended field service for several of the surgeons. Local hospital regulations forbade such pastimes as drinking and gambling, but a considerable amount of both undoubtedly took place. Senator Louis T. Wigfall of Texas favored an adequate guard system "to prevent convalescents from straggling off and poisoning themselves at whiskey shops." And even officers sometimes showed up at wayside hospitals under the influence of liquor to the extent that they were not always amenable to hospital discipline. Gambling was also regarded as a serious offense, and hospital inmates were occasionally placed under arrest as a result of their indulgence in games of chance. Unruly conduct was prone to manifest itself at mealtime; and sometimes the pushing, crowding, and plate-throwing reached such proportions that guards had to be stationed in the mess hall.[22] Kate Cumming concluded that the "most unruly and dastardly in our hospitals have been from Louisiana." Another hospital matron, Phoebe Pember, heaped especial praise upon the Virginians for being "intelligent, manly, and reasonable, with more civilized tastes and some desire to conform to rules that were conducive to their health." North Carolinians, in the eyes of Mrs. Pember, "were certainly most forlorn specimens," and she described their drawl as "insufferable."

Some members of Congress, satisfied that general hospital administration was weak and ineffective, proposed a bill which would have placed these institutions under more stringent military control. As finally drafted the measure proposed that troops on their way to and from general hospitals should be

[22] Frank Hawthorn, surgeon in charge of the Academy Hospital, Chattanooga, punished his offenders by "bucking and gagging."

sent under guard. Senator James L. Orr of South Carolina contended, however, that the bill would make prisons of the hospitals, and opposition to such an innovation was strong enough to block its enactment.

Problem of Monotony in the Hospitals

Hospital life had a tendency to be monotonous. As a matter of fact the unchanging routine of such existence was undoubtedly productive of restlessness, particularly on the part of the convalescents, and a desire for change. This, in turn, was surely responsible for some of the wandering off, drinking, gambling, and general unruliness. Modern facilities for the entertainment of the sick were not then available and entertainers were not known to visit the hospitals, although some efforts were made by authorities to relieve the sameness of hospital life by encouraging religious services, library projects, and other wholesome activity.

Revival meetings sometimes lasted for weeks in the hospitals, and medical authorities were anxious for chaplains to minister to the inmates. Medical Director Carrington believed that chaplains could do much to discourage immorality, intemperance, and profanity "in which," he wrote, "the chaplains should be required to render obedience also." Attempts were made to establish libraries "for the instruction of the patients and the diversion of the mind from the ennui of hospital confinement," and in the summer of 1863 surgeons in charge of hospitals were authorized to draw on the hospital fund to buy newspapers for the benefit of their patients.

Hospitalized men were encouraged to make toys, wood carvings, and the like; they were also humored as much as possible in their preferences at certain seasons for particular colors of hospital clothing and in such diversion as dyeing their canvas shoes with pokeberry juice. When patients in Richmond complained that they could not get their hair and whiskers cut, medical officers were instructed to employ a barber for each hospital division. Nothing was more important to the inmates than letters from home, and it was extremely important that mail call should be conducted properly. An interesting petition from the Chimborazo occupants to Surgeon McCaw asked for the removal of the postmaster in that institution because he miscalled the names on more than half the letters, took too long to complete the call, and made unnecessary remarks about the writing on the backs of letters.[23]

The most trying time in the hospitals, at least for the more critical cases, was at night. Then it was that the average soldier's horror of a hospital was magnified a hundredfold. Alexander Hunter, a soldier who was confined for some time in a Petersburg institution, remembered the long nights as he would "a hideous dream." His ward, he wrote,

> . . . became like the dim caverns of the catacombs, where, instead of the dead in their final rest, there were extended wasted figures burning with fever and raving from the agony of splintered bones, tossing restlessly from side to side, with every ill, it seemed, which human flesh was heir to.
> From the rafters the flickering oil lamp swung mournfully, casting a ghastly light upon the scene beneath, but half-dispelling the darkness, bringing out dim shadows everywhere and rendering the gloom only more spectral. . . . The sickening odor of medicine, the nephritic air shut in by the closed windows, rendered the atmosphere heavy and unwholesome. . . .

Such scenes were not soon forgotten by the unfortunate sick and wounded—if they lived to remember them.

Movement of Sick and Wounded

Men in hospitals were constantly transferred, returned to duty, furloughed, and discharged; there were, for example,

[23] Surgeons in the field seemed to believe that soldiers were coddled too much in the general hospitals. At any rate Surgeon Lafayette Guild wrote that "when once billitted for a General Hospital, it seems to require almost supernatural efforts to force the men back to their Regiments in the field."

93,107 transferred and 74,008 returned to duty in the Department of Virginia alone during the year 1863. Some of the movement was of a routine character whereas much of it, particularly that pertaining to the transfers, represented transportation of an emergency nature. The former may be illustrated by the assignment of many patients first received at Chattanooga to hospitals south of that center early in the war, and the same sort of arrangement existed later with Atlanta serving as the receiving and distributing center. Most of the emergency movement took place in the midst of active military operations and resulted from the necessity of accommodating large numbers of wounded after major battles. Effort was made to avoid overcrowding, and medical officers in charge of hospitals nearest the scene of operations were instructed to increase the capacity of their institutions by every means in their power. Such personnel were also ordered before operations began to move all those disabled who could bear transportation to establishments located somewhat more remotely or to pursue a liberal policy in the granting of furloughs. When overcrowding resulted despite efforts to avoid it surgeons were authorized to permit certain classes of wounded to be treated in private homes, but such patients were still subject to hospital rules and had to report daily to the hospitals or be visited by a responsible physician; their rations were furnished from the hospitals.

Some idea of the steps taken by medical directors to receive an influx of hospitalized troops may be obtained from the following lucid explanation presented to Surgeon General Moore by Medical Director Stout following the battle of Chickamauga:

> . . . The question naturally arises how were the large number of sick and wounded so suddenly thrown upon my hands provided for in the hospitals under my control with a capacity of only about 7500 beds. -Ist Many were sent out of this department, to Montgomery, Columbus and Augusta. 2nd Private families living convenient to hospitals were permitted to take many of them. 3rd, Those whose wounds did not require skillful surgical treatment but who would be

disabled for more than thirty days were furloughed. 4th Every slightly wounded man who would not be injured by remaining in camp, or who could perform any kind of light duty were immediately sent to the convalescent camps, which exist at almost any post in my department. 5th Malingerers and old *'hospital rats'* were summarily dealt with and promptly turned over to post commandants to be returned to their commands.

Numerous complaints arose from time to time regarding the movement of the sick and wounded from the general hospitals. Criticism was heard early in the war to the effect that furloughed and discharged men were turned loose, occasionally without pay, and placed at the mercy of irregular rail service. Reports reached the Army of the Potomac's medical director late in 1861 that some men had been returned to their regiments before they were recovered sufficiently to endure the exposure and fatigue incident to camp life. Another not uncommon complaint voiced was that at times the sick were transferred or furloughed when they were not strong enough to undertake the necessary travel; and records indicate that some of these died on the cars. Charges were also made that the failure of the railroads to provide adequate accommodations produced much suffering among the men. Wood was not always provided for the stoves in sick cars, and on at least one occasion, seats were torn up and burned to keep the men from freezing. Medical Director Carrington learned in 1864 that the disabled were being transported from Richmond to Greensboro in box cars, many of which offered no toilet accommodations, equipped only with backless plank seats.

It must be pointed out, however, that the medical authorities did their best to prevent untoward incidents associated with the release and movement of men from the hospitals. Hospital authorities were ordered to be absolutely certain that the men they remanded to their regiments were fully able to endure field service, and such officials were also directed to use the utmost vigilance in transferring or furloughing their inmates. Medical officers and attendants were sent with ambulance cars, medical personnel at way hospitals were instructed to visit the cars for the purpose of providing necessary aid in the form of medicines or in removing those who were unable to travel further, attendants were sent to the depots to receive the sick, and pressure was brought to bear on railroad officials to provide suitable cars and better service.

Other Problems

There were numerous other problems of hospital administration. At times medical officers themselves refused to obey orders given by surgeons in charge of hospitals if the latter were junior officers—thus throwing themselves open to charges of insubordination. Quite often, too, medical officers evinced acute reactions of wounded pride on occasions when they received changes of assignments, and it became necessary at such times for those responsible to assure the aggrieved that the orders were for the good of the service. To make matters more difficult, ladies connected with some hospitals, as at Montgomery in the spring of 1864, protested against changes in the assignments of favorite medical officers and carried appeals to the highest authorities. It was also noted that reassigned officers were extremely dilatory in repairing to their new posts, and Medical Director Stout, to quicken their pace, found it necessary to threaten those in his department with courts-martial. He also had to direct them not to carry away records pertaining to the hospitals in which they had been serving. Stout, incidentally, was most desirous that each hospital maintain a complete historical record.

Hospital fires, such as that which caused the destruction of the S. P. Moore Hospital at Griffin, Georgia, in February, 1864, also posed real problems for the officers in charge, while shortages of needed items such as stoves and stove pipes, soap, ice, and wood—though not quite as serious—considerably handicapped the hospitals in administering to their sick and wounded. Stoves and pipes were not always to be had, and late in the war, because of the difficulty in obtaining soap, the Surgeon General directed that wheat straw no longer useful in the hospitals be burned and its ashes used for the manufacture of soap. Arrangements were also made by medical authorities whereby hospitals exchanged grease to manufacturers for soap. Despite the construction of ice houses near many of the hospitals, ice was often critically scarce and generally regarded as a luxury during the summer months. The government ice house in Richmond had a capacity of 58,000 bushels, and those interested in filling it had to send bids to Medical Purveyor Edward W. Johns.[24] Quartermasters were responsible for the building or procurement of the ice houses themselves, and the government was known to have seized for hospital use ice put up by private persons.

The wood shortage stemmed from the inability of quartermasters to supply the hospitals adequately. Surgeon Frank Hawthorn at Chattanooga advised Medical Director Stout early in 1863, for example, that he was finding it necessary to "trespass upon the timber" in that area for the purpose of obtaining the wood he needed. The real pinch, however, came late in the war. An officer of the day's report for December 12, 1864, stated that there was not enough wood furnished Jackson Hospital in Richmond "to warm the stoves." Medical Director Carrington asserted early in 1865 that the Virginia hospitals had suffered from a lack of fuel during most of the winter, and he learned that a petition signed by more than one thousand patients had been sent to each Virginia congressman. Evidence of congressional interest in the situation may be seen in the plan of the Confederate House of Representatives to inquire into the causes of the fuel shortage at Chimborazo.[25] Thus there was an ice shortage in summer and a fuel shortage in winter. Carrington recommended, on the eve of the Confederate collapse, that one single quartermaster be assigned to the duty of supplying the hospitals with fuel, straw, and other materials not provided by the medical purveyors.

[24] The ubiquitous Lieutenant Colonel James Arthur Lyon Fremantle, who traveled through much of the South in 1863, asserted that he did not see ice until he arrived in Richmond.

[25] No report of such an inqury was found.

Conclusion

It may be concluded that the general hospitals of the Confederacy, subsequent to the considerable amount of confusion during the early part of the war, were customarily administered with a marked degree of efficiency. Medical officers responsible for the hospital administration were usually capable and conscientious. Despite the numerous problems with which they wrestled they did their work well, and their attendants, although knowing little of the nursing art, improved in quality after the passage of the law approved on September 27, 1862. It appears reasonably clear that the chief failure of the hospital staff was its inability, as a regular thing, to furnish the patients with a nourishing and palatable diet. For the most part, however, this deficiency was due to causes over which the hospital administrators had little or no control.

CHAPTER VI

Prison Hospitals

Establishment and Control

*M*ost prison hospitals in the Confederacy, like the prisons themselves, were established in warehouses and factories. Since governmental policy dictated that, in general, such institutions be contained within a compact area—primarily for security reasons—they were not very large. All of the prison hospitals in Richmond and Danville, Virginia, were located in tobacco warehouses, and an interesting experiment at Petersburg in the same state saw one hospital used for both Union and Confederate prisoners. Mixing of Confederate and Union disabled also took place elsewhere, and "A Confederate soldier" in the Foard Hospital at Newnan, Georgia, protested at seeing the latter "receive courtesies the same as the wounded Confederates who has fought and suffered *for his country* and *not against it.*" The Salisbury, North Carolina, prison hospital consisted of a two-story wooden structure located near the brick factory used for the prison.[1] At Andersonville, Georgia, the hospital was first located inside a seventeen-acre stockade, but it was moved later to a shady oak grove outside the enclosure. Andersonville's sick, to the extent possible, were accommodated in tents.

Hospitals for prisoners of war came to be placed on the same footing as all other Confederate States hospitals. With the exception of those in Cahaba, Alabama, and Andersonville, Millen, and Savannah, Georgia, late in the war,[2] they

[1] A Northern prisoner referred to the Salisbury prison as "an obsolete cotton factory which some deluded capitalist once tried to establish here."

[2] General John H. Winder was in charge of all prison hospitals in Alabama and Georgia, and such institutions were supervised by Isaiah H. White. The latter received reports from R. Randolph Stevenson at An-

were under the control and supervision of the various medical directors of hospitals although "governed by military law through the military authorities."

Favorable Reports

Early observations upon the hospital facilities for prisoners in the Confederacy were generally favorable. Richmond soon became the hospital center for prisoners as well as for its own troops, and when the special committee appointed by the Provisional Congress to inspect the Medical Department visited the prison hospitals there, it found "no cause of complaint"—the disabled being well cared for and furnished with proper diet. Richmond newspapers gave considerable praise to the Libby Prison Hospital, located in a large four-story warehouse on the James River. It was described as being "admirably arranged" and "clean and neat to the last degree." The entire establishment was pronounced to be "admirably conducted, efficiently officered, and in every way a model prison." A report issued by Surgeon John Wilkins, medical officer in charge of the Libby Prison Hospital, reveals that of 1,660 captives admitted to the prison from February 1, 1863, to January 22, 1864, there were 310 on the sick list and only 13 deaths.[3] Deaths in the Richmond prison hospitals were never attributed to lack of proper attention, and it was sometimes charged that the care of enemy prisoners was receiving too much consideration.

Samuel P. Day, a British correspondent in the South, heard that "Federal prisoners in Southern hospitals have frequently wept, owing to the uniformly kind manner in which they had been treated." Other references were made, some by enemy observers, to the kindness accorded Union troops hospitalized

---

dersonville and operated directly under the control of the Surgeon General.

[3] One of those who died in the Libby Prison Hospital was Major Robert Morris, a grandson of the "financier of the American Revolution."

in the South. Dr. Charles C. Gray, a Federal surgeon held prisoner at Castle Pinckney in Charleston Harbor during the Christmas of 1861, told of the "spirited" Christmas service they had in the hospital room and of the subsequent "singing," "cheering," "tippling," and "chatting." Reflecting on the occasion that night he concluded that he had "never enjoyed a Christmas so much since my Santa Claus days." [4] General J. Bankhead Magruder, after the naval attack upon Galveston early in 1863, reported that the Union wounded were taken to the Confederate hospital and given just as much attention "as if they had been our own men." Two dead Union officers, he added, "were buried [by the Confederates] with Masonic and military honors in the same grave, Major Lea, of the Confederate Army, father of Lieutenant Lea [one of the Union dead], performing the burial services." [5] W. H. Pierson, Union surgeon on the gunboat *Water Witch* which was captured south of Savannah in June, 1864, reported that his wounded were carried to the Savannah Naval Hospital, an "airy and comfortable" establishment, and "there received every care and comfort which the somewhat limited resources of the country permitted." Pierson also related that while the Confederate surgeons at Savannah "denied themselves the luxuries of tea at $30 to $40 per pound, they had it furnished to our wounded, and generally fed them better than they fed themselves." Diary observations by another Union prisoner at Salisbury in 1862, however, illustrate the fact that there were those who had cause for complaint. Early in July of that year he declared: "No medicine furnished worth mention, the C. S. Med. Dept. useless. The hospital & supplies 'O'—the case is a hard one certainly." Nine days later he wrote that the prison

---

[4] The same doctor also reported a very lively Independence Day celebration at Salisbury prison in 1862. According to Gray there were sack, foot, single stick, and wheelbarrow races and "a match game of base ball which excited much interest & upon which considerable money (theoretically) was staked. . . . The cheers given in the game were of a sort never before heard in Salisbury—I opine."

[5] The funeral of a Federal prisoner who died in a Columbia, South Carolina, prison was conducted, according to another prisoner, "with much feeling and good taste by our custodians."

surgeon was "about the weakest specimen of a Dr. I have ever met; & he looks as though he had been a 'dirt eater' from his mother's womb. He is dying of consumption—can't last many months."

Exchange of Prisoners

Holland Thompson and William B. Hesseltine, both noted authorities on Civil War prisons, concluded that, in general, prisoners on both sides received good treatment during the early years of the war. Frequent exchange of prisoners, authorized unofficially at first by field commanders and after July 22, 1862, by agents appointed pursuant to provisions of the cartel entered into between the two governments on that date, took place; prisons were not crowded as a general rule, and there was little legitimate cause for complaint.[6] In Richmond, the surgeon of Libby Prison reported as late as September, 1863, that the diet was abundant, the food of good quality, and the meals well cooked; he also stated that medicines and instruments "of the finest quality" were supplied by the medical purveyor.

Suspension of Exchanges and Results

The suspension of exchanges under the cartel in the summer of 1863 and their subsequent cessation soon caused a crowding of prisons and prison hospitals.[7] An inspection of Belle Isle Prison Hospital in November, 1863, revealed that while the Federal patient received as much food, medicine, and attention as the Confederate soldier in hospital he had only half as much room. The three Richmond prison hospitals, with

[6] Prison hospitals, like others in the Confederacy, were sometimes empty.

[7] See the objective treatment of this situation in James G. Randall, *The Civil War and Reconstruction* (Boston, 1937), 436–43.

102

accommodations for about five hundred patients, contained over eleven hundred on March 14, 1864, and the mortality rate had risen sharply since January. General John H. Winder, who commanded the Department of Henrico, averred, however, in reply to recommendations of the medical staff for additional prison space that mortality was incident to prison life and that an insufficient number of guards made it necessary to concentrate the prisoners within a small area.

Andersonville

Andersonville Prison, established in Georgia early in 1864 to relieve the congestion in the capital and ease the supply problem, soon became the scene of sickness and death on an almost unbelievable scale. The inadequate facilities, the difficulties in procuring supplies and equipment, and the increasing poverty of the Confederacy were the principal factors that go to explain the frightful conditions that existed at Andersonville. Surgeon R. Randolph Stevenson, medical officer in charge, was appraised by one of his colleagues as "a *poor medical man* & no surgeon, but an energetic officer in trying to provide for the wants and comforts of the sick under his charge—but without the means afforded him here to accomplish his desires. He was certainly arduous in his efforts to erect buildings here for the sick and I attributed his non attendance upon the hospital to that." [8]

Stevenson himself attributed much of the responsibility for his problems to unnecessary red tape, particularly in the requisitioning of medical supplies. He complained that there was undue delay in obtaining medicines because his requisitions had to be sent to Atlanta for approval by the medical director and then returned before he could forward them to the purveyor in Macon. It was reported by the surgeon in

[8] G. G. Roy, the assistant who wrote these lines to Samuel H. Stout on March 7, 1865, mentioned in the same letter that "rascality" had been practiced at the prison hospital, but failed to elaborate.

charge on September 16, 1864, however, that almost all necessary medicines had been supplied, and that indigenous remedies were being used with good effect.[9]

Shortages Experienced

The lack of medical officers, hospital tents, and funds were the great shortages experienced by the sick and wounded of Andersonville. There were only 13 doctors on June 30, 1864, to care for 26,000 prisoners, and the supply of tents was sufficient to care for only 800. The hospital ration was commuted just as at other hospitals, but the commissary was frequently without funds to supply the hospital for its purchases. The police was deficient, and the diet was inadequate.[10] Conditions were not happier elsewhere. In November, 1864, the surgeon in charge of the Salisbury Prison Hospital informed Surgeon General Moore that he had not been able to obtain quartermaster supplies—that the post and prison quartermasters were each charging the other with responsibility for supplying the hospital—the result being that the sick were improperly cared for and the hospital "not in a condition to bear inspection."

Conclusion

It appears reasonable to conclude that the Confederacy cared for its disabled prisoners about as well as it did for its own sick and wounded. Both were victims of severe priva-

[9] Stevenson, late in October, 1864, hoped to retain the services of a clerk about to appear before a medical board, should the board pronounce the latter unfit for active duty. The clerk's services were "invaluable," wrote Stevenson, "in procuring Anti Scorbutics so much needed by Sick and Wounded Federal prisoners."

[10] Surgeons E. A. Flewellen and E. S. Gaillard conducted an inspection at Andersonville near the end of the war, and, according to Flewellen, "created quite a sensation" there. He planned to give Medical Director Stout the full particulars when they met again. No report of the inspection has been located.

104

tions in the latter part of the conflict. As Sherman and Grant delivered blow after blow at the heart of the South, the transportation and supply system broke down almost completely; and the shortage of manpower, so apparent on the field of battle, also extended to hospital personnel.

CHAPTER VII

Medical Officers in the Field

Field Organization

The organization of the field and general hospital service of the Confederate Medical Department was interlocking at the top level during the first two years of the war. Surgeon General Moore directed the activities of each, and in addition, the medical directors of armies and military departments had general control over all the medical officers and hospitals within the geographical limits of their commands. It was not until March 12, 1863, that a general order was issued by the Adjutant and Inspector General's Office which altered this latter arrangement. Thereafter general hospitals were removed from the jurisdiction of medical directors of armies and departments and placed under the authority of medical directors of hospitals.

Each army corps had a medical director who was immediately responsible to the medical director of the army. Altogether there were eighteen medical directors on duty in September, 1864.[1] Medical directors, in addition to being generally responsible for medical officers and hospitals under their control, were required to prepare for the Surgeon General two monthly reports: a consolidated report of the sick and wounded and a return of medical officers. Immediately below medical directors in the chain of command came the chief surgeons of the various army divisions; these were appointed upon the recommendation of the medical director and were free from all regimental duties. Directly under the division in the army's

[1] Ordinarily, according to General Orders No. 23, February 25, 1863, the senior surgeons of commands entitled to medical directors were detailed as medical directors, but the directive provided that when the interests of the service required, the Surgeon General would recommend such officers.

organization was the brigade, and each brigade had a senior surgeon—not relieved from regimental service—to oversee its general well-being. Medical directors, chief surgeons of divisions, and senior brigade surgeons were directed to make such recommendations regarding the prevention of disease and the "construction and economy of the hospitals, and . . . the police of the camps, as may appear necessary for the benefit and comfort of the sick, and the good of the service." These officers, incidentally, were general—not personal—staff officers; hence they were not affected by personnel changes at the command level.

Each regiment generally had one surgeon and one assistant surgeon to minister to its sick and wounded. A bill to authorize the appointment of an additional assistant surgeon to each regiment, passed by Congress in August, 1861, was vetoed by President Davis on the ground that existing legislation was sufficient to meet regimental needs. That all medical personnel did not agree may be seen in the view expressed a year later by Lafayette Guild, Medical Director of the Army of Northern Virginia, that every regiment should have at least two assistant surgeons. Guild also contended that senior surgeons of brigades ought to be relieved from regimental duties and that one or more assistant surgeons should be attached to each brigade as supernumeraries "for assignment to field hospitals and . . . to supply deficiencies continually arising from sickness and death of regimental medical officers." [2] Records kept and reports made by medical officers in the field were very similar to those required of their counterparts in the general hospitals.

General army regulations allowed regiments in the field one steward, one cook, and one nurse for each company. Hospital stewards, appointed by the Secretary of War, performed duties similar to those executed by stewards in general hospitals. They took charge of the hospital stores, supervised the cooks and nurses, and acted as medical dispensers and apothecaries. Hospital Steward George E. Waller of the Twenty-fourth

[2] Guild, a native of Alabama, was appointed medical director of Lee's army on June 27, 1862.

Virginia Regiment, for example, was left in charge of the field hospital during the entire winter of 1864–1865. Nurses and cooks were usually detailed from the ranks,[3] and a special committee appointed by the Provisional Congress to investigate the medical department complained of poor nursing and cooking in the camps. The establishment of an army nurse corps and a number of bakeries were both recommended by the committee, but neither of the suggestions was deemed feasible.

Medical officers in the field were faced with many problems similar to those in the general hospitals, and the regulations for the latter applied, as far as practicable, to the field service. It should be pointed out, however, that after the early epidemics the number of sick in the field was never so troublesome and that most of the disabled were usually transferred to the general hospitals. As a rule, the most important work of field medical officers pertained to camp sanitation and caring for the men during and immediately following an engagement. Those functions will receive particular emphasis in this chapter.

Camp Sanitation

Regimental surgeons were responsible for finding out as much as possible about the sanitary condition of the camp site, learning of diseases common to the locality and the means which had been most successful in combating them, keeping a close watch over the clothing needs of the troops, maintaining proper police of the encampment, insisting on strict personal cleanliness, enforcing all hospital regulations, seeing that the water was pure, and suggesting necessary dietary changes. Despite the sanitary regulations, however, actual conditions of camp police frequently manifested, to use the words of a Northern observer in describing Confederate hospitals at

[3] Band members sometimes served as nurses. A few women went into the field, and the Catholic sisterhoods were quite active in this respect.

Gettysburg, "a deplorable want of cleanliness" and at times were "disgustingly offensive." A Union army medical director, examining Confederate field hospitals during the Shenandoah Valley Campaign in late 1864, reported seeing "the most extreme filth and positive indications of neglect. . . ." Confederate inspectors themselves also found police regulations disregarded at times and referred to the necessity of frequent camp inspections. One inspector reported the ground surrounding a division hospital in Petersburg to be "offensive to the sight as well as the smell. In this important feature of cleanliness," he concluded, "there was evident and inexcusable neglect. . . ."

Directives concerning camp sanitation became increasingly strict as its importance became evident. A circular of the Second Brigade, Second Division, Army of Northern Virginia, dated August 3, 1862, ordered regimental commanders to publish and enforce all needful police regulations. Sinks were to be dug at once, and the men were to be compelled by posted sentinels to use them. Nonusers were to be "severely punished." A patrol, in addition to the regular sentinels, was "to prevent the commission of nuisances within the camps." Offal was to be buried away from the camps.

Surgeon General Moore ordered "frequent inspections" each month and a sanitary report to division headquarters. In the Army of Tennessee, pursuant to an order of January 8, 1864, the old guard was directed to clean the encampments daily while company details policed their grounds twice daily and stood inspection after each policing. The brigade officer of the day was responsible for the proper placement and covering of sinks, the isolation of slaughter pens, the daily burning of offal, the policing of places where animals were kept, and for seeing "that nothing offensive to decency or detrimental to health be anywhere visible." In August, 1864, the Army of Northern Virginia's medical director instructed chief surgeons of divisions to make at least one inspection each week of the trenches occupied by their divisions. Chief surgeons and inspectors were directed "to confer and advise with the immediate commanders of troops, and, when deemed necessary, to make such suggestions, as to the observance of the laws of hygiene, as will prevent disease and promote the health and comfort of the soldier."

Naval officers commanding vessels on the Savannah River received a general order in April, 1863, that clothes should be washed three times weekly and hammocks twice each month. Bedding was to be aired when hammocks were washed. When the army was in winter quarters there were usually regular cleaning days or "broom days." During a campaign such days took place during a lull in the fighting. On these occasions the men became almost stifled by the large clouds of dust which resulted from the sweeping and rearranging, but the overall effect was probably salutary—for the moment at least.

Responsibility for lax sanitary practices was often assigned to commanding officers in the field. Surgeon General Moore, in a communication to the Secretary of War, dated October 18, 1861, charged regimental officers with failure to act on the suggestions of medical personnel in effectuating proper hygienic regulations, and he urged that all commanding officers be directed to see that police rules were scrupulously enforced by their subordinates. Brigadier General Earl Van Dorn, commanding the Department of Texas in 1861, was accused of retaining Texan volunteers in an unhealthful location until practically all became diseased.

Surgeon J. Julian Chisolm, writing in 1862, excoriated commanding officers for their failure to appreciate the importance of good hygienic conditions. The Confederate army would continue to suffer heavily from sickness and death, he contended, unless officers "take more interest in the general welfare of their men, and cease to consider professional advice offensive and intrusive. . . . The sick list," he added, "will offer a fair criterion of the military status of an officer and his capacity for taking care of his men, which is one of the first rules in military science." [4] Observers sometimes noticed

[4] Field surgeons were known to have voiced their opposition to orders that might affect adversely the health of the soldiers. One brigade com-

that vigorous enforcement of sanitary measures not only reduced sickness but greatly improved the discipline and spirit of the troops. It was asserted that General Lee's efforts along this line transformed the army which he took over from General Joseph E. Johnston, after the latter was wounded at Fair Oaks, from a mutinous and dissatisfied mob into a well-organized, hard-fighting military machine. There is no question but that when commanders insisted on the frequent striking of tents, the punishment of every man who refused to use properly located privy vaults, the careful disposal of the excreta of the sick, and the correct placement of stables and pens for livestock, the salutary results were clearly evident.

Field Routine

Medical officers in the field held surgeon's call, or sick call, early every morning. In the Army of Tennessee sick call was made fifteen minutes after reveille, and the ailing of each company were marched to the hospital by a noncommissioned officer detailed daily for such duty. William H. Taylor, a medical officer, wrote of the procedure in his regiment as follows: "Diagnosis was rapidly made, usually by intuition, and treatment was with such drugs as we chanced to have in the knapsack and were handiest to come at. In serious cases we made an honest effort to bring to bear all the skill and knowledge we possessed, but our science could rarely display itself to the best advantage on account of the paucity of our resources. On the march my own practice was of necessity still further simplified, and was, in fact, reduced to the lowest terms. In one pocket of my trousers I had a ball of blue mass, in another a ball of opium. All complainants were asked the same question, 'How are your bowels?' If they were open I administered a plug of opium, if they were shut I gave a plug of blue mass."

---

mander was told by his senior surgeon that "We must use prophylactic and hygienic measures to preserve the health of our army, and not attempt to cure men who are made sick by improper management."

The supply table authorized the issuance of tents for field hospital purposes, but medical officers were sometimes unable to procure them. It was reported late in the summer of 1861 that because of the scarcity of tents farm houses were seeing service as hospitals all along the Potomac,[5] and the next summer General Lee requested division commanders, if possible, to establish their field hospitals in rented houses rather than tents.[6] Most surgeons favored the use of tents over buildings, however, and some believed them to be more conducive to recovery than the general hospitals. Included among the latter group was Charles S. Tripler, Medical Director of the Union Army of the Potomac. Surgeon General Moore's sentiments on this subject were reflected during the summer of 1863 by his order that three large tent hospitals be established near Staunton and Winchester to receive all those sick and wounded from the Army of Northern Virginia who required only "temporary assistance."[7]

Medical officers in the field had a considerable amount of time on their hands when the army was not in motion, and some, unable to obtain professional literature and increase their knowledge of medicine in that way, spent their free time writing letters, seeking out attractive members of the fair sex, attending religious services in the camp, and promoting various other social activities.[8] Occasionally medical societies were formed, and the members thereof met to discuss medical and surgical subjects. At least one such group had a dissecting hut which was fitted up by the surgeon of a Mississippi regiment. "We could easily procure subjects from beyond the lines," wrote a member of this society, "and we thought it legitimate to use them for scientific and educational purposes."

[5] Some regiments were unable to obtain any tents at all.

[6] Ailing officers were sometimes quartered in private homes.

[7] Hospital tents were fourteen feet wide, fifteen feet long, and eleven feet high; one could accommodate from eight to ten patients. Several tents could be joined together.

[8] Masonic lodges were operating in some camps.

Battle Preparations

Careful preparations were made by medical officers in the field on the eve of expected battles. Medical Director Lafayette Guild ordered that each division medical wagon should transport 150 pairs of drawers, the same number of shirts, 50 blankets, a supply of tea, and some dessicated vegetables to make soup; these items were for the use of wounded during and after a battle. Guild pointed out, in explaining this order, that the clothing of wounded soldiers almost always had to be cut off to facilitate treatment, and even when that was not the case, he added, it was "improper to permit the wounded men to remain in clothes rendered offensive and stiffened with blood." Guild also explained that men suffering from wounds and loss of blood were extremely sensitive to cold even in the summer and thereby needed the warmth afforded by blankets. It is interesting to note that many men on naval vessels removed most of their clothing prior to an engagement; other preparations on board ship included a distribution of tourniquets to division officers and a thorough sanding of the decks "to prevent slipping after the blood should become plentiful." [9]

The medical director of general hospitals, in close contact with the army medical director, attempted as a rule to clear all hospitals near the expected battle site of those who could bear transportation to more distant institutions, and he advised the army medical director as to the number of vacant beds available in each of the hospitals under his jurisdiction.[10] At times, due to army movements, it was necessary to relocate general hospitals. As the battle became imminent, brigade field infirmaries, identifiable by hospital flags, were established; to the extent practicable these were located in build-

[9] The area around the guns frequently became quite bloody.

[10] Many of the wounded of the battle of Chickamauga were sent by rail to Marietta. To make room at Marietta, the sick in hospital there were sent back to Atlanta, and those in the Atlanta hospitals were moved back to La Grange and other points.

113

ings outside the range of shells but strategically enough to maintain constant communication with both the front and the rear of the army. Brigade medical personnel and supplies were sometimes consolidated for the purpose of setting up division infirmaries.

The Infirmary Corps

An infirmary corps, comprising about thirty detailed men —usually those "least effective under arms"—and the assistant surgeon from each regiment, were responsible for the care of the wounded upon the field and for the removal from the field of those unable to walk. The assistant surgeon, who was in charge of the infirmary corps, was to equip himself with a pocket case of instruments, ligatures, needles, pins, chloroform, morphine, alcoholic stimulants, tourniquets, bandages, lint, and splints. All members of the infirmary corps were unarmed and wore badges to distinguish them from the rest of the command. They were outfitted with one litter to every two men, and each member carried a canteen of water, a tin cup, and a knapsack; the latter was supposed to contain lint, bandages, sponges, tourniquets, four splints, and a pint bottle of alcoholic stimulants. The corps members accompanied the ambulances and were charged with following the action upon the battlefield.[11]

The infirmary corps was no place for cowards. As it advanced with the troops the assistant surgeon kept on the lookout for places suitable as first aid stations; due notice was taken of the topography and gullies deep enough to afford welcome protection were especially sought after. Work done by the corps was usually rather simple, but the members were kept very busy. According to one who served as an assistant surgeon in the field, their service "consisted chiefly of the ap-

[11] It has been said that Hunter Holmes McGuire, medical director of Stonewall Jackson's commands, "perfected" the ambulance or infirmary corps in the spring of 1862.

plication of plaster and bandages and the administration of stimulants, and superintending the placing of the badly wounded in the ambulances for transportation to the field hospital. No elaborate surgical procedure was undertaken unless there was urgent necessity for it. Sometimes a very extended area was fought over, and wounded men, both our own and the enemy's, would be scattered about it, often, if the country was wooded or otherwise difficult, in out-of-the way places, whither they had wandered. When the battle was ended, if our troops had possession of the field, we had to hunt up these unfortunates—a duty willingly performed, though not infrequently an arduous one."

It was especially arduous when the woods caught on fire, as during the battles of Chancellorsville and the Wilderness. A vivid picture of the former's aftermath was related as follows by John Casler, a Rebel: ". . . On the left side of our line . . . the scene beggars description. The dead and badly wounded from both sides were lying where they fell. The woods, taking fire that night from the shells, burnt rapidly and roasted the wounded men alive. As we went to bury them we could see where they had tried to keep the fire from them by scratching the leaves away as far as they could reach. But it availed not; they were burnt to a crisp. The only way we could tell to which army they belonged was by turning them over and examining their clothing where they lay close to the ground. . . ." At the Wilderness the infirmary corps was seriously impeded in its work by the flames and smoke; undoubtedly many wounded men there were cremated also as a result.

Members of the infirmary corps were forbidden to engage in any action which was not strictly in the line of duty; the medical officer was specifically enjoined not to devote his exclusive attention to a wounded officer or leave his post to escort him to the rear. Troops other than the infirmary corps were not permitted to break ranks to care for the wounded or remove them from the field; those who did were liable to receive harsh punishment. Field commanders were always proud when they could boast in their battle reports that "no soldier left the field unauthorized."

The Field Infirmary during Battle

While the assistant surgeons were occupied in attending the wounded on the field, the surgeons remained at the brigade or division infirmaries and administered to those whom the ambulances or litter carriers brought in. Their ministrations consisted of performing all necessary surgical operations, seeing that proper nourishment in sufficient quantities was provided by the cooks, and directing the movement of the disabled from the infirmaries to the general hospitals.

Amputations and other surgical operations were supposed to be performed at the field infirmaries with the least possible delay, and this procedure was usually followed.[12] The Surgeon General, in an effort to increase the strength of the field operating staff, directed, early in 1864, that a Reserve Surgical Corps be organized by medical directors of hospitals for temporary field duty during emergencies. Medical directors were to appoint surgeons to the reserve corps on the basis of one for every five hundred beds in their departments. Those appointed to the corps were to be skillful in the use of the knife, and field medical directors were authorized to request their services whenever they were needed.[13] Lafayette Guild's inability to obtain the services of as many members of the reserve corps as he requested during the heavy fighting in the Wilderness (May

[12] The wounded of the battle of First Manassas, instead of receiving surgical attention on the field, were sent to the general hospitals for treatment. Field surgeons were warned against repetition of this procedure.

[13] W. A. Carrington, medical director of the Virginia hospitals, and Lafayette Guild, medical director of Lee's army, did not see eye to eye on some matters. Carrington proposed early in 1863, for example, that medical officers be detached from field regiments and assigned to hospital service after battles. Guild, however, contended that further engagements would probably occur and that field officers could not be spared. One purpose of the Reserve Surgical Corps' formation was to enable regimental medical officers to remain in the field.

5–12, 1864) caused him to express the fear that they were "too anxious to return to their hospitals." [14] Such comments reflect the almost contemptuous attitude sometimes manifested by field surgeons toward those assigned to general hospitals. "As for the disease to which you refer, as being the chronic condition of the 'Hospital Doctors,' " wrote one of the former, "I am satisfied it is *incurable*. I only regret it is not mortal." Medical Director Stout complained bitterly of the field medical officers' lack of confidence in the labors of their fellows in the general hospitals. "Were the same spirit of recrimination manifested toward surgeons in the field by the surgeons in hospitals," he wrote, "few regimental or brigade or division surgeons in this army could do much else than defend themselves against accusations brought almost every day against them by privates in hospital."

The scenes in and around field hospitals during an engagement were quite grim. One soldier who visited a field hospital near Atlanta during the summer of 1864 remembered years later the sight of a large pile of arms and legs in the rear of the building and stated that there was nothing in his whole life that he remembered with "more horror than that pile of legs and arms that had been cut off our soldiers." He concluded his comments on the hospital as follows: "It was the only field hospital that I saw during the whole war, and I have no desire to see another. Those hollow-eyed and sunken-cheeked sufferers, shot in every conceivable part of the body; some shrieking, and calling upon their mothers; some laughing the hard, cackling laugh of the sufferer without hope, and some cursing like troopers, and some writhing and groaning as their wounds were being bandaged and dressed. I saw a man . . . who had lost his right hand, another his leg, then another whose head was laid open, and I could see his brain thump, and another with his under jaw shot off; in fact, wounded in every manner possible." To make matters more

[14] Guild proposed, early in 1865, that some system of rotation be devised so that all medical officers could have both hospital and field experience.

difficult, hospitals sometimes were caught in the line of fire and both surgeons and patients killed.

The dead, of course, were buried as soon as possible after a battle by burial parties from the opposing armies. A short truce was usually agreed upon after an engagement to enable the armies to recover the bodies, and their interment, in common graves dug for the dead of each army, took place immediately. General Lee, according to Lafayette Guild, readily gave his consent to the removal of enemy dead because "he did not want a single Yankee to remain on our soil *dead* or *alive.*" The offensive odor of dead around the works at Vicksburg and other besieged garrisons created a sanitary problem, and it was sometimes reported that, without a formal truce, Federal skirmishers fired on burial parties. Occasionally, when the army was forced to withdraw after a battle, the dead were left on the field.

Movement to the General Hospitals: The Ambulance Problem

After the wounded had received the necessary attention at the field hospitals, the surgeons were responsible for directing the removal of those who had undergone operations, and were able to stand further movement, to the general hospitals.[15] Ambulances and every other means of wagon transportation were used to transport the wounded to railroad depots, steamer landings, and sometimes the entire distance to the interior institutions. This movement was often handicapped seriously by the lack of a sufficient number of ambulances and animals to draw them, two of the truly serious shortages experienced by medical officers of the Southern Confederacy.

Lafayette Guild could report, even after the bloody battles of the Wilderness and Spotsylvania (May, 1864), that there

[15] Guild advised the Surgeon General after the battle of Chancellorsville that 132 wounded men were not able to bear movement to the railroad depot.

was no suffering among the men from the lack of medical supplies or surgical attention.[16] And an abundance of medical stores and officers was reported at other times by inspectors and high ranking surgeons in the field. Never, however, did the armies appear to have an adequate amount of ambulance transportation. Guild complained of the "present impromptu ambulance system of this army" in his report of the Seven Days' engagements (June 25–July 1, 1862) and in April, 1863, he asserted that one of the two most serious problems confronting the army as a whole was that of transportation.[17] The lack of ambulances sometimes compelled Guild to keep his wounded in the field where they might be unprotected from driving rains;[18] and he stated that the wagons he had were made of inferior materials whereas "the horses appear to have been broken down before turned over to the ambulance train." Guild believed that each regiment should have two ambulances and that an additional number should be held in reserve for each corps and the whole army. He was unable ever to procure a sufficient number, however, and continued to complain of the ambulance trains' "wretched condition."[19] In June, 1863, when Lee's forces invaded Pennsylvania, spring wagons were impressed so that the sick could be carried forward with the army.

The ambulance shortage was felt throughout the Confederacy. Thomas Williams, Medical Director of the Army of the Potomac, wrote of the need for ambulances in his army, asserted that poor materials were being used in those that were furnished, and asked that the War Department adopt regulations necessary to prevent the use of hospital wagons for ordinary regimental purposes. When the special congres-

[16] The health of Lee's army in September, 1864, was reported to be excellent and the supply of medicines abundant.

[17] General regulations allowed each regiment two four-wheeled and two two-wheeled ambulances, but these paper allowances never materialized into actuality.

[18] The Shiloh wounded "suffered greatly" from rain.

[19] There was an ambulance manufactory in Richmond at the foot of 17th Street.

sional committee appointed to investigate the Medical Department completed its inquiry early in 1862, it asserted that the lack of medical wagons had "produced much of the mortality and much of the suffering." A year later, inspecting officers reported only thirty-eight ambulances in the Army of Mississippi, the Army of Tennessee's medical director informed Surgeon General Moore that his army had received "an inadequate supply," and Lieutenant-Colonel E. J. Harvie, Assistant Inspector General in the Army of Mississippi, adverted to the need for surgical instruments in that army but emphasized quite clearly that "ambulances, particularly are required and ought if possible to be supplied."

Transportation facilities confronting medical personnel in the Army of Tennessee became increasingly serious, and early in 1864 its medical director warned "that not half the necessary supplies can be carried and those who are so unfortunate as to be sick or wounded on a march, will have to be left by the road side." In the summer of that year, Medical Inspector Edward N. Covey found the ambulance transportation of Medical Director Stout's department to be "entirely insufficient." And in 1865, entire brigades in the Department of Western Virginia and East Tennessee were found to be without ambulances or medical wagons of any kind. Priorities assigned to the use of wagons for purposes of forage and the movement of subsistence stores during the closing weeks of the war made the problem of transporting medical and hospital supplies almost insoluble.[20]

The wounded usually underwent a most uncomfortable trip even when ambulance transportation was available to move them from the field hospitals. Some spring vehicles were supplied early in the war, but when these broke down they were replaced by ordinary wagons, and as the latter moved over rough, wooded country or on roads rutted by artillery and army supply trains the occupants experienced a rude jolting. Heavy downpours sometimes caused wagons to become mired in the mud, while, at the same time, the wounded were

[20] There was an early shortage of ambulances in the Union army.

drenched by the rain falling through leaky covers. Drivers were not always considerate of their charges, and one officer related that he was compelled to draw his pistol on one to stop him from traveling at breakneck speed over the roughest roads.

Ambulance wagons might also be harassed by the enemy. Two ambulance trains headed south after the battle of Gettysburg were both, according to Lafayette Guild, attacked by enemy raiding parties. The raiders, he asserted, "destroyed many wagons," "paroled the wounded private soldiers," and took with them "all of the officers who fell into their hands." When the Gettysburg wounded reached Williamsport, they were moved across the swollen Potomac on rafts and ferry boats; an ambulance line was then organized to Staunton which made connections with the Richmond trains. Not all, however, were removed to the capital. Many convalesced in the Valley hospitals.[21]

Field medical officers of the Army of Northern Virginia were aided to a considerable extent in the removal of their wounded to the general hospitals by an organization known as the Richmond Ambulance Committee. Established in the capital during the spring of 1862, it was composed for the most part of men exempt from military duty and had an overall membership of nearly a hundred well-known citizens. Headed by John Enders, the committee formed itself into a military company and attempted, at its own expense, to attend, feed, and transport the wounded to the interior hospitals. At the battle of Williamsburg (May 5, 1862), the organization had thirty-nine ambulances on the field, and it functioned effectively in almost every engagement participated in by Lee's army. Seven thousand men passed through the committee's

[21] The movement of the wounded from Gettysburg proved to be a harrowing experience for all concerned. Brigadier General John D. Imboden's cavalry brigade guarded the ambulance train that went by way of Cashtown, and the suffering of the wounded during the jolting trip over rough roads to Williamsport made an indelible impression upon that officer. "During this one night," he wrote, "I realized more of the horrors of war than I had in all the two preceding years."

121

hands at Chancellorsville (May 2, 1863), and after the battle of Gettysburg, a Richmond newspaper reported that "the Ambulance Corps was in Winchester for the entire period of three weeks, at the expense of many thousands of dollars to its individual members, caring for the wounded, facilitating their transportation, and doing all possible offices of humanity." Coordination existed between the Ambulance Committee and the medical directors of the Virginia general hospitals and the Army of Northern Virginia. Lafayette Guild and General Lee both acknowledged publicly the great obligations they were under to the committee for its valuable and humane services.[22]

Transportation of the Wounded by Rail

As a general rule, ambulance transportation was used only to remove the wounded to nearby railroad and water connections. A good many disabled soldiers reached the Richmond hospitals in ambulances or on steamers from Drewry's Bluff, but most wounded throughout the Confederacy were transported by rail. In the decade preceding the war the Southern states had been quite active in railroad construction, and by 1860 Virginia and Georgia ranked sixth and seventh respectively among all the states in railroad mileage. The enterprise manifested by these two states was fortunate for the Confederacy in the movement of its disabled troops since their strategic location caused a large share of the burden to fall upon their lines.[23]

The movement by rail was at times a most disagreeable experience for the wounded and a trying one for the medical officials. After the battle of Chancellorsville, for example, Union

[22] The Ambulance Committee even directed the movement of prisoners at times.

[23] Regular ambulance trains connected Virginia hospital centers throughout the war. General Lee and his medical director preferred the hospitals in Gordonsville, Charlottesville, Lynchburg, Danville, Staunton, and Farmville to those of Richmond, and they insisted that their sick and wounded be sent to those points when possible.

cavalry tore up the railroad tracks in the Confederate rear and occasioned a delay of several days in the transportation of the disabled to Richmond. Unheated cars in winter also caused suffering; the wounds of a group that reached Richmond late in November, 1863, on an unheated ambulance train were almost frozen, and the Ambulance Committee "built a fire on the track" to relieve the intense suffering. It was not unusual for trains to jump the track, and the wounded often died or received additional injuries in such wrecks. A Texan who was wrecked en route to the Stout Hospital in Milledgeville, Georgia, wrote: "I went all through the Tennessee campaign, and I tell you that I saw some hard times, and then to get nearly killed on an old car, is rather disheartening." Inspectors complained also of lack of water in the cars and the tendency of engineers to jerk the cars in starting their trains. "Another evil," wrote an inspector late in 1863, "is in the frequent and most unreasonable delays of trains loaded with sick and wounded; in the present crowded and confused condition of transportation, it is doubtful whether we can effect any removal of this difficulty." Such delays were indeed unavoidable, and a surgeon of the Mississippi Blind Asylum Hospital in Jackson noted that some of the wounded received there were almost "in articulo mortis" when they arrived.[24] Medical Director A. J. Foard of the Army of Tennessee held General Leonidas Polk responsible for much of the suffering borne by the disabled sent back from Murfreesboro because Polk would not allow them to stop at Chattanooga, and Foard spoke of that officer as being "very obstinate."

[24] General Earl Van Dorn, Commanding General of the Army of West Tennessee at the battle of Corinth (October 3–4, 1862), was charged by a brigade commander with, among other things, having caused great suffering among the wounded in their movement after the battle. Van Dorn, it was asserted, "did allow one or more trains of cars, freighted with wounded soldiers from the battlefield . . . to be detained without any necessity at Water Valley, Mississippi, during one or more entire nights, said wounded soldiers having been herded in said cars at Holly Springs without blankets or nourishment and many with undressed wounds, no surgeon, officer, nurse, or attendant with them. . . ." A Court of Inquiry, headed by Major General Sterling Price, found Van Dorn innocent of such allegations, however.

Chickamauga

The problems involved in the large-scale movement of wounded men to the general hospitals and the utter impossibility under certain circumstances of preventing much tragic suffering and very many deaths may perhaps best be illustrated by the efforts of the medical officers to care for the Chickamauga wounded. In the first place, the wounded had to be moved by an insufficient number of ambulances over bad roads from ten to twenty-five miles from the battlefield to the railroad. Rail transportation was deficient, and it was reported five days after the battle that there were still twenty carloads of men waiting to be moved. In the meantime, Medical Director Stout had lost contact with the medical director of the Army of Tennessee, but, learning where the wounded were being concentrated along the railroad, he repaired from Marietta to that point with additional medical officers and hospital attendants to supervise the further care and disposition of the wounded. Other hospital surgeons were sent to the field, and they were replaced by private physicians, many of whom volunteered their services to the government during the emergency. After Stout arrived on the scene, he found it necessary to open hospitals at Dalton and Ringgold and to reopen the Tunnel Hill institution; these points were located approximately fourteen, eight, and twelve miles respectively from the area where the wounded were concentrated and were primarily receiving and distributing centers for the patients. Since the hospitals in Stout's department had a capacity of only about 7,500 beds, it was necessary to send large numbers of the wounded to other departments; many were assigned to the care of private citizens residing near the hospitals, and furloughs were granted to those who would be disabled for more than thirty days but who did not require skilled surgical attention. The slightly wounded were sent to convalescent camps, and malingerers were returned to their commands. Unfortunately, however, chiefly because of the rail situation, most of the wounded, regardless of ultimate destination, had to be sent to Atlanta. According to Surgeon Joseph P. Logan, medical officer in charge of the Atlanta hospitals, more than ten thousand soldiers were received into the hospitals of Atlanta during September alone whereas the capacity of those institutions was not more than eighteen hundred. To make matters worse, the hospitals below Atlanta were just in the process of being reopened after their removal from the Chattanooga area. Both Logan and Stout were of the opinion that the medical officials had done well under the circumstances, but the latter communicated to Surgeon General Moore his need for increased hospital accommodations and more qualified medical officers.

Ordinarily the movement of the disabled to general hospitals took place with much more facility. Almost five thousand wounded men, for example, were received into the Richmond hospitals between May 6 and May 20, 1864, and the total number of deaths during that interval of time was reported as exactly seventy-three. Of this number, it was revealed, ten were dead upon arrival, seventeen died within an hour after their reception, and fourteen died within six or seven hours after admission.[25] The reception of wounded from the Army of Northern Virginia at Richmond was superintended by Francis W. Hancock, surgeon in charge of Jackson Hospital, and a military guard stood by to prevent any interference with the men. Only Surgeon Hancock, his immediate aides, and the Ambulance Committee were authorized to attend the disabled.

Problems of Co-ordination

Two important factors that seriously handicapped the Medical Department in removing the sick and wounded to the rear before, during, and after engagements should be

[25] Of 837 wounded received at the Seabrook Hospital in Richmond during a two-day period after the battle of Fredericksburg (December 13, 1862), only one was reported to have died.

noticed. The first of these concerned a lack of proper staff co-operation between the Medical, Subsistence, and Quartermaster Departments. The second was the failure of the military arm to advise the Medical Department of troop movements.

Surgeon General Moore, in an effort to solve the problem of insufficient staff co-ordination, proposed to the heads of the Subsistence and Quartermaster Departments in November, 1863, that special commissary and quartermaster officers, subordinate only to their seniors in Richmond, be appointed solely for the purpose of supplying the needs of the sick and wounded. It was Moore's contention that during active operations the duties of the chief commissary and quartermaster officers were so onerous and the lines of communication with their juniors were broken so frequently that proper services simply were not afforded medical officers. No response appears to have been forthcoming, and, late in January, 1864, the Surgeon General appealed to field commanders themselves to perfect the best arrangement possible and enclosed his own proposition for their information. No comprehensive plan was adopted, but an arrangement was made in Lee's army near the close of 1863 whereby an assistant commissary in each division gave his entire attention during battles toward providing subsistence for the sick and wounded.[26]

The medical directors of both the Army of the Potomac and the Army of Northern Virginia complained at times of their inability to make adequate plans for the removal of the disabled because of the commanding general's failure to advise them of operations. Thomas H. Williams, medical chief of the Army of the Potomac, complained that unless the commander was "less reserved in his official intercourse with this Department, untoward circumstances will prove of frequent recurrence." Lafayette Guild wrote on one occasion that "everything is done hurriedly and mysteriously" and declared that a

[26] Medical Director Stout experienced similar problems of co-ordination in the West.

knowledge of contemplated troop movements "would add greatly to the efficiency of the Corps."

Treatment of Enemy Captives

Large numbers of enemy sick and wounded often fell into Confederate hands after engagements, and their treatment was one of the problems of the battlefield. Usually enough Federal medical officers were left to render surgical attention to their troops, but, of course, much oversight and material aid was almost always needed. Many Union troops, for example, were so badly wounded in the terrible battle of Malvern Hill (July 1, 1862) that they could not be removed from the field. General Lee, made aware of their suffering, directed Lafayette Guild to assist the Northern surgeons in concentrating their men at a central position "where surgical aid could be more efficiently rendered and where provisions and other necessaries could be issued." Arrangements were sometimes made which allowed the United States commander to send supplies for his wounded, and it was not unusual, under agreement between the field commanders, for the disabled to be paroled and transferred within the Union lines as speedily as possible.[27] Others were transported to interior hospitals to receive treatment and await parole there. Surgeons of Confederate prison hospitals were ordered, in the spring of 1864, not to transfer any man whose life would be endangered by the travel incident thereto.

Confederate forces were not infrequently charged by the enemy with barbarous conduct in their treatment of Union sick and wounded. Colonel Abel D. Streight, who led a Federal raiding party from Tuscumbia, Alabama, toward Rome, Georgia, in April, 1863, asserted that the Confederates, after

[27] The transfer of wounded was a humane action. Major General Henry W. Halleck, General-in-Chief of the Union forces for a time, asserted that it was "impossible for our own medical officers after a battle to attend the sick and wounded prisoners, and usually it is impossible for some weeks to hire citizen surgeons for that purpose."

taking possession of the hospitals he had established for his wounded, seized the medical stores, instruments, blankets, rations, shoes, coats, hats, and money from the surgeons and left the wounded "in a semi-naked and starving condition." Several charges were made to the effect that Confederate officers refused to grant requests, made under flag of truce, for the removal of Union dead and wounded from the field of battle. Such accusations as were made usually condemned the offenders with violating well-recognized principles of war.

There was undoubtedly some mistreatment and neglect of sick and wounded captives by both Confederate and Union forces. Neither side, at any rate, enjoyed a monopoly of accusations against the other. Lafayette Guild, for example, held that "the inhuman enemy invariably, when an opportunity offers, drag our sick and wounded officers (at the sacrifice of their lives) into their own lines." Charges and countercharges notwithstanding, Union officers themselves have testified to many refreshing instances of humane attention accorded their disabled by Southern medical officers. John Swinburne, left in charge of the Federal sick and wounded remaining on the field after the "Seven Days" (June 25–July 1, 1862), informed General Lee that the Confederate surgeons had "performed miracles in the way of kind attention both to us surgeons as well as the wounded." A detail of United States surgeons sent within the Southern lines after the battle of Chancellorsville (May 2, 1863) to effect the removal of their men related that the "rebel surgeons . . . treated our wounded with consideration." During the Wilderness campaign some six hundred Union troops were rescued from hospitals inside the Confederate lines, and Montgomery C. Meigs, Quartermaster General of the United States, informed the Secretary of War that the men were in "generally good condition" and had been "kindly treated by the enemy." Thomas A. McParlin, medical head of the Union Army of the Potomac, reported, after the battle of Cold Harbor (June 3, 1864), that the Federal wounded collected in Confederate field hospitals received the same amount of food, medical attendance, and medical supplies as the Southern wounded.[28]

The kind treatment of many Confederate wounded who fell into Union hands on land and sea has also been attested by Southern officers and other observers. When Lee abandoned his positions at Antietam, for example, many wounded were left behind, and the kindness of the doctors in blue to those wounded received wide recognition. Jonathan Letterman, the Union army's medical director, expressed the sentiment of most army medical officers in the following statement: "Humanity teaches us that a wounded and prostrate foe is not then our enemy." [29]

Exchange of Surgeons

An extremely significant development pertaining to the status of medical officers captured on the field of battle occurred in the spring of 1862. During the opening campaigns of the war captive surgeons, in accordance with the practice that had prevailed throughout the world, were held prisoners in the same manner as other officers. Most medical officers, as well as other military personnel, dreaded captivity, and,

[28] The son of General Albert Sidney Johnston stated that his father's death at Shiloh would have been prevented had General Johnston not ordered David W. Yandell, his chief medical officer, to establish a hospital for and administer to a number of wounded men—many of whom were Federals. Johnston was thus deprived of Yandell's personal services.

[29] Confederate disabled and their medical officers left at Gettysburg also received much attention from Medical Director Letterman and the United States Sanitary and Christian Commissions. Simon Baruch, one of the Southern surgeons who remained with the wounded, reported that he was given a six-mule wagon loaded to capacity with commissary and medical stores. Such kindness extended to the war on the sea. The wounded of the *Alabama*, famous Confederate cruiser that was sunk by the *Kearsarge* (June 19, 1864), were taken on board the latter vessel for treatment. Admiral Franklin Buchanan, who commanded the Confederate naval forces in the battle of Mobile Bay (August 5, 1864), reported that his captive wounded were carried to the United States Naval Hospital at Pensacola, Florida, and received much consideration.

when their armies were compelled to retreat after an engagement, there was an understandable reluctance on their part to remain with the wounded and face months of confinement in enemy prisons. Their incarceration, generally speaking, meant that many sick and wounded comrades would be deprived of their services over an indefinite period of time. When Stonewall Jackson, during his Shenandoah Valley campaign of 1862, entered the city of Winchester on May 25, however, a train of events was set in motion that inaugurated a new departure in the annals of war.

A number of Union wounded had been left at Winchester's Union (Hotel) Hospital in charge of J. Burd Peale, a brigade surgeon, and seven other Federal medical officers. General Jackson ordered that Peale and his colleagues be allowed to continue their ministrations undisturbed, and before Jackson's forces withdrew from the city on May 31, an agreement was entered into between the Union surgeons and Hunter Holmes McGuire, medical director of Jackson's army, which freed the former unconditionally upon their promise to work for the release of the same number of Confederate surgeons. The Union surgeons also agreed to lend their efforts to win support for the principle that all medical officers captured thereafter should be released unconditionally.[30]

The agreement of May 31, 1862, between the Union medical officers and Medical Director McGuire at Winchester was followed by a proposal on June 10, 1862, from General George B. McClellan, commander of the United States Army of the Potomac, to General Lee that medical officers "be viewed as non-combatants" and not liable to detention as prisoners of war. General Lee concurred in this proposition on June 17, 1862. Two days later, General McClellan sent General Lee a

[30] The initiative in proposing the unconditional release of the Union surgeons seems to have been taken by Hunter McGuire. General Jackson's official campaign report is silent in regard to this important arrangement. The written agreement signed at Winchester has not been located, but Philip Adolphus, one of the Union surgeons, made a copy of the document, and this copy was given to the Society of Medical History of Chicago when he died.

copy of General Orders No. 60, dated June 6, 1862, issued by the Adjutant General's Office in Washington, paragraph 4 of which reads as follows: "The principle being recognized that medical officers should not be held as prisoners of war it is hereby directed that all medical officers so held by the United States shall be immediately and unconditionally discharged." [31] The precise relationship between this directive and the Winchester agreement is not known but certainly an important step in the interests of the sick and wounded of both armies had been taken. Complete harmony on the subject was apparently reached when the Confederate Adjutant and Inspector General's Office published General Orders No. 45 on June 26, 1862, which, like its Northern counterpart, directed the immediate and unconditional discharge of all medical officers in Southern prisons.[32]

Release of medical officers pursuant to the foregoing orders proceeded without interruption until the summer of 1863. At that time the orders were suspended due to ill feeling which developed from the case of Dr. William P. Rucker. Dr. Rucker, a staunch Unionist native of Covington, Virginia, was charged by the Commonwealth of Virginia with having committed murder and stolen a horse shortly after the outbreak of hostilities. On July 25, 1862, Confederate cavalry forces captured Rucker, who by that time it seems was a surgeon in the Union army, stationed at Summersville, West Virginia. Rucker was then delivered for trial to the state authorities. Robert Ould, the Confederate Agent of Exchange, refused to consider Union demands for Rucker's release or to concur in a proposal which

[31] "Instructions for the government of armies of the United States in the field," issued as General Orders No. 100, dated April 24, 1863, stated in part that the "enemy's chaplains, officers of the medical staff, apothecaries, hospital nurses and servants if they fall into the hands of the American Army are not prisoners of war unless the commander has reasons to retain them."

[32] Such an order had been issued embracing the Department of Northern Virginia (Lee's command) on June 22, 1862. A Union observer noted after the new arrangement that "many Federal surgeons remained behind, and their services were very much appreciated by the men [left on the field]."

would have permitted the exchange of all medical officers held by both sides with the exception of Rucker and a hostage held for him by the United States. The dreary controversy over Rucker dragged on until October, 1863, at which time he escaped from the state authorities in Richmond. On November 11, 1863, Ould accepted a Union proposal for the immediate release of all medical officers without reservation, and the free exchange of surgeons was resumed.[33]

Cases continued to arise from time to time concerning the detention of Confederate medical officers by the United States, and these were sometimes attributed to the "maladministration of subordinate officers." The detention of medical officers for months at a time in such institutions as the Old Capitol Prison in Washington, the Military Prison Hospital in Louisville, Kentucky, and United States Military Prison No. 21 in New Orleans, however, probably could not be blamed altogether on subordinates. And eight Southern surgeons were detained for four months in Chattanooga Hospital No. 2— during which time all of their wounded had been exchanged. Records indicate also that medical officers of the United States were sometimes subjected to undue detention in the Confederacy.

Medical officers on both sides were always anxious for the speedy exchange of all prisoners, and the case for the neutralization of hospitals, their personnel and materiel was stated by no one any more ably than it was by Surgeon Henry S. Hewit of the United States Medical Department in January, 1865. Hewit, Medical Director of the Army of Ohio, wrote: "The hospital should, under all circumstances, be held sacred. Surgeons and attendants engaged in their legitimate duties should not be subject to capture, and hospital stores and medicines should have free transit and enjoy freedom from capture or confiscation. The question is of the utmost importance in its most obvious view in saving life and mitigating suffering on the field of battle, and taking away the necessity for sudden

[33] There were, according to the Richmond *Examiner*, 115 Confederate surgeons exchanged immediately after the accord reached in November.

and most distressing removals of wounded men according to the exigencies of conflict. . . . It would do more than any measure, either military or political, to realize the desire of every patriot—the restoration of an harmonious Union." [34]

Surely the field surgeon should have been accorded, in the interests of humanity, the utmost consideration. He endured the long marches with the troops and shared their peril on the field of battle. His hospital frequently fell into the line of fire, and, during the din of battle, and after, he was called upon to perform hour after hour the most serious operations. The casualties of major battles were so heavy that neither the Confederate surgeon nor his Northern counterpart ever had enough assistance at such times, and his labors in behalf of the wounded often continued until he was overcome from exhaustion. Battlefield promotions and other rewards might be won by the fighting man, but there was little likelihood that the field surgeon, regardless of his risk and work, would receive more than passing notice.[35]

[34] A resolution offered by Horatio W. Bruce of Kentucky, which instructed the House Committee on the Medical Department to inquire into the feasibility of establishing neutral prison hospitals at the most important prison depots in both the Confederate States and the United States, was adopted by the Confederate House of Representatives on February 5, 1864. There the matter rested.

[35] Some surgeons combined military action with their medical duties, and there are quite a few accounts of heroism on the field of battle. Not all were fearless, however. When shells started falling near the *Arkansas,* a Confederate ram, its long, slim surgeon from Mississippi, according to a veteran of the war, could be heard groaning: "Oh Louisa and the babes!"

CHAPTER VIII

Procurement and Manufacture of Hospital and Medical Supplies

The Problem

*T*he problem of obtaining a sufficient quantity of hospital and medical supplies to prevent disease and treat the disabled was one that tested the ingenuity of the Confederate medical authorities to the utmost extent. A fairly large amount of medical and surgical stores was found in United States depots and other installations when these were surrendered to the various Southern states, but such stores were soon exhausted. To supply the medical and surgical needs of the military establishment during four years of war, supplies were purchased abroad and brought in as contraband through the blockade,[1] obtained through the lines, captured from the enemy, furnished by private and state agencies, and purchased or manufactured within the boundaries of the beleaguered Southern Confederacy.

Supplies Imported from Abroad

Records pertaining to the quantity of supplies imported from abroad are fragmentary, but some idea of the amount brought in can be gained. Caleb Huse, the War Department's

[1] The Union government declared medicines and surgical instruments contraband. This led President Davis, in a message to Congress, to assert: "The sacred claims of humanity, respected even during the fury of actual battle . . . are outraged in cold blood by a government and people that pretend to desire a continuance of fraternal connections." On the other hand, a Northerner concluded that "The worst thing that could have been done to the rebels would have been to send them all the medicine they wanted."

first purchasing agent abroad, contracted for both ordnance and medical supplies, and he alone bought and shipped £13,432 10s. 7d. in medicines during the first two years of the war.[2] The sum of $533,333.33 for the purchase of medical and hospital supplies was placed to the credit of Huse during 1863, and £30,000 of the Erlanger loan, marketed abroad that same year, was allotted to the Medical Department. That there was considerable activity on the part of purchasing agents abroad late in the war may perhaps be shown by the fact that in August, 1864, the medical authorities requested £113,000 to meet their foreign obligations for the next six months. At the same time, the Surgeon General asked that $400,000 be made available to Medical Purveyor Hugh Stockdell at Wilmington, North Carolina, for the purchase of medical supplies arriving there through the blockade.

Despite the fact that arms and clothing were given a priority over drugs in blockade running, drugs could be found on almost every ship entering a Confederate port. The value of medicines received by the state of North Carolina through the blockade has been estimated by one historian of the war as reaching $170,933 in Confederate currency, and it is his opinion that Lee's army, during the last two years of the conflict, was dependent for "chloroform, morphine, quinine, blue mass, paragoric, laudanum, and digitalis almost entirely on the blockade runners." No accurate estimate of the quantity of drugs arriving in Confederate ports during the war can be made, but a survey of seventy-five cargo manifests for vessels arriving in the Confederacy from Nassau between April, 1862, and April, 1865, is most rewarding. Such a survey shows the following drugs in the quantities indicated to have been imported: Acids, assorted—26 carboys, 52 cases; alcohol (beverage)—344 barrels, 90 casks, 3,509 cases, 295 boxes, 2 kegs, 10 quarts, 1 jug, 58 demijohns; alcohol (plain)—157 barrels, 56 casks; alum—10 barrels; arsenic (Trioxide)—3 kegs; bay rum—8 boxes; bicarbonate of soda—240 kegs; borax—1

<hr />

[2] The Surgeon General had complete confidence in the judgment of Huse. Beverly Tucker and A. T. D. Gifford were also purchasing medical supplies in Europe for the Confederacy.

case; calomel—5 cases; copper sulphate—3 barrels, 6 casks; ferrous sulphate—174 barrels; phosphorous—1 case; potassium iodide—2 cases; salt—6 barrels, 500 bushels, 23 cases, 11,038 sacks; sodium carbonate—669 kegs; soda ash (crude lye)—220 casks; sulphur—60 barrels. A study of cargo manifests for blockade runners operating from Bermuda over approximately the same period indicates that the following supplies were shipped from that point: medical stores—9 bales, 8 barrels, 113 cases, 3 kegs, 2 boxes; drugs and apothecaries' wares—305 packages, 14 cases; quinine—39 cases, 1 box; and brandy—1,974 cases, 149 boxes, and additional amounts in other measuring categories as well as smaller quantities of champagne, gin, rum, wine, whiskey, and alcohol.

Additional records reveal that from November 1, 1863, to December 8, 1864, the Confederate government imported 2,639 packages of medicine at Wilmington and Charleston, and that these same ports received, between October 25 and December 6, 1864, 115 barrels of alcohol, 110 boxes of tin plate, 7 cases of silk, and 2 cases of bismuth. The blockade runners were difficult to intercept; one of these, the *Kate*, made over forty successful trips and was referred to in the North as a "regular rebel packet."

Internal Trade

Internal trade with the enemy went on throughout the war. On May 21, 1861, Congress forbade the exportation of cotton except to Mexico and through established Southern seaports, and in the following August these restrictions were extended to sugar, tobacco, rice, molasses, syrup, and naval stores. Such efforts to prevent intercourse with the enemy proved unavailing. Cotton was eagerly sought in the North, and the Southern forces were in need of arms, powder, medicines, clothing, coffee, salt, and food. Surgeon General Moore placed Surgeon Richard Potts, a medical purveyor located in Montgomery, Alabama, in charge of all trade with the enemy on the Mississippi, but the entire business appears to have been poorly managed. Not only did Potts encounter competition from other purveyors anxious to share in the trade, but he was hampered also by a general lack of co-ordination among the Richmond authorities. On one occasion, after Potts had obtained a quantity of medical supplies to be paid for with cotton, the agent in charge of government cotton refused to turn over the agreed amount on the basis of instructions received from the Confederate capital. "Every day," Potts informed the Surgeon General, "cotton is being sent through the lines to New Orleans by different parties authorized by the Govt whose only object is to make money & I see no reason why the Medical Dept should not have the benefit of some of this trade." Potts wanted complete freedom in the conduct of this traffic with the enemy, but he learned in February, 1865, that he had been relieved of his duties in connection with such intercourse by the Secretary of War.[3]

A considerable amount of the internal trade centered around Memphis during the period of Federal occupation from 1862 to 1865. "Memphis," declared one Union general in May, 1864, "has been of more value to the Southern Confederacy since it fell into Federal hands than Nassau." Evidence to support this astonishing remark is not lacking for two months later it was estimated by the Union Congressional Committee on the Conduct of the War "that between $20,000,000 and $30,000,000 worth of supplies had passed through this city into the hands of the Confederacy." It is clear that a large amount of drugs was sent southward in exchange for cotton despite the fact that Union officers made a sustained effort to keep such trade under rigorous control. Proprietors of the drug firms of S. Mansfield and Company and Ward and McClelland were imprisoned because they had sent contraband through the lines; the Ward and McClelland proprietors lost their stock of $65,000 also for engaging in this contraband business

[3] Surgeon General Moore, in a communication to the Secretary of War on February 9, 1865, urged that Potts be allowed to continue his trade through the lines.

—estimated at $60,000—after they had taken the oath of allegiance to the United States.[4]

A surprising quantity of medico-pharmaceutical products was smuggled across the lines at Memphis and elsewhere by those who resided thereabout. Many individuals were engaged in such activity, but very few made it a business and perhaps that is why there is so little documentary evidence available. On occasion drugs were secreted in the bellies of dead horses or mules that were presumably being taken to the boneyards for burial. At least one coffin borne by the hearse in a solemn funeral procession was filled with drugs for General Earl Van Dorn's army. Women were especially adept as purveyors of contraband inasmuch as soldiers were somewhat reluctant to search them, and accounts of their success in carrying quinine, morphine, and other items within the confines of hoop skirts and other clothing are legion. A search of one lady trying to leave Memphis uncovered twelve pairs of boots each full of whiskey and other needed supplies fastened to a large girdle. As a result of the necessity for concealing and disguising drugs in the effort to get them through the lines, serious consequences sometimes took place. According to Pharmacist Charles Theodor Mohr, who opened Mobile's first "Deutsche Apotheke" Shop in 1857 and was charged with the analysis of smuggled drugs after the war's outbreak, "confusions occurred rather often between quinine sulphate and morphine sulphate, frequently resulting in harm in the hospitals." Such "confusions" may in part account for the charge made in the spring of 1862 that the Union authorities had deliberately allowed poisoned quinine to be smuggled into the Confederacy.[5] It is interesting to note that the Adams Express Company guaranteed the delivery to any post office in the Confederacy of a quinine-filled envelope for a two dollar fee, a lucrative service until ordered to be discontinued shortly after it was inaugurated.

[4] Potts had done considerable business with both of these companies.
[5] Mohr stated that French quinine was "highly adulterated" throughout the war.

Captured Supplies

Greatly needed medical and hospital supplies were occasionally captured from the enemy. After the Confederate victory at Manassas (July 21, 1861), a Tar Heel surgeon reported the seizure of "a large number of cases of fine Surgical instruments and a large stock of medicines," and he expressed the view that the medical staff would "not be troubled in this line of preparation for another action." One of the most valuable captures of such supplies was made by General Nathan Bedford Forrest's cavalry during a raid into western Tennessee. Forrest appropriated all that was needed by his own command from three large wagonloads and shipped the rest to Atlanta. There a medical purveyor appraised the value of the shipment alone at $150,000 in gold. A large storehouse in Winchester, Virginia, filled with medicines, instruments, and other medical goods, was seized by Stonewall Jackson's men in May, 1862. Another large haul, estimated at about $20,000, was reported from the Kanawha Valley in September, 1862.

Surgeons with invading armies did not hesitate to visit drug stores and doctors' offices for the purpose of appropriating needed supplies. Enemy surgical instruments were especially prized, and Union medical officers who remained with their captive wounded after the battle of Chancellorsville (May 1–5, 1863) asserted that Confederate surgeons took their instruments and made it impossible for them to render proper assistance to their troops. Confederate medical stores were sometimes seized by United States forces, but the Southern acquisitions by this means were quite noteworthy.

Private Contributions

Patriotic and enthusiastic civilians began making contributions of supplies for the armed forces in the early days of the struggle, and their efforts came to be aided by the states. Two acts were passed by Congress in August, 1861, to make provision for the care of citizen contributions. The first directed the Secretary of War to appoint a clerk to take charge of and distribute all supplies received for the sick and wounded. This clerk was placed under the jurisdiction of the Surgeon General, and the two were authorized to establish a depot. The second law instructed the Secretary of War "to make all necessary arrangements for the reception and forwarding of clothes, shoes, blankets, and other articles of necessity that may be sent to the army by private contribution." To receive and distribute the contributions for the sick and wounded, Surgeon General Moore appointed H. T. Banks as contribution clerk and assigned him to the office of Surgeon Edward W. Johns, medical purveyor in Richmond. The latter repeatedly called upon the people to send in contributions of such items as clothing, blankets, comforts, bandages, fruits, wines, and jellies for the use of disabled soldiers.

It would, of course, be impossible to evaluate the contributions made to the government during the war. Individuals presented gifts and gave unselfishly of their services. Late in 1861, the ladies were asked by Surgeon Johns to collect one or more blankets from every family in the South through the agency of church committees. Richmond was the seat of an enthusiastic drive in the latter part of 1862, and a depot on Broad Street was obtained by the Young Men's Christian Association to receive supplies. President Davis, it was reported, subscribed a liberal amount, and theater managers gave benefit performances for the cause. Within a week almost $40,000 was contributed to collecting agencies. Private citizens of Pulaski, Tennessee, endeavored to provide shoes for the Army of Tennesee's barefooted soldiers after the battle of Franklin (November 30, 1864), and county courts sometimes made appropriations for the men serving from their respective counties. The sum of $5,278.88 was donated by various churches to the government early in the war, and Congress appropriated the money to care for the troops disabled at the battle of First Manassas.

Individuals gave quite generously to hospitals. S. Davis Tonge of Bainbridge, Georgia, for example, donated forty-two bales of cotton to the Macon hospitals, and mill owners sometimes provided sheeting, shirting, and clothing material. Many hospitals would at times have suffered from the lack of the barest food necessities had it not been for the patriotic devotion of nearby families; an examination of hospital account books reveals numerous important contributions. Several hospitals were established or enlarged through contributions made by individual citizens.

Aid and Relief Societies

Soldiers' aid and hospital relief societies sprang up all over the South and in some areas were found in almost every county. The women of the Confederacy were especially active in this sort of work. Soon after the war's outbreak numerous hospitals were established and managed by patriotic ladies such as Mrs. Juliet Opie Hopkins of Alabama, and they continued to administer these institutions until the Confederate government assumed jurisdiction over them late in 1862.[6] Their association with some remained very close thereafter, a fact illustrated by the reference of Medical Director Samuel H. Stout to the Ladies Hospital of Montgomery as "under the patronage of the ladies of Montgomery and its vicinity." And Mrs. Hopkins, aided by private contributions, state appropriations, and her own resources, served the several hospitals for Alabama troops in Richmond throughout most of the war.[7]

Women also aided in numerous other ways. There were three associations of ladies in Atlanta: The Ladies' Soldiers' Relief Society, The Ladies' Hospital Association, and The

[6] The work of Sally L. Tompkins was so valuable that President Davis commissioned her a captain so she could remain in charge of the Robertson Hospital in Richmond.

[7] The Ladies' Soldiers' Aid Society of the Natural Bridge District, Rockbridge, Virginia, invited the Surgeon General to send one hundred wounded convalescents to recuperate in members' homes in the late spring of 1862.

141

St. Philip's Hospital Aid Society. Medical purveyors frequently called upon such societies for supplies, which were usually sent. The first of the Atlanta societies listed above, for example, reported that it had distributed the following items among the various hospitals in that city during the period from April 23 to June 12, 1862: "48 shirts, 41 pairs drawers, 6 pairs pants, 11 coats, 48 pairs socks, 6 dressing gowns, 25 towels, lint and bandages, 32 bottles wine, 6 jars preserves, 13 bottles catsup, jellies, dried fruit, rice, meal, flour, grits, corn starch, cordials, honey, vinegar, pepper, allspice, sage, slippery elm, salves, candles, etc." In addition, several large boxes of hospital stores were sent to medical purveyors in Atlanta and Columbus, Mississippi. Early in 1864 an association at Forsyth, Georgia, headed nominally by Judge Cabaniss, had collected $2,000 along with numerous supplies and was fitting up a room to be used as a warehouse and distributing center. Women in many other communities were active, and their efforts received the praise to which they were entitled. The Congress itself, early in April, 1862, adopted a joint resolution in which that body expressed its gratitude to Confederate women "for the energy, zeal, and untiring devotion which they have manifested in furnishing voluntary contributions to our soldiers in the field and in the various military hospitals throughout the country." It is perhaps not too surprising then to find one Confederate veteran asserting that "General Lee's Army was mainly supplied with clothing by the women of the South."

The establishment of relief organizations on a state-wide basis to integrate the work of the many local societies was exceptional, but there were also state organizations and those in Georgia, Alabama, Louisiana, and South Carolina were extremely active. Illustrative of the work attempted and accomplished were the activities of the Georgia Relief and Hospital Association. Organized in 1861 and aided by state as well as private funds, the association sent physicians supplied with medicines and bandages to field and general hospitals. It equipped four sizable hospitals in Richmond and contributed

142

nurses, medicines, commissary stores, and luxuries to supplement those allowed by the government. The association also furnished the Richmond hospitals with two chaplains, assisted the government in organizing other hospitals in several Georgia cities, including Savannah, Augusta, and Atlanta, and filled requisitions for medical supplies from surgeons in the field when the latter could not procure them through regular channels.

Effort was made by the Georgia association to provide all needy troops from that state with proper clothing, and a large storeroom was maintained in Richmond for that purpose. Several wayside homes to alleviate the discomforts of travel were established by the association at various points in 1862, and in 1863 it began raising a fund for the relief of widows and orphans of Georgia soldiers. The activities of the association were conducted on a large scale. Its Richmond agent reported, for example, that 8,145 shirts, 8,480 pairs of drawers, 4,550 pairs of pants, 2,142 coats, 3,351 pairs of socks, 2,344 pairs of shoes, and 2,082 blankets were distributed from that city during the period between October 1, 1862, and July 23, 1863. Over that same length of time, the association shipped from Augusta to Richmond 9,270 shirts, 11,460 pairs of drawers, 6,340 pairs of pants, 4,210 pairs of socks, 3,331 pairs of shoes and 1,867 blankets. The number of hospitalized Georgians visited during this interval totaled 14,150; and from April 20 to July 23, 1863, an aggregate of 3,231 Georgia soldiers were entertained in the association's Richmond wayside home alone.

State Assistance

All of the states were generous in supplementing the work of relief societies. Surgeon Charles E. Michel, writing from Cleveland, Tennessee, late in 1862, observed that "The property here is almost entirely contributions from States and communities to their *own* troops belonging to General Bragg's army." North Carolina through a special agreement with the

143

Confederate government took such extraordinary care of its troops that there was little necessity for extensive private aid efforts. Medical Director Lafayette Guild asserted that North Carolina showed "more zeal & practical intelligence" in caring for its men "than any other state in the Confederacy."

Praise of Relief Associations

Relief associations, whether local or state in scope, received much acclaim for their labors. In October, 1863, for example, Medical Director Stout publicly acknowledged the "timely and efficient aid" which the disabled troops in the Army of Tennessee had received from "the various relief associations from Atlanta, Cartersville, Marietta, Augusta, LaGrange, Florida, and refugee Tennesseeans," and testified "to the many instances of self-sacrificing effort and liberality of individuals, citizens, and ladies, and private physicians. . . ." As to the aid of relief associations during the period between the battle of Chickamauga and the summer of 1864, Stout pronounced its value as being "incalculable, aside from the highly beneficial effect upon the *morale* of the good and faithful soldier, in convincing him that *he is not forgotten* by the patriotic and generous citizens in the rear. . . ." General John B. Hood also expressed his gratitude for the assistance rendered by the associations to the sick and wounded of the same army. "Were it not for such societies," wrote an observer in Virginia, "there are a great many wounded who would die for want of attention."

The Association for the Relief of Maimed Soldiers

The only relief society that was truly organized on a Confederacy-wide basis appears to have been the Association for the Relief of Maimed Soldiers although Mrs. Felicia Grundy Porter of Nashville, Tennessee, headed a body known as the

Women's Relief Society of the Confederate States. The former association was established in January, 1864. Its objectives, according to the constitution of the society, were "to supply artificial limbs for all officers, soldiers and seamen who have been maimed in the service of their country, and to furnish such other relief as will contribute, to the general objects proposed." [8] Reverend C. K. Marshall of Mississippi was the association's president; included among the vice presidents were George A. Trenholm of South Carolina, Louis T. Wigfall of Texas, Pierre Soulé of Louisiana, and Ely M. Bruce of Kentucky; the Medical Department was represented by Medical Director William A. Carrington, who served as corresponding secretary, and by Surgeon General Moore and Surgeon James B. McCaw, both listed as directors.

Legislation to aid the association's efforts was enacted by Congress on March 11, 1865. Free transportation to and from artificial limb manufactories was allowed by this act to all those eligible for such aid; the association was authorized to purchase materials needed at cost or government prices from government departments; the Secretary of War was to detail such expert workmen and mechanics as might be requested by the directors; and the association's funds and all its contract work were exempted from taxation.

A fair amount of work was accomplished by the association. Medical Director Carrington, the corresponding secretary, reported on October 10, 1864, that he had placed orders with two companies for 499 artificial limbs, and he figured the total cost to be $125,000. The record book of the association lists the names of 769 soldiers who had undergone amputations, and it is likely that all of these men were eventually supplied with artificial limbs. The state of North Carolina insisted upon repaying the association for all limbs furnished its native sons and even founded a manufactory in Raleigh to provide for North Carolina troops.

[8] One Confederate surgeon, Alexander Thom, with an eye to future business, suggested as early as the summer of 1863 that he and his brother establish a factory to manufacture artificial limbs.

Depot Purveyors

The principal procedure by which the Medical Department attempted to procure hospital and medical supplies was put into operation early in the war. A number of medical purveyors—surgeons and assistant surgeons under the authority of the Surgeon General—were appointed by the Surgeon General, and these officers were charged with the responsibility for obtaining and distributing all such supplies within the Confederacy. In the first part of the war, most of these supplies were purchased and stored in some eight or nine depots located at strategic points behind the lines; and such depots were managed by the most experienced and capable of the purveyors.[9] As the war progressed, a growing quantity of hospital and medical supplies was manufactured at or near certain of these depots. Altogether there was a total of thirty-two depot and field purveyors by November, 1864; they were assigned throughout the Confederacy from Richmond to San Antonio. Edward W. Johns, purveyor in Richmond, was the only one of the thirty-two with a commission in the regular army. He acted as chief purveyor for almost two years, but in February, 1863, the Surgeon General, a purveyor in the "old army," assumed such status for himself.

Pharmaceutical Laboratories

Pharmaceutical laboratories were established pursuant to orders of Surgeon General Moore at various points in the South for the purpose of manufacturing medicines; the most important were those located at the depots in Atlanta (moved to Augusta before the fall of the city) and Macon, Georgia; Columbia and Charleston, South Carolina; Charlotte and Lin-

[9] From July 1, 1861, through December 31, 1862, the accounts of Richard Potts, Medical Purveyor of the Western Department, totaled $770,654.96. Purveyors occasionally found it easier to obtain needed supplies through exchange than by purchase.

colnton, North Carolina; Montgomery and Mobile, Alabama; and Tyler, Texas. These laboratories, under the direction of the purveyors, manufactured pharmaceutical products formerly obtained abroad or by contract in the South and also produced many substitutes made from native roots and herbs.[10] Druggists or chemists were employed to prepare the various medicines. The best known medicine maker was Joseph LeConte, who had been professor of chemistry and geology at the South Carolina College from 1857 until its doors were closed after the Seven Days' fighting. LeConte served at Columbia, where Surgeon J. Julian Chisolm was medical purveyor, until just before General Sherman's arrival in that city.

One of the ablest druggists employed by the Confederacy was Charles Theodor Mohr of Mobile. The circumstances of his employment and something of the work carried on at the laboratories are best related in his own words:

> Just as soon as I had lain the foundation for secure and adequate gains, this, with all my valuable property, was thoroughly shaken and finally destroyed by the outbreak of the Civil War. Without previous warning I found myself in Mobile in June of 1861, in the new Confederacy cut off from the rest of the world by the blockade of Northern ships. This, however, through necessity, caused us to rely upon our own resources. This urgency made us individually responsible for the maintenance [relief] of the army with hospital supplies, and the government requested me to meet the challenge by taking an active part in the direction of a laboratory for the preparation of pharmaceuticals and indigenous products. I agreed to do so. There was no lack of materials for the construction of apparatus: a drug grinding mill, a steam distillation apparatus and a contrivance for the production of high-grade alcohol from corn whisky; only glass vessels for the laboratory were largely absent. The task of examining the medical supplies smuggled in through the blockade from Europe, like opium, morphine, quinine, and others, was also assigned to me.

Indigenous and other products manufactured at the depots were also examined closely; hence the laboratories served both

[10] The state of Louisiana established laboratories at Clinton and Mt. Lebanon.

as manufacturing laboratories and as analytical control stations.[11]

Drugs known to have been manufactured at the Columbia plant included, among other products, "alcohol, silver chloride, sulphuric ether, nitric ether, and podophyllin resin." By midsummer of 1864, the official organ of the army and navy surgeons could report: "A most gratifying progress has also been made in the manufacture of chemicals within our own limits. Blue mass of the best quality, nitrate of silver, sweet spirits of nitre, iodide of potas [sic], and many other leading preparations are prepared on a large scale. Botanical gardens and farms are flourishing at various points. Manufactories and laboratories are rising up in every direction, under the wise supervision of our medical chief. . . ." [12]

Native Remedies

With respect to the indigenous products, a prevalent belief at the time of the Civil War was that each country contained medicinal plants from which preparations could be extracted in sufficient quantity to care for the diseases common to that country. Surgeon General Moore may or may not have subscribed to this theory, but certainly he was a most forceful advocate of indigenous remedies. His propensities along this line were so well known that one hospital steward believed that the native remedies "sit like a nightmare upon the brain of the Surgeon General." At any rate, shortly after the beginning of the war, Moore directed F. Peyre Porcher to prepare

[11] Norman H. Franke, an able student of Confederate pharmacy, feels that the military failed to make full use of the skilled druggists in the South.

[12] William H. Taylor, a field surgeon, disagreed somewhat as to the excellence of the output. The blue mass made at the laboratory, he related, "would have been a very satisfactory product could its components have managed to keep themselves in harmonious juxtaposition; but, as it was, it would not be long after the mass reached us before the mercury seceded from the rest and settled off by itself at the bottom of the holder." Taylor was known to exaggerate on occasions.

a treatise on the resources of the Southern fields and forests, a work which Porcher himself planned as "a repertory of scientific and popular knowledge as regards the medicinal, economical, and useful properties of the trees, plants, and shrubs found within the limits of the Confederate States. . . ." "I here introduce," he wrote, "upwards of four hundred substances, possessing every variety of useful quality." Copies of Porcher's book, which has been credited by one enthusiast with having "saved the Confederacy for two years," were sent out to medical officers after publication in 1863, while Southern newspapers, at Moore's suggestion, published extracts from the book to encourage the collection of plants and the preparation of remedies therefrom.

Meanwhile, the Surgeon General distributed a pamphlet to his officers in April, 1862, which described the most important plants and requested that they be gathered and sent to medical purveyors for preparation and distribution. From this time on a sustained effort was made to carry on this work as agents and even circuit riders were employed by purveyors to collect plants and encourage country people to do likewise. High prices were advertised for plants such as Georgia bark, white willow, Indian physic, skunk cabbage, wild cherry bark, pipsissewa, and cranesbill—just to name a few. As a result of such encouragement, Surgeon William H. Prioleau could report from his Macon depot on July 31, 1863, that he had 16,034 pounds of indigenous remedies on hand ready for issue and 64,779 pounds more in a crude state.

Surgeon General Moore insisted that native remedies be issued by purveyors whenever possible, and he published a supply table for them in March, 1863. At that time, Moore called upon medical officers to cast aside any prejudice they might have against these remedies and "give them a fair opportunity for the exhibition of those remedial virtues which they certainly possess." Later, he directed purveyors, when practicable, to substitute indigenous preparations for those drugs indicated on requisitions by as much as fifty per cent. He sent out a general directive requesting reports upon the efficacy of the

149

native remedies, and as he learned of additional substitutes he often asked Surgeon McCaw to investigate their effectiveness at Chimborazo. Moore never turned his back on a new preparation. When a crank sent some medicine to Richmond and claimed that it was superior to quinine and would cure "collick," "Dierhea or Bloody flux," "Dysenterry etc." as well as prevent abortion, the Surgeon General, though skeptical, evinced interest. In October, 1864, he instructed Surgeon Potts, purveyor at Montgomery, to investigate the adequacy of sorghum seed as a substitute for grain in the manufacture of whiskey. Learning that acceptable opium could be extracted from the red garden poppy, Moore circularized purveyors to induce Confederate women to interest themselves in the cultivation of that plant. The appeal was made, and some success was experienced.

The Surgeon General seems to have been generally pleased with the work of the medical laboratories, but on at least one occasion he indicated his displeasure at the failure of some officers on the regimental level to utilize fully the *materia medica* of the South. Too, he was not always satisfied with the quantities of medicinal plants collected by the purveyors. Nevertheless, the *Confederate States Medical and Surgical Journal* declared in July, 1864, that excellent results had been achieved in the development of indigenous remedies. Making due allowance for partisan exaggeration on the part of those close to the Surgeon General, there is little question but that the pharmaceutical products manufactured at the laboratories meant much to the Confederate cause. From a therapeutic standpoint, some of the native remedies—such as the concoction made up of dogwood, poplar, and willow bark that was used as a quinine substitute—were decidedly inferior, but others—such as opium and chloroform—were quite satisfactory. "Generally speaking," concludes a recent historian of Confederate drugs, "the Medical Corps had good preparations and few substitutes." [13]

[13] Dr. Bartholomew Egan, director of the Louisiana laboratory located on the grounds of Mt. Lebanon Female College, held that the opium he collected from native white poppies was equally as good as the commer-

Fruit Juices

It is pertinent to note, especially in view of the comparatively recent importance attached to fruits and juices as a part of the diet of the sick, that the Surgeon General and his purveyors were most interested in the possibilities of orange juice, lime juice, and lemons for hospital use; a goodly amount of the fruits were contracted for by Surgeon Prioleau in Georgia, and it was not unusual for the juices to be prepared at his depot for issue. As early as June, 1862, Prioleau recommended orange juice as a beverage "which would add materially to the comfort of our sick soldiers during the warm season." And he was soon sending small quantities to Richmond for Moore's approval. In November, the Surgeon General authorized Prioleau to contract for 250 gallons put up in five-gallon iron bound kegs provided the beverage could be obtained for $10 a gallon, and the following March he requested that the purveyor send all the juice he had to Richmond. In September, 1863, however, Moore informed Prioleau that the department did not wish to purchase oranges or orange juice; whether this decision was caused by the high price asked or by the failure of the fruit and juice to keep well is not known.

A year earlier, in September, 1862, Prioleau had requested and received approval from the medical head to prepare juice from the Ogeechee lime, a fruit that grew abundantly in his district. The result of the purveyor's experiments is not clear, but the Surgeon General apparently preferred lime to orange juice. Quite a few lemons were purchased and distributed to the sick.

Procurement of Whiskey and Alcohol

The experience of the Medical Department in obtaining whiskey and alcohol is illustrative of the general trend toward

cial product. And F. Peyre Porcher asserted that there were no fatal results from the use of chloroform produced locally.

government manufacture of hospital and medical supplies. Alcoholic "stimulants" were greatly desired by medical officers to combat the effects of exposure and fatigue among their patients, and, during the first part of the war, practically the entire quantity of these items was procured from private distillers. The contract price for whiskey ranged from $1.50 to $3.50 per gallon whereas that for alcohol stood near $3.25 for the same amount. Purveyors were allowed to use grain instead of money to contract for whiskey, but in doing so they were directed to make certain that the government received all the whiskey made from the grain furnished.

Consumption of alcoholic stimulants by the Medical Department increased steadily. In May, 1863, for example, Congress appropriated funds sufficient to purchase the 201,600 gallons required for one year, but the Surgeon General estimated his yearly requirement early in 1865 to be 624,000 gallons. As a consequence of the rising demand, plus the fact that the product of private distillers was often of such an inferior quality that it had to be rejected, the Surgeon General decided to establish government distilleries in Salisbury, North Carolina, Columbia, South Carolina, Macon, Georgia, and Montgomery, Alabama.[14] Purveyors were instructed, however, to continue their purchases from private contractors inasmuch as the combined output would be needed.

Bitter opposition to the use of grain for government distillation in North Carolina and Georgia was manifested by Governors Zebulon B. Vance and Joseph E. Brown, respectively. Despite such opposition, however, Congress, in June, 1864, backed up the Surgeon General by authorizing him to establish manufactories or distilleries and to make all necessary contracts for the manufacture and distillation of the alcoholic stimulants.

[14] Early in 1864 Surgeon General Moore informed Prioleau that the engine and apparatus of a distillery had been purchased in Richmond and would be shipped to Macon. He urged Prioleau to "use every exertion to have the buildings erected, the machinery put in working order, and all arrangements made for getting into operation, without any loss of time."

The Surgeon General, in defending himself against those who condemned his establishment of the distilleries, claimed that a large portion of the grain consumed was damaged and therefore useless for other purposes. Barley, wheat, and rye, in addition to corn, were used in the manufacture of the stimulants, and government purchasing agents and collectors of the tax in kind were requested to turn these commodities over to medical purveyors. Moore estimated that 4,000 bushels of corn, 100 bushels of rye or wheat, and 60 bushels of barley were required for the Salisbury distillery each month; and he asserted in February, 1865, that the distilleries at Salisbury and Columbia were each manufacturing from 200 to 500 gallons of the alcoholic stimulants daily.[15]

Supply Activities of Purveyors

Depot purveyors were kept exceedingly busy with their supply function. Articles on the supply table which they needed to keep on hand in large quantities for the most part included, besides medicines, such articles as bedsacks, pillowticks, sheets, boxes, canisters, bottles, jugs, paper envelopes, wrapping paper, lint, brandy, wine, whiskey, tea, cans, mosquito nets, pencils, pill boxes, vials, pots, pans, jars, trusses, forceps, operating tables, dissecting cases, amputating instruments, candles, candlesticks, knives, forks, spoons, dishes, tumblers, medicine chests, buckets, sponges, bandages, corks, comforts, cuspidors, cots, sacks, and bed pans. Late in the war, purveyors were instructed to add crutches to the supply table and to have a supply made for issue. Some idea of the responsibility resting upon the shoulders of depot chiefs may be gained from the order, not an unusual one, given by Surgeon General Moore on March 3, 1862, to Purveyor Richard Potts, then at Memphis, to have field supplies for 20,000 men for six months

[15] At this time, Moore expected his Georgia and Alabama distilleries to commence operations in "two or three months, when all contracts for stimulants throughout the country will be canceled."

packed and ready for shipment. To assist them in their work, depot purveyors usually had a chief clerk, a chief druggist or chemist, a number of other clerks, stewards, detailed men, Negro workers, and perhaps couriers to convey shipments of supplies to their destination. An inspection of the small purveying depot at Demopolis, Alabama, early in September, 1864, revealed that Surgeon E. H. C. Bailey, the officer in charge, had at the time no more than two or three clerks and four other employees, the latter being disabled soldiers.

Routine supply activity of an important depot purveyor over a period of several months may be seen from records kept by Surgeon William H. Prioleau at his Macon, Georgia, location. From June 21 to September 1, 1862, Prioleau sent 138 shipments of supplies from that center to various consignees in south Georgia and east Florida; and during the interval from April 4, 1863, to April 11, 1865, the same purveyor forwarded 675 shipments. Included among the goods issued by Prioleau for three months, from April 4 to July 4, 1863, were 3,169 bottles of whiskey, 226 bottles of wine, 77½ bottles of alcohol, 375 gallons of orange juice, 120 gallons of lime juice, 1,200 lemons, 1,426½ pounds of Georgia bark, 22 ounces of iodine, almost 10 pounds of chloroform, 583 ounces of quinine sulphate, 93 drams of morphine sulphate, 6 operating tables, 30 sets of teeth extracting forceps, 75 field tourniquets, and 136 bandages. During the month of August, 1864, Prioleau received calls for approximately 5,252 items on a total of 166 requisitions; there was thus an average of almost 32 items on each requisition arriving at his depot during that month.

Monetary Accounts of the Purveyors

Previous mention has been made of Congressional appropriations for the Medical Department, and it should be observed that practically all of this money passed through the hands of medical purveyors. The latter were instructed to make quarterly, then monthly, estimates of the funds required for their procurement activities; the Surgeon General received the estimates, and, if they were approved, requisitions were made in the purveyor's favor on the Treasury Department. That large sums were needed may be seen by a glance at some of these estimates. Surgeon Potts, purveyor at Jackson, Mississippi, in 1862, figured that he required $300,000 for the quarter ending September 30, 1862; for April, 1864, alone, however, Potts (then in Macon) asked for $600,000. For the quarter ending December 31, 1862, Surgeon Prioleau, in Savannah at that time, requested $150,000; but his estimate for the month of September, 1864, also reached the sum of $600,000.

The largest single warrant issued in favor of a medical purveyor by the Treasury Department from the war's beginning through June 17, 1864, was one for $850,254.57; this was granted to Surgeon J. Julian Chisolm, stationed in Columbia, on April 13, 1864. Altogether, thirty-two warrants totaling $4,829,139.90 were registered in Chisolm's name during the entire period. Over the same interval, fifty-four warrants were issued in favor of Surgeon Edward W. Johns, purveyor at Richmond, and these totaled $4,143,478.58.

Naval accounts concerning procurement activities are fragmentary, but Surgeon W. A. W. Spotswood, the Navy's chief medical officer, reported in 1863 and 1864 that the purveyor's department was operating efficiently. He stated that valuable assortments of medical stores were being brought into the Confederacy from England, via Bermuda, and purchased in Richmond and elsewhere. Comfortable bedding, blankets, furniture, crockery, and like items had been obtained at auction sales, he declared, for 200 per cent less than they could have been bought in Richmond wholesale houses. He also alluded to the fact that employees in the purveyor's department were engaged constantly in making, packing, and conveying medical supplies to the naval stations south of Richmond.

The principal offices of the Navy's purchasing staff were located at Richmond, Charleston, Savannah, and Mobile.

Treasury records reveal that, from July 11, 1861, to September 22, 1863, an aggregate of forty-two warrants, totaling $200,-449.17, was issued in favor of agents and paymasters located at those points and elsewhere for the purchase of medical supplies. Largest of those issued was one for $50,000 registered on March 20, 1863, in favor of the paymaster at Charleston. It is also known that issues of hospital and medical supplies to the amount of $133,892.58 were made to the seven naval stations from October, 1863, to October, 1864.

Statements of Shortages

Many who have written of the Civil War have stressed the Confederacy's shortage of hospital and medical supplies. It is true that there was much comment made on this score by those who engaged in the conflict; observations as to shortages were recorded by participants from the Sea Islands to the Trans-Mississippi Department and the Indian Territory. A Yankee surgeon, captured at the battle of First Manassas, asserted that the Rebels were without medicines, instruments, dressings, and supplies of any sort; and a precedent was thereby set for the subsequent reiteration of similar assertions throughout the war by friend and foe alike.

Frequent reports of the need for medicines were made during the first year, and a congressional investigating committee stated in January, 1862, that the medical stores of the army were generally "incomplete and insufficient in many of the leading and necessary articles for the prevailing diseases." Such a condition might have been expected in the early months of the conflict, but even more effective organization and administration of the Medical Department may not have solved this problem since, as noted above, complaints continued. Assistant Surgeon William G. Piggott advised his medical superior in the summer of 1862 that the hospital under his control, Poplar Lawn in Petersburg, was in real need of medicines and "badly furnished." "As regards Medical Supplies," asserted the medical officer in charge of Atlanta's Gate City Hospital early in 1863, "we never have had a sufficiency." That fall and winter a deficiency of medicines was deplored by surgeons in the Trans-Mississippi Department's District of Arkansas and the Indian Territory. Surgeon James Mercer Green, the head of Macon hospitals, remarked in January, 1864, that his requisitions to medical purveyors "are cut down so that I frequently get out of medicines & almost always of spirits." And in December, 1864, there was reported to be the "most pressing" need for medicines and other stores in General Beauregard's Military Division of the West. Certainly then, on the basis of this and other evidence, the student of the war might be justified for concluding that a shortage of medicines existed in the Confederacy throughout the Civil War.

Wartime correspondence appears to indicate that the supply of quinine caused more concern than that of any other single medicine. Medical Director Lafayette Guild advised Surgeon General Moore in the summer of 1864 that the shortage of quinine was becoming increasingly serious in the Army of Northern Virginia, and such statements were commonplace. As a matter of fact, the Surgeon General, recognizing fully the importance of this drug, urged as early as September, 1861, that it be used economically. Medical purveyors found that the cost of quinine increased sharply during the war despite the effort of the government to establish a military monopoly with respect to its purchase—but the recollection of one soldier to the effect that quinine was selling for $60 an ounce in Richmond during July, 1862, would seem to be faulty since purveyors were obtaining the product at the same time for not more than $14 an ounce. Nevertheless, subcutaneous injection of quinine was resorted to at several general hospitals as an economy measure, and indigenous remedies were issued freely by purveyors as quinine substitutes.

The same congressional investigating committee that noted the army's need for medicines also found "a great deficiency

157

in surgical instruments," and noted that those in use were "often very inferior and ill adapted to the service." Evidence of any real improvement along this line is lacking, and shortages of surgical appliances were reported constantly. Medical officers in the Army of Northern Virginia were poorly equipped, and, according to Medical Director Guild, those who had instruments manufactured in the Confederacy "might as well be without any, for those they have are entirely useless." Some units in the field were found to be without any kind of surgical equipment. The lack of such equipment is illustrated by the apparent failure of Surgeon E. W. Johns, medical purveyor in Richmond, to obtain any surgical instruments for issue from January, 1864, throughout the year ending in January, 1865.[16]

Speculators and Shortages

It is clearly evident that the activities of speculators made procurement matters more difficult for the medical purveyors and thereby contributed to shortages. Supplies obtained through the blockade or from localities vacated by the enemy were often held for resale by speculators at much higher prices. The situation became so flagrant that some impressment of medical stores took place in the spring and summer of 1862; and in September, General Lee informed the Secretary of War that he had ordered the seizure of medicines found in the possession of speculators. Some generals were not so co-operative, however, and on October 1, 1862, a general order was issued which directed commanding generals to "authorize their medical purveyors to impress all medical supplies held by speculators, paying them the cost price for the articles." The problem was thereby lessened but not solved. There were also other annoyances. In the fall of 1864, Medical Director Guild, charging that people were converting their apples into

[16] Shortages of beds, bedding, hospital shirts and drawers, surgical dressings, and alcoholic stimulants were also reported frequently.

brandy and selling it to the troops, recommended that the brandy be seized, turned into vinegar, and used in the manufacture of medicines.

Contrasting Statements

Despite the observations on shortages of hospital and medical supplies set forth above in scattered reports, it is hardly possible to conclude, except with regard to surgical instruments, that striking deficiencies existed generally throughout the war. As a matter of fact, some Confederate medical officers have gone so far as to state that at no time during the struggle did they fail to have a sufficient quantity of the essentials needed. Surgeon Deering J. Roberts, one of these, found that many of the doctors in gray always had an abundant supply of quinine, morphine, and chloroform—the most important drugs of all. With respect to quinine, generally considered to have been the most difficult to obtain, it is interesting to note that the District of South Carolina was reported "superabundantly supplied" with that drug during the summer of 1864 at the same time that it was held to be scarce in the District of Georgia. Yet quinine seems to have been issued almost uninterruptedly from the medical purveyor's depot at Macon, and an inspection of the Demopolis, Alabama. depot in October, 1864, revealed that included among the medicines on hand were 1966 ounces of quinine sulphate plus 34 pounds of chloroform and 245 drams of morphine sulphate. The prices paid for these products at Demopolis per unit of measurement, also revealing, was $2.00, 1.00, and $4.87 respectively; and it is also pertinent to note that the officer in charge was not regarded as either "active" or "enterprising." Surgeon John H. Claiborne, head of the Petersburg hospitals during the siege of that city late in the war, declared that "the sick and wounded did not suffer for anything necessary to their comfort." And John S. Cain, chief surgeon of a division in the Army of Tennessee, maintained that the difficulty of obtaining supplies in the field, while by no means negligible, was "frequently overdrawn." Cain even contended that Southern medical officers "did not suffer materially for the want of surgical instruments." In this connection a surgeon of Lee's army may be found informing his wife in June, 1864, that "I drew a very excellent set of instruments yesterday, so I will not need mine at all."

No little importance must be attached to the report made by the Surgeon General to the Secretary of War in February, 1865, in which he stated that his department had a year's supply of some articles and a limited amount of others on hand. The Surgeon General believed that if the department were "allowed to retain its skilled employes at the various laboratories, purveying depots, and distilleries, and to import medicines freely through our lines in Mississippi and Alabama, no fear need be entertained that the sick and wounded of the Army will suffer for the want of any of the essential articles of the supply table."

The Surgeon General's report, considered alongside the testimony of such medical officers as Roberts, Claiborne, and Cain, and with such inspection reports as those from South Carolina—where quinine was so abundant that it was being used as a prophylactic—and Demopolis, Alabama, leads one to doubt that any very acute shortage of medicines existed, at least until late in the war. At certain times supplies could not be moved from the depots simply because of the lack of packing boxes and bottles, and unsuccessful efforts were made at some of the laboratories to produce the latter. Surgeons were instructed repeatedly to return all empty boxes and bottles to the depots to avoid shipping delays.

Shuttling of Supplies

Medical supplies were also delayed from reaching their destination at times by the sudden movements of the armies in the field; and when an army moved from the district served

160

by one purveyor to that served by another, the latter was not infrequently somewhat hard pressed to meet the increased demand upon his stockpile of supplies. In such cases, however, the Surgeon General ordered that supplies be shuttled between the various depots as the exigencies of the situations demanded. It was as a result of the problems caused by these developments that Medical Director A. J. Foard of the Army of Tennessee requested that field purveyors be supplied with wagon transportation adequate for them to accompany the army on the march and recommended the assignment of one purveyor for the Army of Tennessee alone; the latter would have as many assistants and depots as needed and the depots should be located, he believed, at positions agreed upon by the medical directors of the armies and hospitals concerned. Foard thought that purveyors should be assigned to armies and departments rather than to particular districts. Surgeon General Moore was in agreement with Foard only with respect to the desirability of field purveyors being supplied with wagon trains, but whereas this plan was effected in the Army of Northern Virginia, it was unfortunately not adopted in the Army of Tennessee. It is difficult to ascertain wherein Foard's plan for army purveyors was more meritorious than that system worked out by the Surgeon General.[17]

Transportation Breakdown—Conclusion

The entire complex problem of procurement and supply was complicated many times over late in the war when the Confederacy's transportation system collapsed. Wagon as well as railroad transportation broke down almost completely, and needed supplies arrived tardily at their destination, if at all. There was also at least a shred of truth in the charge made by Surgeon F. Peyre Porcher that some medical directors and purveyors "cling to their stores as if they were a part of them-

[17] Bills having for their object the establishment of a Purveyor General's Office were occasionally proposed in the Confederate Congress.

selves, carefully preserve them at points remote from battlefield or beleaguered cities, and will rather see them burned
than used." Yet, at least until near the war's end, it would
appear that the Medical Department, assisted as it was by
private and state efforts, was reasonably successful in supplying its sick and wounded with medical and hospital supplies.[18]

[18] Confederate naval vessels sometimes complained of inadequate medical supplies, but there appears to have been no alarming shortages or
supply problems.

CHAPTER IX

Causes of Disease

General

T he causes of disease during the Civil War were both numerous and complex.[1] John Julian Chisolm, the noted
South Carolina surgeon, declared, "Continued exposure and
fatigue, bad and insufficient food, salt meat, indifferent clothing, want of cleanliness, poor shelter, exposure at night to sudden changes of temperature, infected tents and camps, form a
combination of causes which explains the fatality of an army
in the field." The causes set forth by Chisolm as explaining
army fatalities in general were among the foremost causes
of Southern disease and death. On the other side of the lines,
Charles S. Tripler, Medical Director, United States Army of
the Potomac, asserted that "To bad cooking, bad police, bad
ventilation of tents, inattention to personal cleanliness, and
unnecessarily irregular habits we are to attribute the greater
proportion of the diseases that actually occurred in the army."

Inadequate Physical Examinations

One major cause of the large amount of sickness was the
early failure to prevent many who were unqualified for military service from being inducted. Medical regulations prepared in 1861 directed surgeons to strip and examine recruits
and screen out those who were not physically and mentally fit,
but by the time an examining system was established many
volunteers had been accepted who were ill-prepared to endure
the rigors of camp life. The volunteer system, asserted a lead-

[1] The major emphasis in this chapter is on conditions that produced
disease and death in the fighting forces.

ing newspaper, "brings to the field the most patriotic, but the most excitable and nervous portion of the population. These people, however gallant in the field, have rarely the constitution to stand the real burden of war." This problem was not peculiar to the Confederate service. The Medical Director of the Union Army of the Potomac complained: "It seemed as if the army called out to defend the life of the nation had been made use of as a grand eleemosynary institution for the reception of the aged and infirm, the blind, the lame, and the deaf, where they might be housed, fed, paid, clothed, and pensioned, and their townships relieved of the burden of their support."

With the increasing difficulty of fielding sufficient numbers to stand against the ever-expanding forces of the enemy, the program of physical examinations undoubtedly fell far short in screening out the unfit. On February 23, 1863, orders informed examining officers that defects such as "general debility," "slight deformity," partial deafness, speech impediment—"unless of a very aggravated character," functional heart trouble, muscular rheumatism, epilepsy—unless clearly proved, varicocele—"unless excessive," myopia, hemorrhoids —"unless excessive," "opacity of one cornea, or the loss of one eye," "loss of one or two fingers," and "single reducible hernia" were "not deemed sufficient and satisfactory for exemption."

Examining officers were advised on December 10, 1863, that dyspepsia and urethral stricture would not be recognized as grounds for exemption unless of an aggravated character. They were also informed that "The mere determination and announcement of the existence of such diseases as scrofula, hepatitis, spinal irritation and cachexia, do not warrant exemption: their special seat, degree of development, and the consequent disqualifying condition, as well as the general state of the system, must be discerned and intelligibly reported." Doubtful cases of all kinds were to be decided upon the principle that "When a conscript is found equal to, or in the performance of the active duties of the various occupations of civil life, he is able to discharge the duties of a soldier."

New Troops

New troops would have come down with disease in the 1860's regardless of the nature of their physical examinations. Surgeon General Moore explained to the Secretary of War in the fall of 1861 "that while there has perhaps been much sickness which could have been avoided, yet the experience of all military life shows that new troops, whether regulars or volunteers, are sick in vast numbers during the early period of their service." The amount of sickness around Manassas and other camps in 1861 was staggering. On August 17, 1861, General Joseph E. Johnston, at Manassas, reported 4,809 sick of 18,178 present. Recruits fell such easy victim to disease that General Lee, asserting that conscripts were proving burdensome rather than advantageous to his army, requested that they "be assembled in camps of instruction, so that they may pass through these inevitable diseases, and become a little inured to camp life."

Conscription of Older Men

The Conscription Act of 1864, requiring military service of all men between the ages of seventeen and fifty, brought into the army many men who were too old to be of much real value and who were quite susceptible to disease. The surgeon of a regiment made up largely of these older men found more sickness in that regiment than in all the others of the division. It soon became apparent that men over the age of forty could not easily make the transition from civilian to soldier without being harassed by sickness.

Preponderance of Troops from Rural Areas

Another important lesson taught by the Civil War was that men from rural and upcountry districts suffered more from disease than did those with an urban background. Since most Southerners were rural residents this helps to explain why there was so much disease within their ranks. Paul Fitzsimons Eve, who in 1831 had practiced military surgery in Warsaw, Poland, and who served as surgeon general of Tennessee and in the Gate City Hospital of Atlanta during the Civil War, concluded that "at the organization of the army, one town regiment was more efficient than two or even three from the country." Many recruits from rural districts, unlike those from cities, had never experienced the infantile diseases so prevalent in camp, and many had never been vaccinated. The various irregularities in living to which townspeople become accustomed also probably helped urban recruits orient themselves more rapidly and effectively to the exigencies of life in the field than those from the country.

Ignorance

The lack of a formal education appears to have been a definite handicap in the soldiers' efforts to keep well. "A company of soldiers, who made their signatures to the pay-roll largely with cross-marks," according to one Confederate surgeon, "was sure to suffer much from disease." Thousands of illiterate troops contributed to the elevation seen in disease statistics. The ignorant soldier was almost always a phlegmatic soul, contended an observant doctor in gray, who could not be made to comprehend "the dangers of dirt and filth, or the importance of cleanliness in all things pertaining to health and life. Neither could his dull intellect understand why one method of preparing his food should be more conducive to digestion and health than another. He burned his bread and fried

166

his food saturated with grease, and suffered from indigestion, colic, and diarrhoea, but was ignorant of the cause."

Chisolm, the Confederate surgeon, claimed that occasionally men who had been in the service for as long as six months received their first bath during that period upon admission into a Southern hospital. Henry W. Bellows, president of the United States Sanitary Commission, reported that Southern prisoners on Governor's Island had to be compelled to wash and exercise, and he believed them to be extremely careless in their personal habits.

General Lee was distressed at the extent of sickness which he thought his troops brought upon themselves through negligence. "They are worse than children," he wrote, "for the latter can be forced." Officers generally understood the importance of hygiene better than men in the ranks and suffered less from disease.

Ignorance, of course, was not the sole reason why troops often seemed dirty and unkept. Soldiers in the field sometimes became separated from their supply wagons and were unable to effect a change of clothing. Moreover, there were occasions when the Commissary Department was unable to furnish the army an adequate supply of soap. Early in 1865 General Lee informed the Secretary of War that there was a great amount of suffering in his command from cutaneous diseases, and he attributed it to the lack of soap. At the same time, however, in view of this observation by Lee, an entry was made in the diary of John Beauchamp Jones, a War Department clerk. "The government," stated Jones, "allowed Lee's army to suffer for months with the *itch*, without knowing there were eight hundred barrels of soap within a few hours' run of it."

Neglect of Camp Hygiene

Early in the war the neglect of camp cleanliness was as noticeable as the disregard of personal cleanliness. Overall sanitary arrangements having to do with such matters as the

167

choice of camp sites and the location of latrines, neglected at first because of the rapidity with which troops were assembled and the early optimistic belief that the conflict would be a short one, received increasing attention as the war progressed. The police of camps left something to be desired, however, as proper hygienic practices were sometimes forgotten.

A source of considerable sickness in many camps was the improper disposal of excrementitious matter. An army of 17,000 under the command of General Lee in the fall of 1861, encamped in a healthful locality, was devastated by such diseases as typhoid fever, dysentery, and pneumonia. Within a very short time the morning reports showed some 4,000 cases of disease and an extremely high mortality rate. Investigation revealed that the camp excreta was being carried by heavy rains into the sources of the water supply. Moreover, field inspection reports indicate that latrines were often either dug improperly or not at all, and there was sometimes a failure on the part of commanding officers to enforce the use of those provided. Compulsion as to the use of latrines was necessary in view of the somewhat peculiar unwillingness to visit them manifested by many soldiers. Surgeon Chisolm believed that the lack of latrines and the reluctance to use those that did exist was one of the major causes for the Army of Northern Virginia's extensive sick lists during the summer of 1862.[2]

Inspection reports show also that men in trenches were careless in disposing of melon rinds, fruit peelings, and other such scraps; the easiest way was simply to scatter them about the works. More serious perhaps as a factor in the breeding of disease was the improper burial of offal and the failure to remove dead cattle from the camps. It was asserted in the fall of 1861 that "At Manassas, the whole atmosphere is impregnated with the vile and disgusting smells of the offal of the camp and of the carcasses of dead cattle lying about on the fields immediately on the line of the railroad." This same com-

[2] The following entry was made in one soldier's diary: "On rolling up my bed this morning found I had been lying in—I wont say what—something though, that didn't smell like milk and peaches."

plaint was made by the Army of the Potomac's medical director late in January, 1862. At nearly the same time inspecting officers in the West reported that the careless disposal of kitchen offal was productive of much camp fever. It was also recognized by inspectors that poorly ventilated quarters were an important cause of illness.

Insects and Vermin

The great number of insects and vermin found in camp was due in part to the neglect of personal and camp cleanliness. and these pests played an important role in the promotion of epidemics. Few soldiers in any great conflict have been safe from the menace of these vexatious and perilous disturbers of the peace. They seemed "born with national prejudices against all Southern flesh," wrote one sufferer.

One of the most annoying insect pests was the ubiquitous fly. A soldier stationed on the South Carolina coast complained that "sand flies and miserable fleas devour my hide like a mangy cur would a nice slice of old Virginia ham." And another, in reporting on a night attack by sand flies, admitted that "although we killed a great many we got pretty badly whipped."

Night attacks were also made by mosquitoes, and one victim concluded from their determined efforts that they "seem resolved to take me dead or alive." Since clothing and blankets were insufficient protection against these enemies fires were often built by the defending soldiery; yet nothing devised by the latter seemed able to prevent the chills and fevers that followed in the wake of these unwelcome raids.

There were other unwanted guests also. "I want you to send me some smoking Tobacco," wrote a North Carolinian. "The nats are so bad here that we will have to smoke tobacco to keep them from eating us up." Chiggers and roaches did their part to make life unbearable; but the least welcome of all, certainly the one most widely discussed, was the army louse—

generally referred to in soldier correspondence as the gray-back. "Every soldier had a brigade of lice on him," reflected one veteran, "and I have seen fellows so busily engaged in cracking them that it reminded me of an old woman knitting." This observation was verified by Surgeon Samuel H. Stout in a report made early in 1863 that "the whole army is louzy." "The grayback was never here until Lincoln's soldiers came," held another Confederate, "and the easy assumption is that they brought him along with them, and turned him loose on us." Soldier accounts of lice so tough that they could hardly crack them and so strong that they carried off articles of clothing were perhaps not strictly true, but the revulsion for them felt by most wearers of the gray is a matter of solemn record. Their sentiments were summed up succinctly by a Georgia surgeon when he declared with much fervor: "I detest them worse than any body."

Exposure

Another source of ill health, one that was generally mentioned by Confederate surgeons in explaining the long lists of names on hospital rolls, was exposure. Armies in the field have always had to contend with exposure, but, due to the inability of the government to supply the men in gray with an adequate amount of clothing and camp and garrison equipage, it is doubtful whether any body of men ever suffered more from this condition. Diarrhea, dysentery, continued fever, rheumatism, catarrh, bronchitis, pneumonia, frostbite, and glandular swellings were some of the ailments attributed by surgeons and commanders to exposure.

Winter campaigns were especially rigorous. One of Stonewall Jackson's troops had a vivid recollection of the march from Romney to Winchester, Virginia, and back in January, 1862. As the men "marched along," he wrote, "icicles hung from their clothing, guns, and knapsacks; many were badly frost bitten, and I have heard of many freezing to death along the road side. My feet peeled off like a peeled onion on that march, and I have not recovered from its effects to this day. . . . The soldiers in the whole army got rebellious—almost mutinous—and would curse and abuse Stonewall Jackson; in fact, they called him 'Fool Tom Jackson.' " This same Confederate chronicler also related that eleven members of the Fourteenth Georgia and Third Arkansas regiments froze to death while on guard duty near Hampshire Crossing during the same campaign. "Some were sitting down," he recalled, "and some were lying down; but each and every one was as cold and as hard frozen as the icicles that hung from their hands and faces and clothing—dead! They had died at their post of duty. Two of them, a little in advance of the others, were standing with their guns in their hands, as cold and as hard frozen as a monument of marble—standing sentinel with loaded guns in their frozen hands!" That winter also Brigadier General Gideon J. Pillow reported that prior to his surrender of Fort Donelson in February, 1862, the men "had been in the trenches night and day for five days, exposed to snow, sleet, mud, and ice and water, without shelter, without adequate covering, and without sleep." Frostbite was sometimes so severe that amputation was necessary.

Soldiers in winter quarters even found it difficult at times to protect themselves against exposure. "We are having a spell of bitter cold weather," wrote one of Lee's men in December, 1862, "& I have to take a dog in bed with me every night to keep warm." Another explained in December, 1864, that "instead of undressing for bed (as citizens do) we put on *all* the clothes we had, viz: 4 shirts (2 flannel, 2 cotton) 2 pair pants, 1 pair socks (yarn) 1 vest, 1 coat and hat—and slept tolerably warm—considering." Crude log huts, cabins, and pine poles covered by tent flies were erected; the architecture and construction were not impressive as a rule, but the houses contained fireplaces and were usually very liveable. Winter quarters were reasonably pleasant and healthful if the site was carefully chosen and there was an adequate supply of wood and water nearby.

Troops who spent the winter in comfortable quarters frequently suffered more from exposure during the summer campaigning when they were without tents to keep off the rain. Major General Daniel Harvey Hill, commanding at Yorktown in April, 1862, advised the Secretary of War that "Two-thirds of our men have no tents" and declared that "our men are kept in the wet trenches and are harassed day and night." Hill was of the opinion that disease would "destroy a hundred fold more [than] the Yankee artillery." Near Gordonsville, Virginia, at about the same time, troops went through one of the "severest experiences" of their lives when they were exposed to four days of a cold, drenching rain without shelter of any kind.

The exposure of the Vicksburg defenders to torrential rains for the greater part of five weeks certainly helped produce physical debility and extensive sickness during the latter stages of the campaign. And after the battle of Gettysburg the Army of Northern Virginia experienced similar exposure as the troops "slept in the rain, got up in the rain, cooked and ate in the rain, and marched and sometimes fought in the rain." General Lee had a tent, an early issue, but he informed the Quartermaster General in July, 1864, that time had dealt so harshly with it that it might not survive the summer. Further testimony as to the misery caused troops in the field by unusually heavy rainfall may be seen in the diary entry for October 23, 1863, by a soldier camped near Chattanooga: "This days duties and toils may be summed up as follows: mud ancle [sic] deep, mountain rivulets swolen [sic] to boisterous streams, rifle pits full of water, camp fires all out, and the north wind sends a chill through our bones, and to 'Cap the Climax' we go to bed supperless."

Tents, of course, provided no guarantee of protection against rain. Heavy downpours often caused water to run under the tents, saturate everything therein, and drive the occupants to seek haven elsewhere. "Night before last," related a Virginia veteran, "we were blest with a tremendous rain which flooded our camp or part of it, and part of us have been ditching ever since. . . . In some tents I saw this morning the water was a foot deep and had been deeper." With or without tents the soldier found no adequate refuge from rain, and much sickness was the result. "If our 'dear Mamas' could look in on us now," opined a Tar Heel after one deluge, "our deplorable condition would fetch the big tears to their eyes."

Soldiers were also put out of action at times by a blazing summer sun, especially when they were on the march or engaged in battle. It was reported by one of its members that there were several deaths from sunstroke in the Stonewall Brigade during a march from Orange Court House across the Rapidan River just before the battle of Cedar Mountain (August 9, 1862). Another soldier's account, reporting a clash on the Charles City Road in Virginia two years later, revealed that the heaviest loss sustained by the Texas Brigade during that encounter was caused by sunstroke. At about the same time a board of naval surgeons reported that boat crews were suffering exposure because of the lack of awnings for protection against the sun.

Lack of Clothing and Shoes

The unpleasantness and sickness caused by rain and cold weather was much more severe when the men lacked clothing, blankets, socks, and shoes. Procurement of these essential items never seemed to keep pace with the demand and need for them. An Atlanta newspaper asserted in October, 1862, that "a large majority" of Southern troops were in no condition to face the winter season as there were thousands who had "neither shoes nor stockings, nor more than one suit of clothes, and that a summer suit, and dirty and ragged at that." That same month the commander of a cavalry brigade in the Trans-Mississippi Department reported a strength of 2,319 men but only 1,068 fit for duty; many of his brigade, he declared, were "without a blanket, overcoat, shoes, or socks." This was no isolated case. On November 13, 1862, Lieutenant

173

General John C. Pemberton notified the Richmond officials that his army was generally "very deficient in clothing, shoes, and blankets"; and a report for the next day listed 6,466 bare-footed troops in Lieutenant General James Longstreet's Corps. Of 1,500 men in Hays's Brigade, Army of Northern Virginia, early in 1863, the assistant adjutant revealed that 400 were without shoes, many had no blankets, and some were "without a particle of under-clothing, having neither shirts, drawers, nor socks; while overcoats, from their rarity, are objects of curiosity." In November of 1863 General Lee informed the Secretary of War that many soldiers in his army were bare-footed, and he considered it necessary to emphasize the importance of good shoes to good health. Near Bean Station, Tennessee, on December 21, 1863, Surgeon Robert Myers wrote: "I saw on the 20th soldiers marching barefooted and feet bleeding leaving the marks on the frozen ground. . . . Many of the brigade deserted for want of clothing and sufficient food to satisfy their hunger. . . . This morning as I put water on my tooth brush, it froze before I put it to my mouth." And during the Knoxville campaign in Tennessee it was reported on January 8, 1864, that a "very large proportion" of Longstreet's cavalry, including officers, were "ragged and barefooted, without blankets or overcoats."

A plaintive letter to the editor of a Richmond newspaper in December, 1864, from "Many Sufferers" near Richmond, asked: "Why does the Government allow so much destitution in the line of clothing among the troops who are camped around the capital? . . . Many of us are almost destitute of pants, and the cold, chilling blasts of approaching winter urges us to call upon the Government and the people to use every means at their command to supply the wants of the men who have for four long years battled in defence of the sacred rights of our young nation." In January, 1865, Tennessee troops were observed to be in real need of clothing; [3] and an inspector

[3] Considerable clothing had been issued, however. According to the Augusta *Daily Constitutionalist*, February 24, 1865, which claimed to have an official statement from Major W. F. Ayer, Chief Quartermaster of the Army of Tennessee, the following items of clothing were issued to the Army of Tennessee from October 1, 1864, to February 7, 1865:

found the post at Danville, Virginia, considerably "deficient in clothing, shoes, etc, many men being entirely barefooted, and much sickness caused thereby."

Navy personnel not infrequently complained of sickness due to the shortage of pea jackets, blankets, and shoes. "It should be remembered," wrote an officer, "that exposure to bad weather on shipboard is worse than in camp life, where the men can have the advantage of exercise and cheerful fires; hence the wants of a sailor in clothing are greater than those of the soldier in the field." Prisoners of the Confederacy also were subject to exposure, and in February, 1865, William A. Carrington, Medical Director of Virginia Hospitals, was impelled to attribute the great amount of sickness partially to insufficient clothing.

The lack of clothing and shoes not only contributed to the long lists of names on hospital rolls; it also hampered the success of some important military operations. General Lee admitted that the Antietam campaign was undertaken in spite of the shoe and clothing needs of his troops, one consequence of which was an excessive amount of straggling. The hard roads of Maryland, according to Douglas S. Freeman, Lee's biographer, ruined what was left of the soldiers' shoes and inflicted painful cuts on their feet. Most of the straggling, concluded Freeman, "was due to bad shoes and good roads." That the overall situation with respect to shoes failed to show much improvement is attested by a circular issued to the Army of Tennessee late in 1864 which ordered field commanders to see that sandals were made from "green beef-hides" for all barefooted soldiers.

Poor and Insufficient Food

A large amount of sickness in the Rebel ranks resulted from the failure of the men to obtain good, well-prepared food in sufficient quantity and variety with any degree of con-

---

35,602 blankets, 78,900 pairs of pants, 50,687 jackets, 73,441 pairs of shoes, 102,769 pairs of socks, 25,134 shirts, and 61,327 pairs of drawers.

sistency. General Lee was constantly on the march to find food, and Lafayette Guild, medical director of Lee's army, asserted in May, 1864, that "the impoverished ration, without vegetables or vegetable acids, is, in my opinion, the prime source of disease." "It is perfectly useless," echoed the surgeon in charge of Walker Hospital, Columbus, Georgia, "to attempt to treat such diseases as prevail most commonly among soldiers unless suitable diet can be provided, as a great proportion of the diseases arise from the exposure and diet of the camp." And from the Trans-Mississippi Department early in 1863, Lieutenant General Theophilus H. Holmes informed President Davis that the extensive sickness and mortality in his command was caused by the inadequate diet—poor beef and corn bread—and exposure. The Navy also ascribed much of its sickness to a dietary insufficiency, and there was some complaint of "the substance now issued as coffee" having an injurious effect. At times too the prison ration was impoverished, and in January, 1865, Belle Isle occupants captured and ate the commandant's pet poodle.

The food ration itself was oftentimes short or lacking altogether. During campaigns the wagon trains were not infrequently separated from the troops or several days' rations cooked by special details in the rear were sent up and eaten at one sitting. As the conflict dragged to its close the overall system of supply gradually deteriorated with the result that men went days without food. One such unfortunate Rebel, a member of the Thirty-sixth Virginia, opined: "I have had nothing to eat for four days & I don't feel very hungry now but I know d——ned well I'm starving to death." Actually, however, most of the suffering and disease was caused by the lack of proper food in sufficient quantity and by poorly prepared food.

General Beauregard informed President Davis that one major cause for the large amount of sickness at Corinth in 1862 was the lack of proper food, "the salt meat furnished to the troops being often not fit to eat; also the almost total want of fresh beef and vegetables, beef having been furnished once a week or every ten days, instead of five times a week, as

SAMUEL PRESTON MOORE

SURGEON GENERAL, CONFEDERATE ARMY

SAMUEL HOLLINGSWORTH STOUT

MEDICAL DIRECTOR, CONFEDERATE ARMY

CHARLES E. JOHNSON

SURGEON GENERAL,
NORTH CAROLINA

E. BURKE HAYWOOD

SURGEON IN CHARGE OF
PETTIGREW HOSPITAL, RALEIGH

PETER E. HINES

MEDICAL DIRECTOR OF GEN-
ERAL HOSPITALS, NORTH CAROLINA

MEDICAL & SURGICAL JOURNAL.

EXPERIENTIA DOCET.

JOURNAL.

Vol. I.   RICHMOND, FEBRUARY, 1861.   No. 2.

CONFEDERATE STATES MEDICAL & SURGICAL JOURNAL

CHIMBORAZO HOSPITAL, RICHMOND, MAY, 1865

(FORM 13.)

ARMY OF THE CONFEDERATE STATES.

CERTIFICATE OF DISABILITY FOR DISCHARGE.

Private John Bradford of Captain
Company ( ) of the *Gordons Arty* Regiment
of
of the
was enlisted by
at on the
day of to serve
years.
He was born in in the State of
is years of age, feet inches high,
complexion, eyes, hair, and by occupation, when enlisted.
a

During the last two months said soldier has been unfit for duty
days*

The above man was sent to this hospital, being a complete Idiot, unable to give the slightest rational account of himself. From information received, four of his sisters are similarly afflicted.

STATION: *2 No. 64 Hospl. Columbia S.C.*
DATE: *October 25th 1864.*

Commanding Company

*Note.—The Company Commander will here add a statement of all the facts known to him concerning the disease or wound, or cause of disability of the soldier; the time, place, manner, and all other circumstances under which the injury occurred, or disease originated or appeared; the duty, or service, or situation of the soldier at the time the injury was received, or disease contracted, or supposed to be contracted; and whatever facts may aid a judgment as to the cause, immediate or remote, of the disability, and the circumstances attending it.

CERTIFICATE OF DISABILITY FOR DISCHARGE

"The above man was sent to this hospital, being a complete idiot, unable to give the slightest rational account of himself. From information received, four of his sisters are similarly afflicted."

Surgeon General's Office,

RICHMOND, VA., APRIL 2ND, 1862.

It is the policy of all nations at all times, especially such as at present exist in our Confederacy, to make every effort to develope its internal resources, and to diminish its tribute to foreigners, by supplying its necessities from the productions of its own soil.

This observation may be considered peculiarly applicable to the appropriation of our Indigenous Medicinal Substances of the Vegetable Kingdom—and with the view of promoting this object, the enclosed pamphlet embracing many of the more important Medicinal Plants, has been issued for distribution to the Medical Officers of the Army of the Confederacy, now in the field.

You are particularly instructed to call the attention of those of your Corps within your district, to the propriety of and necessity for, collecting and preparing with care such of the within enumerated remedial agents, or others found valuable, as their respective charges may require during the present Summer and coming Winter, with directions to forward to the Medical Purveyors of their districts, for preparation and distribution, such amounts of those articles as they may be able to have collected, as well as their own supply, for which they may not have storage.

Our forests and savannahs furnish our *Mat: Med:* with a moderate number of Narcotics and Sedatives, and an abundant supply of Tonics, Astringents, Aromatics and Demulcents, whilst the list of Anodynes, Emetics, and Cathartics, remains in a comparative degree incomplete. The attention of the profession should therefore be especially directed to a determination of the relative value and specific application of such of the last mentioned classes, as have been adopted in practice, as well as to the discovery of curative virtues in others of the same classes, not yet introduced to public notice.

Information thus elicited when of sufficient importance, should be communicated through the Medical Director of the Army Corps or Military Department, to this Office.

Instructions relative to the procuration of a proper supply of Indigenous Medicinal Substances will be forwarded to Med. Purveyors.

(Signed,)

S. P. MOORE,
Surg'n. Gen'l.

SURGEON GENERAL'S OFFICE CIRCULAR

Warrant for $500,000.00 for medical supplies signed by George W. Randolph, Secretary of War ordered." One result was incipient scurvy. Men sometimes went for months, particularly during the winter, receiving such rations as salty bacon, rice, flour, and an occasional piece of tough beef. "Horse beef was issued sometimes," recalled a veteran of Lee's army, "and we found it a difficult dental proposition."

During the latter stages of the Vicksburg siege the rations issued were barely able to sustain life, and emaciated troops scoured the works for food of any description. After the beef and bacon gave out the soldiers slaughtered and consumed the mules and horses, turned loose because of the lack of forage to feed them. Large wharf rats were also caught and eaten. A petition, dated June 28, 1863, and signed by "Many Soldiers," warned General John C. Pemberton that the army was ripe for mutiny unless it could be fed. "If you can't feed us," said the petition, "you had better surrender us, horrible as the idea is, than suffer this noble army to disgrace themselves by desertion." "They are feeding us horrible," wrote a truer patriot near Dalton, Georgia, early in 1864, "but when one thinks of the Cause he forgets all other things."

The threat of mutiny was not to be taken lightly. Protesting against a ration that consisted only of beef, sour molasses, and corn meal, the last item being "sour, dirty, weevel-eaten, and filled with ants and worms, and not bolted," the Third Regiment of Texas Infantry mutinied in Galveston early in August, 1863. Sometime later, troops of the Army of Tennessee intercepted one of their own provision trains in Dalton, Georgia, broke into all the cars, and made off with all the bacon, meal, and flour on board; General Braxton Bragg was blamed by one Confederate chronicler for the fact that rations in that army "were always scarce," and, according to him the troops "became starved skeletons; naked and ragged rebels." Near Richmond, in December, 1864, several noncommissioned officers of the Thirty-first North Carolina Regiment were court-martialed for leading a "charge" against the commissary to obtain increased rations.

General Lee manifested much anxiety over the insufficiency

of rations for his army and informed the Secretary of War late in 1862 that the only part of the ration supplied to his men for some time was bread and meat and this in small quantity. Early in 1864 he reported that short rations were "having a bad effect upon the men, both morally and physically." Desertions to the enemy, he asserted, were increasing, and it was his opinion that the army could not remain effective unless the ration was increased. The troops could not "continue healthy and vigorous," Lee wrote, "if confined to this spare diet for any length of time." A few months later he became so distressed over continuing shortages that he apprised President Davis of his inability to apprehend how the army could be kept together much longer. Food was more badly needed than men, wrote a defender of Fort Fisher early in 1864; and Nat Wood, a young lieutenant in the Army of Northern Virginia, recalled that rations were so deficient in his brigade that several of his fellow officers boiled a cat for two days only to experience frustration when they found it still too tough to carve. Deficient rations would also appear to be illustrated by the following entry for April 8, 1864, in a North Carolinian's diary: "Had fried *rat* for breakfast & never ate better meat." It was not until June, 1864, that Lee's medical director could report: "We are now getting vegetables for the troops, and I feel assured that the health of the Army will be greatly improved."

Rations in the army became short once more during the winter of 1864–1865. As one underfed soldier put it: "Our ratons [sic] is pretty short now & we dont get them regular . . . it seems that evry thing goes against us of late." A rather general observation, made by the Commissary-General of Subsistence in December, 1864, is also revealing: an admission that for more than two years it had been impossible to meet the requirements of the ration table for the Army of Northern Virginia. "As time advances," he explained, "the funds for procuring subsistence becomes less and less devisable and available, and the obstacles to collecting what is in the country increase in like ratio." It is quite understandable then why a battle-scarred veteran felt justified in breaking into his minister's prayer that the Lord would give them more courage with the admonition: "Hold on there, Brother Jones! Hold on! There's no sense in asking God for more courage, for he knows we have got plenty of it. Ask him for more grub—that's what we need most of all." [4]

Poorly prepared food in the field was also a source of disease although soldiers sometimes liked to brag that "We can cook as good as any woman." The frying pan was used altogether too much, and the cooked food was generally greasy. Surgeon General Moore early in the war inveighed against small company messes and their culinary deficiencies, but little was done to substitute anything better for them. Occasionally the government received criticism for neglecting to organize a corps of cooks and bakers from which assignments could be made to each regiment. "American soldiers have not an inherent taste for cooking like the Frenchman," ran the argument, "and certainly, until they are taught how to prepare their food so as to make it healthy and palatable, they ought to be furnished with cooks competent to attend to this department." Sometimes troops were able to find Negroes or residents in the vicinity of camp who would cook for them; others gave their digestive apparatus some respite when they could take meals at nearby farmhouses.

More criticism seems to have been directed against badly baked bread as a cause of sickness than against any other single item. President Davis, on August 20, 1861, notified General Joseph E. Johnston at Manassas that the main complaint made to him regarding the army "is of bad bread, and inattention to the sick." A few days later Congress enacted a law directing the Secretary of War to furnish "well baked bread"

[4] As Joseph Jones pointed out after the war, however, it is difficult "to correctly appreciate the full effects of the scant rations upon the Confederate troops, from the fact that throughout the entire war, they received an immense amount of extra supplies from their friends and relatives, and through various State agencies and benevolent institutions; and much extra food was also gathered during foraging." The Quartermaster-General's Department effected a special arrangement with the Southern Express Company concerning the shipment of boxes to soldiers containing food and clothing.

in lieu of the flour ration to field troops upon the latter's requisition, and he was authorized to establish bakeries or make contracts necessary to supply such bread. Little improvement followed, however, as the Surgeon General was informed in November, 1861, that "the bread baked in camp and used by the soldiers . . . is generally of the worst possible description, and most prolific of disease." The issue of portable bake ovens was recommended. Two months later further complaint was made against "the badly baked bread eaten by our soldiers." And a congressional committee appointed to examine into the Quartermaster, Commissary, and Medical Departments reported on January 29, 1862, that "The indifferent as well as the unwholesome food provided for the sick . . . attracted the attention of the committee." The cooking, especially that of bread, was condemned. Said the committee: "Bread hastily made up of flour and water and imperfectly baked, almost incapable of being digested, was deemed a most fruitful source of disease. It was apparent at those camps where well-baked bread was served to the men that the amount of disease was greatly reduced." Several portable bake ovens appeared in the field during the latter part of the war, but appetizing and wholesome bread remained a scarce commodity.

Impure Water

Bad water was also a cause of disease among troops in the field. Good water was not always to be found in the vicinity of camps, and efforts at purification were generally neglected. A soldier campaigning in York County, Virginia, stated that "we drank more mud and wiggle tails than water." And troops in the Army of Tennessee used water "filled with animaleulae that requires no microscope to detect their presence." At Vicksburg the water was "hot, scarce and only to be procured from the ponds or river, under fire, and at the risk of life." The mortality from disease at Corinth during its siege, estimated by Joseph Jones as equal to or greater than the number of casualties from the battle of Shiloh, appears to have been due as much to impure water as to inadequate diet. A common soldier at Corinth remembered that "All the water courses went dry, and we used water out of filthy pools." It therefore occasions no surprise to learn that in reply to President Davis' query as to the cause of sickness at Corinth General Beauregard cited first the lack of good water. Even the surface water available soon became polluted by excrementitious matter. According to a newspaper report the odor of the water at Corinth was such that the men had "to hold their noses while drinking it." Another problem was presented by the fact that soldiers stationed near the coast and sailors on long cruises sometimes suffered from drinking salt water.[5]

Efforts were sometimes made by the commanders of troops stationed in areas where the water was bad to obtain their supply from the water works of nearby cities or towns. Surgeon J. Julian Chisolm advised either the boiling of water found in such places or its filtering through straw. The recommendation of F. Peyre Porcher was more popular with the troops: the serving of blackberry cordial to victims of bad water.

The Mental Problem

Monotony and boredom produced by inactivity also appeared to cause sickness. A Richmond newspaper, hostile to the administration, charged that the defensive policy pursued by the government in its conduct of the war had produced "that ennui which is the fruitful mother of diseases, discontents and demoralization in the camp"; the "dirt digging industry," echoed Medical Director Samuel H. Stout, as practiced by General Beauregard was responsible for much illness,

[5] On August 25, 1863, Raphael Semmes, commander of the *Alabama*, famous Confederate raider, reported that his fresh-water condenser was giving out.

especially typhoid fever, among Confederate troops. It was generally observed that an army in motion was healthier than a stationary one and those in favor of an aggressive, active policy were highly elated when "the spade and the ditch" were discarded by Lee's army in the fall of 1862.

During the long winter months spent in camp the soldiers complained continuously of their barren, monotonous existence, and they welcomed almost any diversion. This boredom was undoubtedly more responsible than any other single factor for the excessive drinking which at times caused the War Department considerable concern. A general order issued in January, 1862, went so far as to declare that "the largest portion of our sickness and mortality" resulted from drunkenness. This assertion, of course, was an exaggeration, but good surgeons were quick to advise exercise and work when their sick lists increased in stationary quarters. "My habit was," related one of these, "when I found my sick list increasing, to advise all hands, except the sick, to be put to work. . . . When there was no work I studied to make work, and I was amply repaid."

Very little is known about the neuroses of Confederate troops but there is every reason to believe that some, like soldiers of other wars, became psychoneurotic. Recent psychiatric thought has advanced the theory that neuroses are caused by a combination of past experience and the sympathy soldiers know that they will receive behind the lines. Actual battle experiences, it appears, are not as important as secondary mental processes in the causation of disordered nervous systems. It is also clear that some diseases of the brain and nervous system had a traumatic origin.

Disease in Confederate Prisons

Most of the causes set forth above as explaining much of the disease and death in the Confederate military establishment may also be cited as producing sickness and death among Union troops confined in Southern prisons. Inadequate sanitary regulations, crowded conditions, negligence of personal cleanliness, vermin and insects, lack of proper shelter, insufficient clothing and blankets, poor food, bad water, boredom, and secondary mental processes—all combined to fill prison hospitals and graveyards.

CHAPTER X

Prevalence and Treatment of Disease

Classification of Diseases

Confederate medical regulations published early in the Civil War listed a total of 130 diseases under the following main headings: "Fevers," "Diseases of the organs connected with the digestive system," "Diseases of the respiratory system," "Diseases of the circulatory system," "Diseases of the brain and nervous system," "Diseases of the urinary and genital organs and venereal affections," "Diseases of the serous exhalent vessels," "Diseases of the fibrous and muscular structures," "Abscesses and ulcers," "Diseases of the eye," "Diseases of the ear," and "All other diseases." Twenty-three ailments, including "Debilitas," "Nostalgia," and "Scorbutus," were enumerated under the last-named heading. This classification of diseases known to the medical officer was "remodelled," according to the Surgeon General, but forms reflecting any change were never published.

Diarrhea and Dysentery

The great enervating ailments of the Southern fighting men were the intestinal disorders, diarrhea and dysentery. Since diarrhea actually is a symptom of many diseases rather than a "disease" and since many cases diagnosed as dysentery were certainly nothing more than cases of loose bowels, it is obvious that the disease statistics leave something to be desired. Diarrhea no doubt prevailed to a greater extent than dysentery, but the two terms came to be used almost interchangeably. Surgeon Paul F. Eve considered these maladies to be "the diseases" of the Confederate forces.[1] According to Eve, "Chronic diarrhoea was very prevalent and quite difficult of management. Indeed, so common was looseness of the bowels in the army, that few soldiers ever had a natural or moulded evacuation. The camping grounds, privies everywhere, and too often the depots, streets, etc., of villages and towns presented disgusting evidences of this fact." Diarrhea struck early. Bedford Brown, another Confederate medical officer, asserted that nine-tenths of all recruits were attacked by this condition and so weakened physically that they became easy victims for other ailments. Surgeon F. Peyre Porcher believed that almost every patient admitted to a hospital for treatment had a previous history of diarrhea or was suffering from it at the time of admittance. "No matter what else a patient had," wrote another doctor in gray, "he had diarrhoea."

Some idea of the high incidence of the intestinal disorders may be gained from the fact that 226,828 of the 848,555 cases of disease entered on Confederate field reports east of the Mississippi during the first two years of the war were reported as diarrhea and dysentery. And of the 50,350 soldiers admitted to Chimborazo Hospital suffering from some specific illness, 10,503 were diagnosed as having one or the other of these disorders. The two ailments were also rampant among Union prisoners of war in the Confederacy and appear to have helped cause more than half of all deaths due to disease. Surgeon Joseph Jones, after considerable observation throughout the Confederacy, concluded that "Chronic diarrhoea and dysentery were the most abundant and most difficult to cure amongst army diseases; and whilst the more fatal diseases, as typhoid fever, progressively diminished, chronic diarrhoea and dysentery progressively increased, and not only destroyed more soldiers than gunshot wounds, but more soldiers were permanently disabled and lost to the service from these diseases

[1] John Duffy, well-known authority on colonial epidemics, concludes that dysentery shared with malaria "first place among the colonial infections."

than from the disability following the accidents of battle." [2]

Jones hardly exaggerated. A patient in a Tennessee hospital wrote that he had never seen men so nearly reduced to skeletons as those who suffered from diarrhea. "The disease that seemed to break down the will power more than any other," wrote a Southern minister, "was chronic diarrhea, and the patients seemed to lose not only desire to live but all manliness and self-respect. They whined and died in spite of all we could do." The story is told of a haggard and unhappy Confederate soldier who, seeing a vigorous and healthy-looking Yankee cavalryman near the end of the war, exclaimed: "Oh my, oh my! you look like you wuz sich a happy man! You got on sich a nice new-uniform, you got sich nice boots on, you ridin' sich a nice hoss, an' you look like yer bowels wuz so reglar."

Medical officers were of the opinion that the inadequate ration, poor cooking, impure water, fatigue, and exposure were prime causes of diarrhea and dysentery, but they were not always in harmony as to which was the most important. Medical Director Guild, for example, believed that the increase of these two affections in the fall of 1863 was primarily due to exposure, but some of his medical colleagues ascribed it to the poor water. In May, 1864, while alluding to fatigue and exposure as productive of bowel disorders, Guild expressed the opinion that "the impoverished ration" was the chief cause of disease. Nothing was known, of course, about the dysenteries caused by definite protozoal or bacterial agents or the transmission of these infections by contaminated milk or food.

Various remedies were used in the treatment of diarrhea and dysentery. Some medical officers found nitrate of silver injections to be effective. One surgeon introduced an anal speculum, lubricated with soap, and freely cauterized the mucus membrane of the rectum for a distance of several inches from the anus. Others fed their patients raw beef, with the fibers scraped out, covered with a "little vinegar, salt and

[2] According to statistics pertaining to the Union forces, these ailments "produced more sickness and mortality than any other form of disease."

pepper" and reported "considerable success." Hospital prescription books reveal that "Blue Mass," "Astrgt Pills," and
"Diarrhoea mixture" were some of the remedies most frequently prescribed. Calomel, strychnia, opium, and acetate of
lead were also administered rather freely. There was some
criticism of the use of mineral astringents on the basis that
they interfered with the integrity of the gastro-intestinal surfaces "disturbing the functions of absorption, and consequently of digestion." This feeling contributed to the widespread popularity of indigenous astringents such as the
blackberry, chinquapin, dogwood, cranesbill, sweet gum, marsh
rosemary, pomegranate, knot grass, and black oak. An Alabama medical officer and his assistant concocted a pill containing equal amounts of red pepper and crude resin. The
"Diseremus Pill," as they called it, was handed to the weakened men with the instruction to "take two after each loose
operation." Another surgeon administered "an infusion of
raspberry leaves or whortleberry leaves (both of which act
finely on the kidneys and bladder)."

Some medical officers realized that proper diet and rest
were probably more important than medication in the treatment of diarrhea and dysentery. The misdiagnosis of many of
these cases may be seen in the fact noted by a few that most
were "associated with a scorbutic condition and . . . improve
best under an invigorating corrective diet and but little medicine." Surgeon James A. Bowers, stationed at Port Hudson,
Louisiana, noted early in 1863 that rations of potatoes, turnips,
turnip salad, and onions were having a more salutary effect
in his treatment of patients with intestinal troubles than "all
the astringents etc that I can give them." And Joseph Jones
believed that almost all of the diarrhea and dysentery sufferers, except those with "extensive ulceration and destruction of the mucus membrane of the colon and rectum, would
have been greatly benefited and cured by the proper diet." [3]

[3] Bedford Brown, an observant Confederate surgeon, blamed fried food
for much of the intestinal trouble and noticed considerable improvement
in health when "the stew-pan was substituted for the frying-pan."

After the patient had been administered "chalk mixtures, with demulcents, milk, eggs, arrowroot, jelly, with small quantities of brandy or other stimulants," according to Surgeon Porcher, he should "be trusted to time, rest, the recumbent posture, to the recuperative powers of his constitution and to nature." The waters at Cherokee Springs, Georgia, were considered beneficial in the treatment of chronic cases, and patients in that area were ordered to be sent there.

Measles

Measles, caused by a filter-passing virus, was recognized as another great scourge. Long regarded as a disease of children, it is a matter of record that more havoc was caused by measles, an extremely infectious sickness, during the early months of the war than by any other ailment. Regiments made up of rural troops were especially hard hit, and the training program was so thoroughly disrupted by the epidemic that companies, battalions, and even whole regiments were disbanded temporarily and the men sent home. Over 8,000 cases of measles were reported in the Army of the Potomac during the months of July, August, and September, 1861; one out of every seven men in this command contracted the disease. In a camp near Raleigh, North Carolina, 4,000 cases of measles developed among 10,000 troops, and hospitals in the cities as well as those in the field were filled with men suffering from this sickness. When Samuel H. Stout took charge of the Gordon Hospital in Nashville, for example, he found 650 patients—most of whom had the measles. And the sick who filled the Overton Hospital in Memphis early in 1862 were mostly victims of measles and exposure. Measles struck its most devastating blow in the first part of the war, but the disease never subsided completely as is evidenced by the fact that 2,207 cases of this ailment were reported by the Virginia general hospitals from October 1, 1862, to January 31, 1864.[4]

[4] There were 76,318 cases of measles reported in the Union army, and the deaths therefrom totaled 5,177. "An Alabama Volunteer," as early as

188

Bad hygienic conditions no doubt contributed heavily to the early outbreaks, and one of the lessons taught by the war was that careful sanitary control was more effective than medication in the treatment of measles. Medical officers learned that drugs were of little value in limiting the duration of the disease, and most of them recommended abundant ventilation for those affected. There was, however, some "indisposition to give such patients an abundance of fresh air, there being a fear that the eruption would be driven in, as it was termed." [5] In addition to the usual treatment one hospital surgeon found that a solution of ammonium acetate "given in doses of 40 or 50 drops, 3 times a day, in a cup of warm tea, seems to possess a particular eliminating action." The redoubtable Porcher recommended a tea made from the roots and leaves of sassafras.

Measles Sequelae

A soldier stationed near Hopkinsville, Kentucky, noted during the first winter of the war that fifty men of his regiment had died "principally from backset in measles." This was not an unusual development. As a rule few men died from measles alone, but the sequelae of the disease produced fearful results. On this subject a special committee appointed by the Provisional Congress to examine the operation of the Quartermaster, Commissary, and Medical Departments reported on January 29, 1862: "It is the peculiar characteristic of measles that the system is left liable to the invasion of the most formidable diseases, upon exposure a short time after under-

---

December, 1861, proposed that "recruits, especially from the country, be kept at least two months in camps of instructions," by the end of which time he thought "epidemic camp diseases will have run their course; the troops will have acquired some knowledge of drill and camp life, and be prepared for effective service." General Lee made practically the same proposal nearly a year later.

[5] Union surgeons also found that the treatment of measles "involved measures of sanitary supervision rather than clinical instructions or pharmaceutical formulae."

going an attack. Fever, pneumonia and diarrhoea . . . follow in the wake of measles where the convalescents are exposed to cold and wet; and when to this we add unsuitable diet, badly-ventilated tents and hospitals, there can be no surprise at the number of sick in the Army, as well as the great suffering and distress."

Ophthalmia, bronchitis, persistent otorrhoea, dysentery, typhoid fever, and phthisis, in addition to pneumonia and diarrhea, were some of the other diseases that were observed by medical officers to follow in the wake of measles. It was asserted early in the war that nine out of ten cases of serious illness stemmed from an attack of measles, and Surgeon Bedford Brown was so concerned over the weakening effect of the disease that he proposed furloughs of from two to three weeks duration for all measles convalescents. Brown went on to contend that "The disease consequent to and traceable to measles cost the Confederate Army the lives of more men and a greater amount of invalidism than all other causes combined; and if this method of general furloughs could have been adopted after an attack of this disease, it would have resulted in preventing a vast loss of life and time, and would have proven a decided means of economy." The incidence of measles sequelae decreased as the epidemics of measles subsided, but the problem was one that continued to plague medical officers.

Malaria

"I have been having the chils & fevers & I tell you that I dont like the chaps atol," wrote a soldier from Salisbury, North Carolina, in the fall of 1862. "I had one yestaday," he continued, "that like to shook me clean out of the garrison." This Confederate was just one of the many who suffered from malaria, a disease which had long been both endemic and epidemic in the Southern states due to the presence of the anopheles mosquito and an infected population. It was generally believed that malaria was caused by "miasms" emanating from

190

areas covered by stagnant waters, and certain practices, such as the burning of tar in the vicinity of hospitals, were followed to prevent the malady. It was also noted that when soldiering near a swamp at night "there is no danger so long as the party keeps on the windward side of it." A student of malariology has pointed out that the movements of the armies during the war "must have profoundly disturbed the balance between infection and resistance in the indigenous population of the invaded areas," and he concluded that the incidence of malaria increased considerably during and after the war as a result.

There was, according to reports, one case of malaria in every seven cases of disease among Confederate troops east of the Mississippi during the years 1861 to 1862, and the Department of South Carolina, Georgia, and Florida was especially hard hit. This department, for example, with a mean strength of 25,723 troops, reported 41,539 cases of malaria and 227 deaths from January, 1862, to July, 1863. During the same period Confederate troops in and around Mobile, with an average strength of 6,752, recorded 13,668 malaria cases.[6] And Major General Dabney H. Maury, who commanded the District of the Gulf, informed the Adjutant and Inspector General on November 10, 1864, that six-sevenths of the strength in some of his garrisons had been incapacitated by chills and fevers during the past two months. The malarial fevers also caused a considerable amount of sickness in the Confederate States Navy. In the late summer of 1864, for example, the James River Squadron was crippled seriously by malaria. Union prisoners in the Confederacy appear to have suffered less from malaria than the Southern military forces. The register of Andersonville and other prison hospital records do not indicate a particularly high incidence of the disease among the imprisoned.

Quinine had been isolated from cinchona by French chemists in 1822, and it soon became a favorite remedy of Southern

[6] The incidence of malaria seems to have been greater among Confederate than among Union troops, but the mortality rate was probably lower.

physicians in the treatment of malaria inasmuch as it was more effective than crude cinchona and lowered the mortality rate. Confederate medical officers naturally employed the drug whenever possible, but the amount of quinine that found its way through the ever tightening blockade gradually diminished and led to the search for other antiperiodics among native plants. Georgia bark and dogwood were given a trial, and late in 1862 the Surgeon General, after concluding that both were adequate substitutes, ordered that a compound tincture of dogwood, poplar, and willow barks mixed with whiskey "be issued as a tonic and febrifuge and substitute as far as practicable for quinine." Late in the war Medical Director William A. Carrington requested the surgeons in charge of the major Richmond hospitals to place their intermittent fever cases under the supervision of one medical officer in each institution for the purpose of trying various native remedies and other expedients. "I especially desire," wrote Carrington, "that you try the Ext. of American Hemp, Fodder Tea, application of heat to various parts of the body, coffee and pepper." Malaria convalescents were sometimes issued one gill of medicated whiskey daily.[7]

Southern practitioners had long adjudged turpentine to be a valuable remedial agent, and its use as a quinine substitute to combat malaria is not particularly surprising. Several doctors, including the able Josiah Clark Nott of Alabama, pointed up the effectiveness of external applications of turpentine during the 1850's, but such therapy found little favor so long as quinine was obtainable. In mid-September of 1863, however, Surgeon General Moore instructed his medical officers to substitute external applications of turpentine for quinine in the treatment of malaria cases "as far as practicable." Declared Moore at this time: "Satisfactory experiments have been instituted to show that the local application of this remedy

[7] Joseph Jones was of the opinion that malaria was affecting the results of treatment in the gangrene hospital at Macon, Georgia, during the fall of 1864, and Jones was there, according to a colleague, "making copious drawings of specimens of ill-conditioned wounds, of pus, urine and everything he can subject to microscope. . . ."

has proved amply sufficient to interrupt the morbific chain of successive paroxysms—one application only being required, in the majority of cases, whilst in the remaining ones, it has proved fully successful in preventing the more serious stage of the paroxysm viz: the chill. . . ."

The above treatment enjoyed considerable vogue. Reports of its successful use in over four hundred cases were sent to the *Confederate States Medical and Surgical Journal* from January to August, 1864. "With few exceptions," stated the editor, "the remedy is regarded as one of great power, if not positive efficiency, in preventing a return of paroxysm." His own conclusions, however, were not so enthusiastic. He thought that "experimental medicine will be very likely to mislead us" and decided that turpentine "is one of the large class of agents which may be rendered useful in the treatment of periodic fever, as an adjuvant to other remedies, but that it does not deserve to be regarded as a specific in the treatment of such affections." Experience upheld the validity of these conclusions. The medical officers at Raleigh's Pettigrew Hospital, for example, discovered that the use of turpentine along with quinine proved effective and also reduced the amount of quinine to be administered.

One valuable lesson learned from the war was that malaria could be prevented. Joseph Jones, aware of the prophylactic use of quinine by English seamen stationed off the African coast, recommended such use of the drug for Southern troops. Although the scarcity and relative high cost of quinine precluded its use as a prophylactic on any wide scale, it was used in certain localities with positive results.

The prophylactic employment of other medicinal agents against malaria was also attempted. In July, 1862, the Surgeon General called for the administering of "the Dogwood, Tulip-bearing Poplar, Willow, Boneset, Centawolf and other indigenous tonics" as prophylactics to soldiers serving in malarious areas. Whiskey saturated by dogwood and other indigenous barks was another remedy thought to possess prophylactic power. The troops manifested high approval of this latter prescription, observed one medical officer, "and were careful to remind their physicians of the hours appointed for receiving their favorite medicine."

As was the case in regard to diarrhea and dysentery, many soldiers afflicted with other diseases were probably diagnosed as malarial cases. The investigations of Charles Wardell Stiles early in the present century, for example, make it reasonably certain that many patients listed under the heading of malaria were undoubtedly suffering from hookworm.

Typhoid Fever, Typhus Fever, and Common Continued Fevers

The so-called "continued fevers" appeared on hospital and field registers with considerable frequency. This term encompassed typhoid fever, typhus fever, and common continued fevers. Diseases similar to typhoid but which could not be identified clearly as such appear to have been assigned to the category last named. Typhoid fever had long been prevalent in America, and its symptoms were like those of both typhus and the intestinal ailments. The disease had an extremely high incidence for some time and was one of the most deadly.

After a careful analysis of official reports, Joseph Jones calculated the approximate number of deaths from all causes between January 1, 1862, and August 1, 1863, to have been 68,838, and he believed that typhoid fever took the lives of at least 25 per cent of this total. Other statistics support the claim that typhoid was a "killer" disease. There were 1,619 deaths from 4,749 typhoid cases in the general hospitals of Virginia, exclusive of those in and around Richmond, between January 1, 1862, and April 1, 1863, and Chimborazo reported 1,388 cases and 661 deaths for the entire war. Further south, between December, 1861, and January, 1864, typhoid and pneumonia cases comprised only about eight per cent of the total but caused approximately two-thirds of the mortality in Savannah's General Hospital No. 1. It should be pointed out, however, that there was a diminution of typhoid subsequent to the early epidemics. According to Joseph Jones, typhoid "progressively diminished during the progress of the war, and disappeared almost entirely from the veteran armies."

Few records of value are available as to the incidence of the continued fevers among Union prisoners in Confederate hands. At Andersonville, however, Joseph Jones made note of 753 cases of continued fever and 199 fatalities during the period from March 1 to August 31, 1864.

Some uncertainty seemed to exist as to the proper treatment of the continued fevers. There was a tendency though to isolate victims of these disorders in well-ventilated rooms or tents. "Typhus cases particularly," wrote J. Julian Chisolm, "should, if possible, be isolated in tents, and ample room be given to each." Hospital wards, he thought, could not "be protected by too many hygienic regulations." In the treatment of typhoid it was observed that saline purgatives followed by stimulants were successful in counteracting the asthenic effects of the disease. Felix Formento, surgeon in Richmond's Louisiana Hospital, found that the oil of turpentine produced dramatic results in typhoid cases accompanied by "much tympanitis, dryness, and fuliginous condition of the tongue and fauces, gurgle and pain in the right fossa iliaca, and moderate diarrhoea." Externally, much reliance was placed upon cold cloths and sponge baths.

Smallpox

Smallpox, a disease whose cause is still unknown, was one of the most dreaded of the sicknesses that harassed the Confederate soldier. Brought to the New World early in the sixteenth century from Europe, it had become both endemic and epidemic. Brigadier General Henry H. Sibley, commanding the Army of New Mexico, reported that this scourge had thinned his ranks as early as January, 1862, but the first great wartime epidemic reached its full fury during the following fall and winter. Reports of its elevated incidence were made

195

at that time from the Army of Northern Virginia, the Valley District, the Gulf area, and the Army of Tennessee. The worst epidemic took place in the Army of Northern Virginia.

The contagion in the Army of Northern Virginia followed upon the heels of the Antietam campaign in the fall of 1862, and the infection's source was never definitely determined— the medical director of the Virginia general hospitals contending that the soldiers came into contact with smallpox in Maryland and the army's medical director arguing that it originated in the Virginia hospitals or prisons.[8] At any rate, all available space was soon filled with smallpox victims, and the infection took a heavy toll of lives. During the single week of December 12 to December 19, 1862, the Smallpox Hospital in Richmond reported 250 admissions and 110 deaths, although 29 of those who died were also suffering from some other ailment. Records extant indicate that there was a second epidemic in Virginia during the winter of 1863–1864 with the same heavy mortality. Of 2,513 cases of smallpox treated in Virginia's general hospitals from October 1, 1862, to January 31, 1864, the fatal cases numbered 1,020. There were, in addition, 1,196 cases of varioloid with 39 deaths.

Many Union prisoners also fell victims to smallpox. Joseph Jones recorded only 236 cases of all the eruptive fevers— smallpox, measles, erysipelas, and scarlet fever—80 of which terminated fatally at Andersonville between March 1 and August 31, 1864; but there were 818 cases of smallpox out of 4,168 ailments reported as having been admitted to the Danville, Virginia, Prison Hospital from November 23, 1863, to March 27, 1865. This latter report probably suggests a truer picture of the overall situation.[9]

Medical authorities had not been unaware of the danger of smallpox epidemics. As early as May 3, 1861, the Surgeon General of Virginia, perhaps aware of epidemics in that state

[8] According to another theory, Confederate prisoners returned from Fort Delaware brought the disease with them.

[9] The surgeon in charge of a division in the Danville, Virginia, General Hospital claimed early in 1864 to have 800 prisoners under his care, 285 of whom had smallpox.

prior to the Civil War, ordered the immediate vaccination of all troops not already vaccinated. And although it had been over sixty years since Jenner, the English physician, had demonstrated that smallpox could be prevented by vaccination, most individuals had not been vaccinated. The Confederate Surgeon General instructed medical purveyors in the fall of 1861 to procure vaccine virus for medical directors, and practitioners throughout the Confederacy were called upon to collect fresh, genuine virus and send it to Richmond for the use of the Medical Department. [10] On February 6, 1862, the Surgeon General directed that all hospital patients undergo vaccination, and three months later that same official instructed his medical directors "to have detailed in each Department or Army, an efficient Medical Officer to superintend the vaccination of the soldiers of the Command." [11] Such medical officers appear to have been very active.

Surgeon Edward N. Covey, one of the superintendents of vaccination, requested medical officers to send him not only the vaccine crusts obtained from their patients but also those taken from the arms of children for the purpose of obtaining vaccine. Human vaccination scabs proved to be the source of most vaccine, and crusts from the arms of children were especially desired. To procure more vaccine virus in 1864, the Surgeon General ordered medical directors, if practicable, "to promptly assign one Asst. Surgeon in each of the larger cities of the Confederacy to the temporary and special duty of vaccinating gratis, in such cities and precincts, all healthy children, white and black, who have not been previously vaccinated." [12] Less than a month before Lee's surrender, medical officers were advised that the large amount of reliable virus needed for the army must be obtained from the scabs of healthy children, and they were authorized to pay private

[10] Advertisements were run in the Richmond press and other newspapers were asked to copy.

[11] During the following August the post commander of Atlanta ordered the vaccination of all civilians and of all soldiers in hospitals.

[12] Surgeon James Bolton collected some 800 crusts, most taken from the arms of healthy Negro children, late in the war.

physicians $5 for each reliable scab they would furnish. Unfortunately, the supply of vaccine virus never quite met the demand, and much of the matter proved to be inert. A record of 307 vaccinations in one of the divisions of Chimborazo Hospital during the months of June and July, 1864, for example, showed the number "taken" to have been 134 and the number "not taken" to have been 173.

Some effort was made to procure animal virus. Surgeon Hunter Holmes McGuire, a corps medical director in the Army of Northern Virginia, attempted to obtain vaccine virus from the udder of the cow early in 1863. Lafayette Guild, the army's medical director, expressed the fear, however, that virus procured from the cow "may develop in the persons to whom it is immediately applied, a form of the disease in itself infectious" and was "unwilling that the Army should be promiscuously vaccinated with it." The Confederate Surgeon General, in a postwar article, wrote that experiments conducted for the purpose of obtaining virus from cows terminated unsuccessfully, but Medical Director Samuel H. Stout's superintendent of vaccination referred to vaccination in Tennessee practiced with virus taken from the udder of the cow and the heel of the horse.

Vaccination was only one of the steps taken to avert the spread of smallpox. Surgeon General Moore, in November, 1862, ordered that all sick and wounded from Lee's army must undergo a fifteen-day quarantine in a special receiving hospital, and similar directives went out to other armies and departments. Men in infected areas were not allowed to leave their camps, and in December, 1862, the Surgeon General announced that leaves of absence or furloughs would not be given to those officers and enlisted men who had been exposed recently to the infection in field or hospital. Communities sometimes became greatly alarmed when cases of smallpox were reported at nearby army camps.[13]

[13] Mayor Thomas Atkinson and the people of Danville, Virginia, were quite worried in the fall of 1862. The surgeon in charge of the general

198

The smallpox victims themselves were promptly isolated in remote buildings and tents, sometimes called pest houses, and medical officers were assigned for their special care. In the treatment of the disease, considerable emphasis came to be placed on providing patients with an abundance of fresh air and properly ventilated rooms or tents. Several years after the war the General Inspector of Confederate Hospitals recalled that the smallpox camp at Macon, Georgia, had the lowest mortality of any coming under his observation; no medicines were administered there, and the patients lived in small tents. "The mortality at that camp, from the most malignant cases," he recalled, "was less than that existing in the oldest and best hospitals in Europe." Some surgeons, however, relied rather heavily on medication. One prevented clothing from sticking to the sores by covering the latter with an ointment made from linseed oil and limewater. F. Peyre Porcher recommended the flex opaca, a native plant, as a diaphoretic. The treatment administered to smallpox victims at Richmond's Louisiana Hospital seems worthy of special note. According to Felix Formento, its chief medical officer:

Our treatment consisted principally in saline purgatives, cooling drinks, and enemata in the view of abating the force of the eruptive fever and keeping down the number of pustules when these were confluent; in cases in which the eruption seemed deficient, the liq. [uid] acet. [ate] ammon. [ia] readily promoted it. Opiates given once or twice a day had an excellent effect in moderating the restlessness, tremors and delirium which generally occured.

During the period of suppuration, the strength of the patient was supported by a nourishing diet, by wines and cordials, . . . The eyes were carefully washed with water and vinegar, and the pustules of the eye lids touched with the lunar caustic to prevent dangerous ophthalmia. As to the prevention of the pitting or seaming of the face, which was not so important in our class of patients, mercurial ointment smeared from time to time, was the only thing used.

---

hospital there wrote of "the silly, meddlesome complainings of the sapient Mayor of Danville."

Spurious Vaccinia

A phenomenon generally referred to as "spurious vaccinia" followed in the wake of the general vaccination program and made matters all the more unpleasant for the long-suffering Confederate soldier. Large, repulsive-looking ulcers supposedly caused by impure vaccine virus began to appear at the place of vaccination or on other parts of the body, and many showed no disposition to heal. This trouble produced a devastating effect upon the military forces. In May, 1863, when the battle of Chancellorsville was fought, five thousand men in Lee's army were reported unfit for duty because of spurious vaccination. Surgeon General Moore also received reports that it was having a crippling effect upon both the Army of Texas and the Army of Tennessee. The latter's medical director, when requesting genuine vaccine virus from Moore early in 1864, explained that there had been "so many cases of Spurious Vaccination throughout this region that it is not considered prudent to use the virus that can be obtained here if it can be avoided." The Surgeon General ordered a thorough investigation of this "particularly annoying and disgusting disease," but many men continued to become disabled from "impure vaccination." [14]

As time went on many soldiers and some medical officers came to believe that spurious vaccinia owed its origin to crusts taken from persons having syphilis. This thesis gained strength after three hundred cases of supposed syphilis in Semme's and Cobb's Georgia Brigades were traced to the crust of a soldier who admitted to having been vaccinated while on furlough by his hostess in an Augusta house of ill fame,[15]

[14] Of 165 patients admitted to the First Mississippi Hospital at Jackson in June, 1864, for example, there were 27 cases of "impure vaccination."

[15] Joseph Jones concluded that constitutional syphilis could be transmitted by the vaccine lymph. Some Union doctors diagnosed an outbreak of spurious vaccinia in the Northern army as syphilis, but most concluded that incipient scurvy was responsible. Smallpox was confused with syphilis as early as the seventeenth century.

and when the Association of Army and Navy Surgeons of the Confederate States met on February 27, 1864, its president appointed a special committee to investigate and report on "Syphilitic inoculation, its relation to vaccination." The origin of these infections, however, was never definitely determined. Surgeon O. Kratz contended that "the principal cause of the deterioration of the vaccine virus" and the consequent spurious vaccination had been the "indiscriminate vaccination and re-vaccination from arm to arm." This may have been true, especially since soldiers often vaccinated each other with almost any sharp instrument that came to hand, but Joseph Jones believed that in many cases the untoward effect of vaccination was due to incipient scurvy. Jones thought that the same vaccine which produced grave effects upon those men suffering from the results of poor diet, exposure, and fatigue produced no ill effects among those who were healthy and well-fed.[16]

Some surgeons believed that spurious vaccinia could be arrested by cauterization soon after its appearance, but it was usually necessary to resort to constitutional treatment. Proper diet, the administering of stimulants, chlorate of potash, and iron and bark plus local applications of chlorinated soda or nitrate of silver generally proved successful in controlling this trouble.

Scarlet Fever

The Surgeon General asserted after the war that Southern troops "suffered severely" from scarlet fever, another eruptive fever, but his assertion is not borne out by the records. A "dreadful and loathsome" disease referred to as "malignant scarlet fever," during the paroxysms of which "blood gushes from the nose, eyes and ears of the patient," was reported in Richmond late in 1862, and Atlanta faced a near epidemic of

[16] There were thousands of cases of spurious vaccinia among both Confederate and Union prisoners.

scarlet fever in the early part of 1863. There is, however, practically no account of the disease among the military commands.

Pneumonia

Numerous respiratory ailments attacked the Confederate soldier; of these, according to reports, the most deadly was pneumonia, although here again the problem of diagnosis was a difficult one. Joseph Jones estimated that over seventeen per cent of the troops contracted pneumonia during the period from January, 1862, to August, 1863, and he observed that in general "the cases of Pneumonia diminished as the temperature became more elevated, and the vicissitudes of the season less marked." During the period under consideration, Jones figured that pneumonia caused between 17,209 and 21,474 deaths or about one-fourth of those which occurred from all causes in the Southern contingents. The general hospitals of Virginia, excluding those in and around Richmond, alone reported 4,864 cases of pneumonia and 1,261 deaths from January, 1862, to March, 1863, inclusive. And one hospital, Chimborazo, recorded 1,568 cases of pneumonia and pleurisy—583 of which proved to be fatal—for the entire war. Further south the percentage of fatal cases was not so high. Confederate troops operating in the Gulf area, with an average mean strength of 6,752, listed 1,161 cases of pneumonia over an eighteen-month interval, but the number of deaths from the disease totaled only 151. The incidence of pneumonia and the number of deaths therefrom were naturally greater among men subjected to constant exposure and privation.

The number of patients suffering from pneumonia in Confederate prisons was probably not large, but the percentage of fatal cases corresponded rather closely to that in the Southern armies. Of the 41,974 sick found by Joseph Jones at Andersonville only 979 were diagnosed as having pneumonia and pleurisy, 266 of whom died. There were 314 cases of these two ailments among the 4,168 sick in the Danville Prison Hospital, and the number of recorded deaths therefrom totaled 88.

Prior to the war pneumonia had nearly always been of the sthenic type. Consequently, in the treatment of the disease, practitioners had relied heavily on antimony and the lancet. But when this same treatment was administered to pneumonia victims during the war it met with little success, and the mortality rate was alarmingly high. The infection, it was noted, became asthenic and demanded a "sustaining" rather than a "depleting" treatment. The tartar emetic, other preparations of antimony, and bleeding, all thought effective before the war in civil practice, were dispensed with in favor of a carefully regulated diet, brandy or whiskey, opium, and quinine. Surgeon Felix Formento recommended "dry or scarified cupping according to the general condition of the patient . . . followed by very large blisters on the chest" and "expectorants combined with chlorhydrate of ammonia . . . and often with carb. ammonia." Porcher considered snakeroot an excellent remedy "for promoting expectoration." And one treatment sometimes prescribed called for the use of other indigenous remedies consisting of local applications of mustard seed (or leaves), stramonium leaves, and hickory leaves along with "butterflyroot and sanguinaria."

Tuberculosis, Catarrh, and Bronchitis

Pulmonary tuberculosis, catarrh, and bronchitis also harassed the Confederate fighting man. J. Julian Chisolm stated that the amount of tuberculosis as a sequelae to measles was "truly fearful," and troops thought to have tuberculosis were not infrequently discharged from the service. Furthermore, as the health of numerous others became impaired, the notation "Incipient Pythisis & Gen. Debility" as a reason for granting furloughs was seen increasingly often on furlough registers. Of 189 cases of consumption with known results at Chimborazo there were 52 deaths. The Army of the Potomac reported

19,455 cases of catarrh and acute bronchitis from July, 1861, to March, 1862, and the Twenty-first North Carolina Regiment alone experienced 232 "Catarrhus" cases from April, 1862, through September, 1863. Needless to say, coughs and colds were rife throughout the armed forces.

Joseph Jones recorded 33 deaths from 114 cases of consumption at Andersonville, and at the Danville Prison Hospital the cases and known deaths numbered 18 and 7 respectively. There were 3,004 cases of sickness recorded in the Salisbury, North Carolina, Prison Hospital during the month of October, 1864, and 656 of that number were afflicted with catarrh. Bronchitis also figured as a disease among prisoners held in the Confederacy. Jones found 2,808 cases and 90 deaths therefrom in Andersonville whereas at Danville 31 known fatalities resulted from 269 cases.

Early in 1865 Medical Director William A. Carrington set aside a separate hospital in Richmond, General Hospital No. 24, in which those who required better food and care than they could get in the larger institutions, "especially men with Pulmonary complaints," might be treated. Standard treatment for tubercular patients included nourishing food, tonics, and stimulants. Porcher proposed a decoction made from the black snakeroot and iodine for the treatment of phthisis in its early stages; and for coughs and colds he knew "of no better remedy . . . than the juice of horehound sweetened and given during the day." Other indigenous remedies for coughs and colds included lobelia, the leaves of the bené, the bark of the holly root, and button snakeroot.

Several medical officers concluded that camp life itself did much to improve the health of many who had histories of tuberculosis or scrofulous diseases. After the war, for example, Surgeon Paul F. Eve, while conceding that there may have been some, could not remember any "cases of impaired constitutional health from tuberculosis or scrofula, who experienced injurious effects from exposure in the camp." And S. S. Satchwell, another medical officer, recalled that those threatened by tuberculosis and some "with tuberculous formations and the hectic glow of consumption on their cheeks . . . were as a general rule either greatly relieved or finally restored by the exactions of army life and the roughness and open air of field service." [17]

Rheumatism

Another disease that incapacitated numerous soldiers was rheumatism. A total of 59,772 cases of rheumatism was reported on the field and hospital registers of Southern forces operating east of the Mississippi River during the first two years of the war, and 1,842 men suffering from the ailment were discharged as unfit for service. The Army of Tennessee, from June, 1862, to May, 1863, recorded an aggregate of 9,927 rheumatic ailments, and there were 1,984 cases of rheumatism with known results at Chimborazo during the war, of whom 80 succumbed. On a smaller scale, out of 312 admissions to the Post Hospital, Dalton, Georgia, for the month of August, 1862, 18 were diagnosed as suffering from rheumatism, and 2 of the 18 became fatalities. A Southern editor, perhaps striving to discourage the consumption of intoxicants, warned that heavy drinkers were "particularly liable to bad attacks."

There were 866 cases of rheumatism and 20 deaths therefrom recorded by Joseph Jones in Andersonville although the prison hospital register at that point listed fewer cases and a higher mortality rate. The number of cases and recorded deaths at Danville reached 348 and 18 respectively.

Treatment for rheumatism or what was diagnosed as rheumatism seldom brought much relief. As a matter of fact some chronic rheumatics received no specific treatment at all. Near the close of the war, however, Medical Director Stout authorized all surgeons in charge of hospitals in his department to transfer their chronic cases to the Bell Hospital in Eufaula, Alabama, at which institution Surgeon H. V. Miller was pre-

[17] An assistant surgeon at Dalton, Georgia, was believed by his fellows to have tuberculosis.

pared to treat such cases "with a good Galvanic Battery." Colchicum and iodide of potassium appear to have been standby remedies for those who received medicinal preparations. The latter drug, it was observed, enjoyed "very fair success."

Scurvy

Dietary deficiency was not long in producing scurvy throughout the Confederate Army and Navy. Thomas Williams, Medical Director of the Army of the Potomac, reported the appearance of this disease as early as January, 1862, and Surgeon Paul F. Eve believed that the first alarming cases in the West appeared early in 1863 although General Beauregard advised President Davis that some of his men showed symptoms of scurvy during the siege of Corinth in the spring of 1862. The year 1863 was just beginning when Lafayette Guild detected "a tendency to scorbutus throughout the whole army" of Northern Virginia, warned that unless the vegetable ration was increased "scurvy must make its appearance," and predicted that "our next campaign may be a disastrous one, simply for the want of antiscorbutics." With the commencement of spring, General Lee ordered a daily detail from each regiment "to gather sassafras buds, wild onions, garlic, lamb's quarter, and poke sprouts" to supplement the ration, but the supply obtained was not sufficient to overcome the deficiency. Guild continued to complain of the lack of vegetables, and both Guild and Eve referred to the increasing frequency of secondary hemorrhage, following surgical interference, caused by the scorbutic tendency among the troops. Guild became alarmed over this development during the spring of 1863, and, in the West, Eve observed that secondary hemorrhage occurred with greater regularity after the battles of Chickamauga and Missionary Ridge later that year. Scorbutic symptoms were also noted at times among seamen on Confederate cruisers.

The prevalence of scurvy and other deficiency diseases is not reflected in the Chimborazo records where only 119 cases and 8 deaths were reported; there is little doubt, however, but that incipient scurvy was widespread and was responsible for a considerable amount of the sickness and death ascribed to other ailments. The probable misdiagnosis of many cases of incipient scurvy as diarrhea and dysentery has been mentioned previously, and the oft-listed "Debilitas" on both field and hospital reports, a "disease" which was responsible for numerous furloughs granted by the Richmond authorities, was certainly in many instances incipient scurvy.[18]

Joseph Jones thought that the Andersonville prisoners "were in the condition of a crew at sea, confined upon a foul ship upon salt meat and unvarying food, and without fresh vegetables." He discovered 9,501 prisoners afflicted with this wretched disease and concluded that it was responsible for nine-tenths of the mortality, "either directly or indirectly," in the prison. Only 91 cases of scurvy and six fatalities, however, were recorded at Danville. A surgeon of the United States Army, held captive in the Salisbury prison, noticed a scorbutic taint in many of his fellow prisoners during May and June, 1862, and two years later it was reported that a number of the prison guards at that institution had fallen victim to the disease.

The importance of a well-rounded diet in the prevention and treatment of scurvy was generally recognized. J. Julian Chisolm urged the issuance of fresh meat and vegetables and recommended that they be cooked in soup. Medical Director Carrington requested extra issues of fruit, molasses, or sorghum for the hospitals twice a week during the winter months, and he suggested that extra issues of "Sour crout as an antiscorbutic" be furnished prison hospitals. In addition to vegeta-

[18] "Debility from Acute Dysentery," "Debility from Chronic Diarrhoea," "Chronic Dysentery and Debility," "Chronic Diarrhoea with Debility" were remarks entered often on furlough records. Of 1,334 patients admitted to the Robertson Hospital during the war, 97 were listed as suffering from debility. There were 5,780 cases of debility and anaemia at Chimborazo and 117 deaths ascribed thereto.

bles and fruits, Paul F. Eve favored buttermilk, lime or lemon juice, wine, and brandy. Newspapers at times urged their readers to supply the army with food, and it was pointed out that "Apples, peaches, pears, figs, okra, peppers, etc., can all be readily and cheaply dried, and would thus materially aid to supply, throughout the year, not only nutritious food, but that variety in diet which is essential to health."

Soldiers themselves did the best they could to obtain nutritious foods. Not only were frequent forays into the woods made in the search for edible plants and herbs, but when Lee's troops moved into Pennsylvania the search for fresh meat and vegetables was entered into with alacrity. During this latter venture a Confederate surgeon wrote that the "only limit to the appropriation of the fowl, sheep, pigs, vegetables, etc., which can be found" was "to avoid detection by the higher officers," and he believed that "our soldiers will soon cease to have scurvy or other diseases."

Little medication seems to have been used in treating scurvy. Citric acid and a decoction from pine tops was used with good results in Winder Hospital, and a Union surgeon in Salisbury prison extracted the gallic and tannic acids from the bark of oak wood to make a scurvy remedy. On the other hand, Surgeon Eve found that "Clorate of potash was certainly our best medicine." Scurvy, wrote Eve after the war, was "an obstinate affection, requiring a long course of treatment, calculated to improve the general system."

A strange malady associated with scurvy and exposure to sunlight was nyctalopia or night blindness. The prevalence of this disorder in the Army of Northern Virginia assumed almost epidemic proportions during the latter stages of the war. Troops affected were unable to see after sunset, and one of Lee's soldiers remembered seeing "men led by the hand all night . . . go into battle with the command in the morning." Medication was of little help; surgeons found that the influence of home—"its cleanliness, improved diet and relief from mental anxiety and physical exhaustion, never failed of effecting a speedy cure." Restoration of sight followed an improvement in general health.

Camp Itch

"I believe the health of the company is very good excepting those that have . . . the itch," wrote a soldier camped at Kinston, North Carolina, in the fall of 1862. And in the Army of Tennessee before Missionary Ridge at about the same time, a soldier complained that the troops "were starved and almost naked, and covered all over with lice and camp itch and filth and dirt." "Camp itch," as it was commonly designated, was one of the most annoying and prevalent army diseases. Lafayette Guild and Surgeon John Herbert Claiborne, who for a time had charge of the Petersburg hospitals in Virginia, noticed that the army itch was not scabies but a nonparasitic skin irritation. Explained Claiborne, "Camp itch . . . is not a disease in which the animalcule of scabies, the acarus, is ever seen. It is not even a vesicular disease. It is papular, and whilst almost a *sui generis,* is more nearly akin . . . to lichen, some cases to prurigo, than to any other skin disease. When chronic, subjected to the irritation of scratching and to neglect and a hundred influences, unpropitious and aggravating . . . it changes its character—seems almost pustular, sometimes vesicular, occasionally squamous. . . ."

When the Association of Army and Navy Surgeons of the Confederate States met on April 19, 1864, the Surgeon General, president of the organization, appointed Surgeon J. C. Baylor to investigate and report on the topic "Camp Itch—its distinctive character—its differential diagnosis from true scabies and its most efficacious treatment." Despite Guild, Claiborne, and the association, medical officers generally failed to distinguish between scabies and the nonparasitic inflammation. As a matter of fact, the former was more common among the civilian population and the troops in close contact therewith.

Numerous experiments were conducted in the effort to find a cure for camp itch. In March, 1864, Medical Director Carrington, in a letter to Surgeon James B. McCaw at Chimborazo, adverted to the general lack of success in healing cutaneous diseases and asked McCaw to isolate patients afflicted with such ailments in separate wards and try "any plausible, and well recommended mode of treatment." Almost a year later Carrington was making the same request to surgeons in charge of other hospitals in the Confederate capital. Claiborne himself introduced a new therapy early in 1864, the results from which he considered to be as good as could be obtained "by sulphur, arsenic, or the alkaline baths, which are the routine treatment, and which are now so difficult to procure." He proposed in treating mild forms of the disease a strong decoction of poke root used as a wash once or twice daily. In the treatment of chronic cases, Claiborne favored decoctions of broom straw or slippery elm applied three or four times each day. He also recommended a vegetable diet. In January, 1865, S. R. Chambers, an assistant surgeon, brought forth a remedy which, he claimed, "has never failed in my hands to accomplish a cure." Chambers used an ointment made from the inner bark of the elder, lard, sweet gum, basilican ointment, olive oil, and sulphur flour. The bark was first boiled down and then the other items were added. Porcher declared that the *Melanithium Virginicum* was a sure but dangerous itch cure.

Venereal Disease

Venereal disease may have been more prevalent than has been generally supposed.[19] Surgeon Eve listed it as one of the prominent disorders observed in the Southern army, and it was seen frequently on hospital registers. Eight of 312 patients admitted to the Post Hospital in Dalton, Georgia, during August, 1862, for example, were diagnosed as suffering from either syphilis or gonorrhea, and 47 venereal admissions were reported by Virginia's Emory Hospital from January 1, 1864, to April 12, 1865. Such statistics are revealing inasmuch as

[19] E. Merton Coulter and Bell Irvin Wiley have concluded that there was comparatively little venereal disease in the Confederate army.

only those cases with "some complication or concomitant disease requiring the regimen and treatment of a hospital for its removal" were admitted, the "simpler cases" being kept in the field. One medical official thought "that many soldiers would voluntarily expose themselves to such contagion if it became generally understood that it was a sufficient cause for removal to hospital, or a continuation therein." Medical records of one regiment, the Twenty-first North Carolina, listed an aggregate of 59 cases of venereal infection from April, 1862, to April, 1864.

Many hospitals set aside separate wards for the treatment of patients with venereal disease, and Medical Director Stout opened a venereal hospital at Kingston, Georgia, in the early part of 1864 which administered to those with serious cases in his department. Remedies used in the treatment of these disorders included poke roots or berries, elder, wild sarsaparilla, sassafras, jessamine, and prickly ash. One surgeon discovered that "Silk weed root put in whiskey and drank, giving at the same time pills of rosin from the pine tree, with very small pieces of blue vitrol" would cure stubborn cases of gonorrhea.

Alcoholism

"George Slone died last Wendsday withe delearam tremens," wrote a soldier from Fort Macon, North Carolina, in the summer of 1861, and this ailment was not unknown in either of the opposing armies. Statistical data are fragmentary as to the extent of alcoholism, but Joseph Jones found 194 cases of delirium tremens listed on the field reports and 57 cases reported by the general hospitals during the period from January, 1862, to July, 1863.

Liquor was eagerly sought by many of the soldiers, and it was frequently available. "Molie tell your paw that if I had his brandy out here, I could with ease sell it for forty dollars per galon," a wearer of the gray instructed his wife from a camp near Fredericksburg. And, he added, "Some men will give the last dollar for a drink of liquor." Canteens were sometimes filled from stills located along the line of march in secluded mountain areas, and hospital patients purchased whiskey from nearby distillers and shipped it out to the camps in boxes marked "Soldiers' Supplies." Soldier correspondence is full of references to the heavy drinking, and this activity was not confined to the army. Raphael Semmes, commander of the *Alabama,* famous Confederate cruiser, complained that some of his "rascals" got drunk at every opportunity and could "be trusted with everything but whisky." [20] Some imbibing even took place within Confederate prison walls. "Quite a general spree in evening (the new officers have brought the 'sinews of war')," a Salisbury occupant confided to his diary in June, 1862, "in which my digestion, or rather 'indigestion,' organs allow me to take no part; even had I the inclination." [21]

Congress, confronted by assertions that whiskey was "demoralizing and ruining our army," and causing "a bloody list of blunders and disasters," was compelled to take action. In April, 1862, following an impassioned speech by Senator William Lowndes Yancey of Alabama, in which he proclaimed that the cause was "suffering morally from the disorganization of the army from liquor," that body passed "An Act to punish drunkenness in the Army." Under the provisions of the act all officers found guilty of being drunk were to "be cashiered or suspended from the service of the Confederate States, or be publicly reprimanded, according to the aggravation of the offence," and officers cashiered might "also be declared incapable of holding any military office under the Confederate States during the war." Controls over the issuance of whiskey were also tightened by the authorities in Richmond.

[20] While off Martinique in November, 1862, one of Semmes's "thirsty rascals" jumped overboard and was apprehended in a grog shop.

[21] Medical records of the United States white forces list 5,589 cases of inebriation, 3,744 cases of delirium tremens, and 920 cases of chronic alcoholism; the fatal cases numbered 110, 450, and 45, respectively.

Mental Depression

Psychosomatic medicine was unknown at the time of the Civil War, but some surgeons apparently were aware of the acute mental depression of many soldiers and of "the dominating and controlling influence of the mind or will over the functions and recuperative energies of the physical system." All men were naturally subject to spells of homesickness, or "nostalgia," but homesickness, mental depression, and anxiety developed among some to a morbid degree and probably did more than anything else to cause death in certain cases. According to one veteran of the conflict, "many, very many, of the sick died in the hospitals simply from nostalgia or homesickness." Hospitalized troops chafed under military restrictions and became immersed in self-pity. One Winder Hospital inmate in the fall of 1863 opined that "our authoritys dont hav aney simpathy for us" and later must have depressed his wife with the statements that "ther is nothing that is any pleasure or satisfaction to me hear" and "my life is becoming a burden to me and is giting more so every day." Nostalgia was almost always noticed among prisoners and certainly was a factor in the Andersonville suffering.

To the Confederate soldier suffering from mental depression or nostalgia no remedy was so effective as the furlough. According to Porcher, "the promise of a furlough was found to be superior to the whole pharmacopoea, and would literally rescue a sick or wounded soldier from the jaws of death. We have seen them turn to the wall to die, and yet leave for their homes a few days after the revivifying influence of hope and a return to their families and all which it implied." Porcher was critical of the Surgeon General's opposition to a liberal furlough policy and ascribed such opposition to the fact that Moore had been accustomed in the "old army" to troops "on the average much less sensitive and high strung" than those of the Confederacy. In a report made to the Surgeon General near the close of the war, Porcher suggested certain modifications in the treatment of sick and wounded soldiers. He placed considerable emphasis upon proper food as "the principal agent which assists in the cure," excoriated the excessive use of internal medication, and called upon medical officers to encourage the disabled soldier and "reinstate hope and cheerfulness in his heart." [22]

"Mania" and "Dementia"

Such ailments as neuralgia, meningitis, headache, chorea, cerebritis, apoplexy, paralysis, and mania were classified as diseases of the brain and nervous system. Hospital and field reports covering the period from January, 1862, to July, 1863, show that neuralgia and headache occurred with much more frequency than other diseases in this grouping. It was not until the conflict entered its final year that the number of soldiers suffering from mania or insanity increased enough to cause much concern. On June 16, 1864, Medical Director Carrington informed Surgeon General Moore that, according to reports, there were soldiers at various hospitals and in the homes of friends "in various stages of Mania and Dementia." He therefore requested that a Confederate hospital "for cases of lunacy and Dementia be established in North Carolina on the line of RR or at some central location." [23] No action was taken, and Virginia surgeons were advised on September 5, 1864, to take all troops of unsound mind before justices of the peace, pursuant to the Virginia Code of 1860, "and send them in accordance with his decision to the nearest Asylum along with the

[22] "Nine physicians out of ten," asserted a newspaper correspondent with the troops in Tennessee early in the war, "scare their patients by long faces, looking at the tongue often, thumping the chest, shake their heads significantly, and dosing them with quinine and ipecac. The first makes you deaf and dumb, the other turns you inside out."

[23] Douglas S. Freeman in his biography of Lee (Volume IV, 7–8) refers to a conversation that took place on March 3, 1865, between Generals Lee and John B. Gordon on the condition of the army. One topic, according to Gordon, was the extensive amount of temporary insanity among the troops.

papers resulting from the examination." Such procedure seems not to have worked satisfactorily and several weeks later a Danville medical officer was instructed to investigate the possibility of procuring a suitable building in which to house the insane soldiers. Satisfactory housing was unavailable in Danville, and it was not until February 2, 1865, that the chief surgeon at Lynchburg was asked to advise whether or not the college building there could be utilized for this purpose. Finally, on March 27, 1865, Surgeon W. C. Nichols, officer in charge of the Louisiana Hospital in Richmond, was notified by Carrington that troops of unsound mind would be confined and treated in that institution. Similar steps looking to the establishment of a hospital for such unfortunates in the West were also being taken, but the end of the war precluded further development of this program.

Other Diseases

Numerous other diseases made their appearance on hospital registers. One of the most "fashionable" ailments at times was the mumps, and a camp comprising many men with their jaws tied up was not unusual. Occasionally there were reports of yellow fever. An epidemic of cerebrospinal meningitis occurred in the Camp of Instruction at Raleigh, North Carolina, in February, 1862. Eye diseases were of sufficient incidence and import to warrant the establishment of hospitals and the opening of wards for their treatment. Such a ward was opened by Medical Director Stout at Forsyth, Georgia, in the late summer of 1864 and placed under the direction of Surgeon Bolling A. Pope; medical officers in Stout's department were authorized to send the men afflicted with such maladies to that point. Pope appears to have established the Ophthalmic Hospital in Athens, Georgia, soon afterward.[24]

[24] A worker in the Hill Hospital, Cuthbert, Georgia, commented on the large number of patients with sore eyes in the summer of 1864, many of whom "were almost blind." Some of these were believed to be "beyond restoration; and doubtless will have to grope their way."

Complaints of sore mouth, asthma, poison oak, seasickness, and other disorders were also mentioned from time to time. Some of the ailments noted on the register of Richmond's Robertson Hospital appear to be rather unusual. Charles Albright's difficulty was diagnosed as "badness"; Charles McMullen had "pains all over"; and W. W. Langhorne's disease was described as "wife." Hamilton Foster, a soldier from a Maryland regiment, was discharged from this same institution "for bad behavior," R. Saunders of the Twenty-sixth Mississippi was "transferred for complaining," and W. T. Peace, organization unknown, simply "disappeared."

Malingering

Armies have always had their malingerers and that of the Confederacy was no exception. Surgeons and others referred frequently to malingering in their correspondence, and Medical Director Stout spoke of "very many who have no other disease than want of heart which medicine and regimen will not cure." Some men suffered so much from "battlesickness" and "shell fever" that they shot themselves in the hand or prevented their wounds from healing so as to escape service.[25] There is reason to believe that malingerers sometimes disposed of their shoes, particularly during the months of battle, in order to avoid duty. In late September, 1863, a circular was issued in the Army of Tennessee to the effect that barefooted men would not be excused from "any duty whatsoever," and officers extending exemptions to those without footgear were to be held to "strict accountability." One of General Joseph E. Johnston's last orders, dated March 25, 1865, directed that no privileges be granted to barefooted troops merely because they lacked shoes.[26]

Medical officers were warned by regulations to be cautious

---

[25] Kate Cumming adverts to a soldier who "rather than be returned to duty, cut three of his fingers off with an ax, and a bad job he made of it."

[26] One ingenious goldbrick, according to George Cary Eggleston, stayed on the sick-list throughout the war.

216

in granting disability certificates to soldiers who had not been under their care, inasmuch as disorders such as rheumatism, epilepsy, and deafness could be easily feigned.[27] J. Julian Chisolm advised medical officers to exercise their ingenuity in exposing deception. Pretended deafness, he suggested, might be revealed by making "loud noises, such as discharging a pistol near the ear of the unsuspecting person." Occasionally, men suspected of feigning certain diseases were subjected to the influence of chloroform and given a thorough examination.[28] The number of malingerers was perhaps not unusually large. Lafayette Guild boasted in May, 1863, that only about 50 had been found out of 9,325 sick and wounded in the Army of Northern Virginia.

Conclusion

The Confederate soldier was stalked relentlessly by sickness throughout the war years. Despite their deficiencies in many respects, medical officers met the diseases they encountered with all the knowledge, experience, and skill they possessed. Generally speaking, they labored courageously, but they were up against almost overwhelming problems created by the military situation. All of the knowledge of more recent years would not have sufficed to save the lives of many who died from disease in the great conflict of the sixties.

[27] Medical officers commented on the rather singular fact that most of the men in certain units complained of chronic rheumatism.

[28] The mother of one Private William J. Orrell complained to the Surgeon General that her son had been chloroformed, pinched, and stuck with pins by the examining board at Chimborazo. Moore demanded a report of the case.

CHAPTER XI

Surgery and Infections

The Surgical Problem

Southern practitioners who became Confederate medical officers after the outbreak of war in 1861 had little prior training or experience in military surgery. A few fortunates, including the Surgeon General and Paul F. Eve, had seen service in the Mexican War while Eve, St. George Peachy of Virginia, and several others had employed their professional abilities in the Crimean War or other European conflicts. This is not to say, however, that Southern doctors as a whole were complete strangers to operative surgery inasmuch as, for reasons mentioned earlier, there had been an increased use of the lancet and scalpel by physicians all over the United States in the years before the war's outbreak. Nevertheless, it is not unreasonable to conclude that most doctors in the prewar era had never treated a gunshot wound.

A number of publications to instruct the Confederate medical officer in the art of military surgery made their appearance soon after the outbreak of war. The first of these was a scientific treatise entitled *A Manual of Military Surgery for the Use of Surgeons in the Confederate Army* by John Julian Chisolm. Chisolm's book, published in 1861, underwent several revisions. George H. B. MacLeod's *Notes on the Surgery of the War in the Crimea* was edited by Alexander Nicholas Talley, another Confederate surgeon, and published in 1862. A third Southern medical officer, Edward Warren of North Carolina, prepared *An Epitome of Practical Surgery, for Field and Hospital,* which was issued in 1863. Also published that same year was *A Manual of Military Surgery* written by a group of officers assigned to such duty by Surgeon General Moore. The Surgeon General ordered the preparation of several other works on military surgery, but these were never completed. All of the published works appear to have been circulated widely among medical officers. One Confederate surgeon, writing after the war, remembered that Chisolm's and Warren's books were "in 'the pockets'" of medical officers, and early in 1864 the Army of Tennessee's medical director acknowledged receipt of 433 copies of the manual written pursuant to the Surgeon General's orders.

Large numbers of men received various types of wounds —caused chiefly by small arms—during the many engagements of the war, and, as would be expected, a considerable amount of surgical intervention was absolutely necessary. During the first two years of the conflict, 77,293 Confederate soldiers, excluding those in the Trans-Mississippi Department, received treatment for gunshot wounds; and in 1863 the Army of Northern Virginia alone reported 27,206 cases that were hospitalized as a result of wounds. It was recognized that wounded men were a greater liability to the opposing army than were its dead, and soldiers were sometimes instructed to aim their fire at the feet of the enemy.[1] After one engagement a Southern correspondent noticed that the enemy's cartridges contained, in addition to the usual charge, a number of large buckshot. During particularly sharp encounters troops might receive multiple wounds. Of 110 Confederate wounded treated in a Union hospital during the fighting around Atlanta, for example, many had from three to five wounds, and a soldier with but a single wound was the exception. It was reported that General Patrick R. Cleburne, "the Stonewall Jackson of the West," was hit with forty-nine bullets at Franklin near the end of the war. And one Southern colonel wounded on the field at Shiloh, when asked where he had been struck, replied: "My son, I am wounded in the arm, in the leg, in the head, in the body, and in another place which I have a delicacy in mentioning."

Many of the wounds suffered by both Confederate and

[1] Nearly two-thirds of the wounds and injuries classified by the Union Surgeon General were located in the extremities.

Union troops differed to a considerable extent from those experienced by soldiers in previous conflicts and created new surgical problems. This was the result of the introduction of a relatively new element in modern warfare known as the Minié ball which was fired from a rifled musket, and most of the wounds were caused by this bullet. The Minié ball was conical in shape, heavier than the old round ball, and of increased velocity. The round ball caused numerous fractures of the extremities, but it never caused such severe comminution and likelihood of infection as did the new one. According to Deering J. Roberts, a surgeon in the Army of Tennessee, "The shattering, splintering, and splitting of a long bone by the impact of the minie or Enfield ball were, in many instances, both remarkable and frightful, and early experience taught surgeons that amputation [to avoid infection] was the only means of saving life. In the vicinity of a joint, the ends of the bone being more spongy, softer, and less brittle, the damage to the shaft of the bone was not so great, and the expedient of resection, largely resorted to and greatly developed by the surgeons, in many instances afforded a comparatively, if not perfectly, restored limb. . . ."

It was also pointed out that the shock caused by Minié ball wounds was greater than that produced by the round ball and might have influenced unfavorably the results of amputation. The fatality rate for abdominal wounds, already quite high, was pushed still higher by the conical ball inasmuch as the intestines were almost always perforated thereby. As to wounds of the chest, however, it is believed that the round ball may have been more deadly due to its more bruising and lacerating effect on extensive areas of lung tissue.[2] At any rate, the character of the wounds was such that in those cases where life could be saved amputation or resection was often demanded. "All cases of gun shot wounds interesting large

[2] Surgeon John R. Buist of Chimborazo Hospital thought that "nearly all of the head and abdominal wounds were quickly fatal." The mortality in the French and British forces from abdominal wounds during the Crimean War was over 90 per cent.

joints that came under my observation," stated Surgeon Felix Formento, "required either resection or amputation." Still another surgeon remembered that "as to bruised, 'contused' or lacerated fractures, not a moment was wasted, but amputation was at once done."

Surgery in the Field

Such operative surgery as appeared essential should, it was generally thought, be performed as soon as possible after the wound was received. Chisolm, for example, asserted that "all needful operations must be performed within twenty-four hours, or the wounded suffer from neglect." The scenes in and around the field hospitals where most of these operations were performed became increasingly grim as the wounded were brought in for surgical attention. After engagements in which extensive casualties were experienced the surgeons were frequently overwhelmed with patients; many were laid in the woods and yards around the hospitals. Night often fell before the operators finished their work, and torches or candles were then lighted to provide illumination although operations were known to have been performed with no light other than that provided by the moon. Sometimes, in extremely cold weather, surgeons found it necessary to heat water and warm their near-frozen hands therein. A graphic description of General John B. Hood's division hospital after the battle of Second Manassas (August 29–30, 1862) was given by a war correspondent at the scene of the engagement. The casualties, he wrote, "were lying upon the ground awaiting their turn with patience, some dead and some dying, but the great majority with only painful wounds in the extremities. The operating tables . . . were slimy with blood . . . and as fast as one patient was removed another took his place to be anethized by the merciful chloroform and undergo the necessary surgical treatment. The men all appeared to bear their wounds cheerfully, and it was only now and then when the knife cut deep that a smothered groan revealed the sharp pang of pain." [3]

Surgeon Simon Baruch recalled that after the battle of Gettysburg he spent two days and two nights "in constant operations and vigils." The tail gate of a wagon, the communion table of a church, a door laid upon barrels or boxes, and other such makeshifts, were often employed as operating tables.[4] A distinguishing feature of all field hospitals at such times, according to one veteran surgeon, was "that ineffable smell of gore which no man can fail to recognize who has passed through the experiences of four years of a bloody war." [5]

Primary and Secondary Amputations

Primary operations where amputations were involved, the purpose of which was to amputate within twenty-four hours after the wound was received "before inflammation and its results had ensued," appear as a rule to have had a much more favorable prognosis than secondary amputations—those performed more than twenty-four hours after the injury. There were, for example, 272 primary amputations and 308 secondary amputations reported in and around Richmond from June 1 to August 1, 1862; the operative statistics reveal 82 deaths from the former and 163 from the latter.[6]

An examination of the number of operations with known

[3] "This is a horrid night," wrote a Confederate soldier held captive in a Federal field hospital at Gettysburg, "cold and wet and rainy. Groans and shrieks and maniacal ravings; bitter sobs, and heavy sighs, piteous cries; horrid oaths; despair; the death rattle, darkness; death."

[4] Temporary hospitals in the navy were sometimes established on flatboats.

[5] The same surgeon, John H. Claiborne, found on a table in a field hospital near Appomattox "an open anatomy, from which some surgeon had evidently been refreshing himself during the work of mutilation."

[6] There were 419 primary amputations and 220 secondary amputations performed at the Dolona Bagtche Hospital in Constantinople from May 1 to November 1, 1855. The number surviving the former operation was 221 while only 72 recovered from the latter.

results that were performed in the Confederate States Army from the beginning of the war until October, 1864, is most informative. Altogether 1,142 cases of primary and 546 cases of secondary amputations occurred, and the number of subsequent deaths totaled 315 and 284, respectively. Some of the most interesting and significant operative results were those which pertained to amputation of the thigh. During the Crimean War the mortality rate for such operations was 64 for every 100 attempted, and in the Polish and Mexican Wars not a single successful thigh operation was performed. Yet Confederate surgeons, prior to October, 1864, reported 213 successful primary amputations of the thigh of 345 cases attempted; of 162 secondary amputations only 43 proved successful.

Some success was reported even in amputations of the upper third of the thigh following compound fractures of the femur. Such famous surgeons as Baron Guillaume Dupuytren and George H. B. MacLeod had recommended amputation for such wounds, but the operation was regarded as almost surely fatal. Of 77 cases of primary amputation at the upper third of the thigh reported by Confederate surgeons, however, 40 recovered and 37 died. Among those who recovered from amputations just below the hip joint were Generals John B. Hood and Richard S. Ewell. Such daring surgery as disarticulation at the hip joint was occasionally attempted with moderate success although apparently the prognosis was more favorable for such operations when some time was allowed to elapse between reception of the wound and amputation since few men could undergo the successive shocks produced by the injury and the required surgery.

Other operative statistics for the Confederate Army reveal that 219 of 314 primary leg amputations and 252 of 294 primary arm amputations were reported to have been successful during the period up to October, 1864. At the same time, the reports of secondary operations show that 74 of 150 leg amputations and 53 of 140 arm amputations ended in death. More favorable results from primary amputations were also obtained in other operations. The case then in favor of such surgery was quite strong. In this connection it is interesting to notice a Union surgeon's observation that "almost every case of secondary amputation performed in Stanton Hospital [a Union general hospital] during the months of May and June, 1864, proved fatal." "Poor food and great exposure," wrote Phoebe Pember, Chimborazo matron, "had thinned the blood and broken down the system so entirely that secondary amputations . . . almost invariably resulted in death, after the second year of the war." In other words, soldiers weakened by field service and incipient scurvy were not fit subjects for elaborate surgical procedure. Mrs. Pember went so far as to state that the only cases under her observation who survived secondary amputations "were two Irishmen, and it was really so difficult to kill an Irishman," she claimed, "that there was little cause for boasting on the part of the officiating surgeons." [7]

Resection

When amputation was deemed unnecessary surgical intervention not infrequently consisted of resection, that is, the removal of joints with preservation of the extremities. Resection was found to be more successful when applied to the arms than when it concerned the legs. A total of seventeen resections were performed in and around Richmond from June 1 to August 1, 1862, six of which proved to be fatal. And on file in the Surgeon General's Office were the complete histories of 131 resection cases which had been performed during the first three years of the war. Exactly 70 of these were primary operations, and 52 were reported to have been successful. Of the 61 secondary operations, 46 were regarded as having terminated satisfactorily. A more comprehensive summary, prepared from reports of resection cases in Confederate hospitals,

[7] About three-fourths of the operations classified by the Surgeon General of the United States were amputations.

1862 to 1864, indicates that there were 647 such surgical cases listed during this period of the war. No distinction was made as to what number were primary and what number were secondary cases, but the known deaths numbered 117; some 150 cases were reported without information as to their final outcome. The wisdom of some of these operations may be called into question inasmuch as the reports show that they were made on patients already weak from diarrhea, scurvy, and other ailments.

There was some feeling that resection, except for small joints, was questionable if not reprehensible surgery. It was pointed out that, in addition to the often unfavorable physical conditions and surroundings of the patients, many who recovered from the operations had little use of the extremity saved. Only one successful resection of the knee joint seems to have been reported in either of the opposing armies. James B. Read, Confederate surgeon of Savannah, Georgia, performed such an operation in 1863 at Richmond. Read also performed a resection of the hip joint successfully, but the limb in both instances was useless, and in the former case the patient requested amputation as soon as his health permitted. Another argument against resection was that it kept the patient in the hospital for a greater length of time than amputation and thereby exposed him for a longer period to tetanus, erysipelas, hospital gangrene, and pyaemia.[8]

Use of Chloroform

Most operative surgery was performed while the subject was in complete anesthesia, and the anesthetic agent administered almost exclusively by Southern medical officers was chloroform. Dr. James Young Simpson of Edinburgh in the year 1847 was the first to use chloroform as a general anes-

[8] Some very successful resection cases were reported nevertheless. Felix Formento removed the whole elbow joint in the left arm of a Captain Myatt, and the latter was said to have gained excellent command of the member within a very short time.

thetic, and the agent's popularity in the South soon came to exceed that of ether. Chloroform, according to George H. B. MacLeod, the English surgeon, was employed in almost every operation performed by British medical officers during the Crimean War, and only one death was attributed to its use. Not a single fatal result was ascribed to the agent during the Austro-Sardinian War, and chloroform's remarkable record in Europe was cited by Chisolm, Warren, and others who recommended that it be employed by Confederate surgeons. "We do not hesitate to say," wrote Chisolm, "that it should be given to every patient requiring a serious or painful operation."

The surgeons appear to have administered chloroform freely. It was usually dropped on a sponge, handkerchief, or cotton cloth and given until complete anesthesia had been produced. In Winder Hospital one surgeon explained that the sponge was frequently removed to allow for the "free admixture of atmospheric air." Such "admixture" in both the general and field hospitals undoubtedly lessened the mortality from an anesthetic regarded by modern surgeons as not without its perils. It also appears that sometimes the product was adulterated. "I remember a lot that smelled like turpentine," wrote one surgeon after the war. Often the supply was scarce and Chisolm, to prevent the loss of the agent by evaporation, employed a common funnel as an inhalor during the process of administration.

Chloroform was preferred by Union as well as Confederate surgeons,[9] but the latter used it almost universally with what apparently were excellent results. "In all our operations," declared the Louisiana Hospital's Felix Formento, "we invariably used chloroform, and . . . we never met with the least accident or even inconvenience." "In every case of operation in this division," related a Winder Hospital surgeon, "chloroform has been used and with invariable good effect." Still an-

[9] It was estimated that anesthetics were employed by Union surgeons in at least 80,000 cases. The use of chloroform was definitely ascertained in 6,784 cases and that of ether in 1,305. There were 37 known deaths from chloroform and 4 from ether.

other hospital surgeon wrote: "I administered chloroform and had it administered for me many scores of times, for all manner of operations and on all sizes and ages and conditions of men, and I never had a serious accident,—never a death from chloroform, nor had a man to die on the table during my whole experience as a surgeon during the war. I do think it remarkable, when I recall the perfect abandon,—the almost reckless manner in which it was given to every patient put on the table, almost without examination of lungs or heart and without inquiry. I can only attribute it in part to the fact that it was given freely,—boldly pushed to surgical anesthesia, and no attempt was made to cut till the patient was limber."

Medical Director Hunter Holmes McGuire asserted that although chloroform was administered over 28,000 times in his corps "no death was ever ascribed to its use." Sometimes there was no resort to anesthetic. Phoebe Pember related that the wounded brought to Chimborazo after a clash at Drewry's Bluff in April, 1863, "were so exhausted by forced marches, lying in entrenchments and loss of sleep that few even awoke during the operations." [10] On other occasions there was no chloroform or ether to be had.

It was a matter of common practice on the part of the surgeons, particularly in cases when their surgical subjects were in a state of shock or run-down, to administer whiskey or brandy. Many of the men showed amazing fortitude, however, and Miss Emily V. Mason, matron at Winder Hospital, related that she had seen man after man "carried to the amputating room, singing a Baptist or Methodist hymn as he passed on his stretcher."

Radical versus Conservative Surgery

Military surgery during the war period, in the words of a present-day medical historian, "was at best a ghastly busi-

[10] One surgeon told an English woman that the surgical patients, during amputations "frequently lay and smoked their cigars, and kept up a conversation with their fellow sufferers."

ness." [11] And it was certainly not made less ghastly by the propensity on the part of some surgeons to operate whenever the slightest excuse presented itself. Too many accounts have survived of wounded men saving condemned limbs from amputation by hiding from the operators for there not to have been some truth in them. The worst offenders appear to have been the young men, anxious to become skilled in this branch of their profession; these could be seen on the field and in the hospitals performing "difficult operations with the assurance and assumed skill of practiced surgeons, and with little regard for human life or limb." One Confederate surgeon, after a visit to the battlefields and hospitals of the Army of Tennessee, concluded that medical officers were much more interested in acquiring or displaying surgical skill than they were in preserving life and limb. Cases of compound fracture, he wrote, were "condemned to the knife with as little hesitancy as if men's limbs, like those of the salamander, were reproduced with great certainty." This penchant on the part of some for lopping off limbs no doubt explained—partially at least—why the Surgeon General, in August, 1863, directed the creation at each hospital of a consultative board to give advice in all important surgical cases; no important operation, when delay was practicable, was to be performed without the approval of this board.

It was easy at that time, however, and it has become customary since, to exaggerate the "butchery" practiced by the field and hospital surgeons. This is one of those subjects in which the most outrageous statements find credulous listeners who in turn become narrators. Circumstances at times necessitated an unusual number of amputations. Many of the Shiloh wounded, for example, lost limbs as a result of the very heavy casualty list of this bloody engagement and the consequent

[11] "Of the thirteen thousand amputations performed by French army surgeons during the Franco-Prussian War," writes medical historian Richard Shryock, "no less than ten thousand proved fatal." Hospital matron Emily Mason recalled how she wrote down the last words of one patient while "he coolly surveyed the instruments, the surgeons with bared arms, and the great tub prepared to catch his blood."

inability of the medical officers to attend the wounded more promptly. In such cases there was little choice: almost certain death without surgery and probable death with it. According to one report, eight of every ten of the Shiloh wounded died when they underwent amputations necessitated by their failure to receive earlier attention.[12] There may well have been a too rapid resort to the knife in such cases as compound gunshot fractures involving the upper third of the femur yet experience had taught the French and English masters that "in rejecting amputation in such cases, we lose more lives than we save limbs." Their experience was relayed to Southern medical officers, but it seems clear that, in general, the latter became more conservative as the war continued. One surgeon who confessed his fondness for the knife claimed that he restricted its application to those cases "in which its use is requisite." Explaining that surgeons performed enough operations each day on "bad subjects . . . to satisfy the most bloodthirsty," one of the operators stated quite simply what was unquestionably the sentiment of many: "I am tired of it." Still another declared: "Our rule is, to put it [amputation] off to the very last day, and if possible save the limb." Surgeon Willis F. Westmoreland of Atlanta's Medical College Hospital received praise for his successful demonstrations in behalf of conservative surgery, and most surgeons, contended an observer, in contrast to the young and reckless, "did their duty nobly." Deering J. Roberts and John S. Cain, high-ranking Confederate surgeons, contended that conservative surgery was never lost sight of during the war. And when the epithet of "butchers" was directed against the surgeons of the Union Army of the Potomac for their conduct during the Antietam campaign, that army's medical director, Jonathan Letterman, attacked such name-calling as gross misrepresentation and expressed his conviction that "if any fault was committed it was that the knife was not used enough." Henry S. Hewit, Medical Director of the Union Army of the Ohio, asserted in his report

[12] Surgeons noted the more favorable results of major operations when the army had been victorious.

of the Atlanta campaign that those medical officers "who had read much and seen little were highly conservative, while those who had read little and seen much were the reverse." [13]

Surgical Improvisation

The surgical achievements of both Confederate and Union surgeons, considering the general ignorance of aseptic and other modern theories and methods, were deserving of much praise. Confederate surgeons, moreover, were especially handicapped by their overall lack of first-class surgical instruments. Their improvisatorial ability came to their aid, however, and they were able to compensate somewhat for this deficiency. Surgeon Ferdinand E. Daniel, in a room lighted only by a smoky coal oil lamp, amputated a patient's hand with the contents of a small pocket case and a carpenter's saw. Another surgeon, confronted with a sudden and profuse secondary hemorrhage, successfully ligated the external carotid artery with the assistance of a pair of retractors improvised from the iron bale of a wooden water bucket. Medical Director Hunter Holmes McGuire believed that the adaptability of Confederate surgeons to the exigencies of army life produced within their ranks some of the most proficient military surgeons in the world, and, if these practitioners of wartime surgery are judged just from the standpoint of their operative ingenuity and dexterity, McGuire's praise of them must surely be allowed to stand. According to McGuire, "The pliant bark of a tree made for him a good tourniquet; the juice of the green persimmon, a styptic; a knitting-needle, with its point sharply bent, a tenaculum, and a pen-knife in his hand, a scalpel and

[13] S. S. Satchwell contended in an address delivered after the war that "a new era in conservative surgery" was being ushered in as a result of the wartime experience. Satchwell emphasized the restorative action of nature. Surgical records available do not indicate undue recklessness. Of thirty-four wounded men treated by R. Randolph Stevenson in June and July, 1864, at Buckner Hospital, Newnan, Georgia, he resorted to operative surgery in only eleven cases.

bistoury. I have seen him break off one prong of a common table-fork, bend the point of the other prong, and with it elevate the bone in depressed fracture of the skull and save life. Long before he knew the use of the porcelain-tipped probe for finding bullets, I have seen him use a piece of soft pine wood and bring it out of the wound marked by the leaden ball. Years before we were formally told of Nelaton's method of inverting the body in chloroform narcosis, I have seen it practiced by the Confederate surgeon. . . . "

Antiseptics

It was part of the tragedy of the Civil War that these surgeons knew nothing of the doctrine of sepsis and the proper use of antiseptics. All Confederate theories as to the repair and restoration of lost tissues were based on inflammatory reaction, and one aim of the surgeon in treating gunshot wounds was to promote suppuration in the form of a creamy pus—called "laudable pus"—that appeared in wounds healing by second intention. The appearance of "laudable pus" on the third or fourth day was viewed with satisfaction, and the atmosphere of Richmond, after the battles around the city, was "heavy and nauseating" with its odor. There was some use of "disinfectants" by Confederate medical officers although these were employed altogether on an empirical basis. Nevertheless, turpentine, the chlorides, permanganate of potash and diluted pyroligneous acid, and powdered charcoal were applied liberally to wounds by some surgeons for the purpose of speeding the process of repair. Few surgeons, if any, however, understood how and when to use these antiseptics effectively.

Dressings

Dressings for wounds were obtained from a number of sources. A fairly good quality of osnaburg from which band-

231

ages were made was manufactured by several cotton manufactories, and the women of the South furnished sheets, spreads, skirts, and other worn goods. Old linen was scraped with a knife to make lint, and a good substitute for the latter was raw cotton baked in an oven until it was charred. Sponges became scarce, and clean linen or cotton rags were used instead —sometimes over and over again as they were frequently boiled, washed out, and ironed. Silk for ligatures and sutures was usually available, but at intervals surgeons had to employ cotton or flax thread and horse hair; the latter was boiled to render it soft and pliant—another accidental aseptic procedure.[14]

Some difference of opinion existed early in the war as to the comparative advantages of cold and warm water applications to wounds, and a committee, whose chairman was Surgeon James B. Read, was appointed in October, 1863, by the Association of Army and Navy Surgeons to prepare a report upon this subject. Read's report, presented early in 1864, pronounced cold water as "invaluable in the treatment of gunshot wounds." It was explained that cold water might be used in three ways: "by direct application, dripping, and by applications covered so as to prevent evaporation and exclude air." The third method, Read concluded, had the "most general utility," but he was of the opinion that to obtain the best results "the application should not be made oftener than three or four times in twenty-four hours." Joseph Jones recalled that the cold water treatment was generally adopted throughout the medical service and even brought about recovery, without operative surgery, in a "fair proportion" of gunshot wounds involving joints. Wrote Jones: "In knee joint injuries, which, when not operated on, have heretofore been considered as almost always fatal, nearly fifty per cent were cured by securing rest, immobility of the injured joint and by employing the coldwater dressing (irrigation being preferred) and by the free use of opium."

---

[14] Kate Cumming was told by field surgeons "that many a time they have had nothing but old tent cloth to bind up wounds."

The superiority of the cold water treatment was echoed by Felix Formento: "Wounds cicatrize much better and sooner by the water dressing. Cold irrigation was used with utmost advantage in all cases where violent inflammation threatened or existed." One of the most effective uses of cold water applications appears to have been in the treatment of bayonet wounds. Surgeon Simon Baruch of the Third South Carolina Battalion treated a number of such wounds successfully, and in two of his cases the bayonet had entered the back, pierced a lung, and emerged through the chest. Baruch found that the chest cases, "though presenting a more extensive track than those of the hand, loins and shoulder, healed more rapidly, for this reason, that the slightly punctured patient would not obey my injunctions to keep quiet."

Despite the general preference for cold water applications to wounds, it is known that the medical officers sometimes applied cloths heated in hot water and even poultices for the purpose of encouraging suppuration, "laudable pus." And, there were other surgeons who changed from the cold water treatment to the warm at the onset of suppuration in order "to promote it." There were also those who complained that the wet dressings led to "sloughing" and some of these resorted to the use of dry dressings with dramatic results. It was reported that one hospital surgeon, for example, "treated six hundred and fifty cases with dry lint and had but one case of gangrene." The only surgical treatment received for several days by Confederate wounded brought to Williamsport after the battle of Gettysburg was exposure of their wounds to the air, and such treatment, according to one account, had a most favorable outcome.

Hermetic Sealing of Wounds

An interesting departure from established policy in the treatment of gunshot wounds was advocated late in the war by Surgeon J. Julian Chisolm. It was Chisolm's recommendation that all wounds be hermetically sealed as soon as possible. Such practice had been recommended earlier in the war by Assistant Surgeon Benjamin Howard of the Union Army with respect to chest wounds, but Chisolm advised that the principle be extended to the treatment of all gunshot cases. Hermetic sealing, contended Chisolm, would exclude the atmosphere and thus effect a cure "by absorption and re-modelling, without the aid of suppuration." Howard received much criticism at the hands of his brother officers, and Chisolm's proposal met with some skepticism as well. The editor of the official journal of the Confederate medical officers thought that the idea had much merit, however, provided there was no fracture involved or that no wad of clothing was carried into the body. It was his opinion that "the cautious surgeon should consider well the general condition of his patient, the character of the wound, the size of the ball and its probable velocity as it passed through the soft parts, before expecting too much from the proposed treatment. . . ." Years after the conflict one ex-Confederate surgeon asserted that "it was the almost universal adoption of this surgical procedure [Chisolm's] in all wounded cases that yielded us our splendid results in wound surgery."

Larval Therapy

Wounds that were neglected often became covered with maggots, and the Surgeon General, in May, 1863, advised his corps that the common elder (*Sambucus Canadensis*) was reputed to be an effective agent for their expulsion. Calomel also seems to have seen some use for this purpose. Joseph Jones noticed, however, that maggots destroyed the diseased tissue and left the wound in a healthy condition. Other surgeons affirmed that gangrenous wounds which had been infested by maggots healed more rapidly than if these scavengers had not appeared. Similar observations had been made during the Napoleonic Wars, but they appear to have been forgotten just as they were after the Civil War.

Splints

Most cases involving fractures would undoubtedly have benefited by the use of more and better splints. A Confederate field surgeon recalled that makeshifts were usually employed, and on one occasion he claimed to have "used a whole fence-rail for a broken arm, being unable to do any better." Other medical officers, however, reported that they were aided considerably in the treatment of fractures of the lower extremities by Dr. Nathan Ryno Smith's anterior wire splint. Smith, who occupied the chair of surgery at the University of Maryland for almost half a century, constructed his splint, a suspensory apparatus, before the war, and it was used by both the Confederate and Union armies. Its use in the Confederate forces was apparently the result of a favorable report concerning the splint's utility made by a commission appointed by the Surgeon General just before the First Battle of Manassas. Surgeon Ferdinand E. Daniel referred to Smith's splint as "a blessing to the Confederate surgeons, a refuge, and a tower of strength. It is so simple," he went on to say, "so easily and quickly made, so cheap, and so easily adapted to almost every fracture that it was generally used." When there was excessive comminution in fractures of the lower extremities the Smith splint was replaced by the pulley and weight.[15]

Orthopedic Hospitals

It is not surprising that many wounds failed to heal satisfactorily, and the medical authorities, in February, 1865,

[15] During this same period two other surgical aids, for the treatment of fractures of the femur, were invented in the United States. Gurdon Buck, a New York surgeon, introduced a device known as "Buck's Extension," and John Thompson Hodgen, Surgeon General of the Western Sanitary Commission and of Missouri during the war, contributed an apparatus which combined the features of Smith's and Buck's splints in one remarkable orthopedic device.

decided to establish orthopedic hospitals "for the exclusive treatment of cases of old injuries and deformities from gun shot wounds." Surgeon James B. Read was instructed to organize such an institution in Richmond, and Lauderdale Springs, Mississippi, was selected as the site for one in that sector of the Confederacy. Another hospital in charge of Surgeon Robert Battey, the Polk at Macon, Georgia, was set aside for the treatment of hernia cases. Surgeon Read, in addition to caring for the unhealed or imperfectly healed wounds and deformities resulting from gunshot wounds, was instructed to treat such ailments as necrosis, sloughing, false joints, ununited dislocations, local paralysis, hernia, stone in the bladder, aggravated varicocele, and chronic hemorrhoids.[16] The interest in those with orthopedic problems extended to men who were no longer in the service, and Congress, in a measure approved on March 9, 1865, enacted that all former soldiers who suffered from old wounds or deformities might, provided their cases presented reasonable prospects of responding to skilled surgical attention, receive treatment. This whole program, although established too late to produce any tangible achievement, is indicative of the general concern felt in Richmond over the Confederate wounded.

The Surgicial Fevers

Infections of wounds were the chief causes of mortality that followed upon the heels of operative surgery, and the so-called surgical fevers—tetanus, erysipelas, hospital gangrene, and pyaemia—were greatly feared. Wartime surgeons never determined the causes of these ailments although some did reach the conclusion that soldiers tainted with scurvy or in a general

[16] Amateur surgery was responsible for some of the abnormalities. Surgeons sometimes left too little flap with the result that the bone protruded through the stump. Supplementary operations were also made necessary at times by "the application of improper dressing or no dressing at all, and to sloughing."

run-down condition were very susceptible to them. The ideas held as to methods of communication and effective treatment of the fevers were less sound.

Idiopathic tetanus—actually an incorrect designation since no such disease existed—was presumed to be caused by "remote or predisposing" factors such as "exposure to cold and damp" and "the suppression of certain natural secretions or adventitious drains." [17] The traumatic variety of the disease, it was believed, resulted from "wounds of all kinds, contusions, luxations, burns, frostbite, surgical operations, and indeed every conceivable form of physical lesion." The incidence of tetanus, actually caused by the bacillus tetani, was not particularly disturbing. Dr. Francis Sorrell, surgeon and inspector of hospitals, found that of 47,724 cases of wounds noted on hospital reports during 1861 and 1862 there were only 66 cases of traumatic tetanus—31 of which terminated fatally. Sorrell suspected, however, that tetanus might have occurred more frequently than the reports indicated since surgeons often failed to record "supervening diseases." It was believed by some surgeons that the rare incidence of tetanus could be attributed to the practice of caring for the wounded in tents or "in hospitals unceiled or unplastered." A more valid explanation by the medical historian of the Union Army, aware of the horse's role as a carrier of the bacillus tetani, points to the fact "that most of the battlefields were on virgin soil untouched by the plow and unmanured." The army and navy surgeons, however, considered the disease important enough to be placed upon their agenda early in 1864.

There was no satisfactory treatment for tetanus. "To enumerate the means used for the relief of tetanus would require a volume," explained one of the surgical manuals, but "to record those entitled to confidence does not demand a line." Recommended though was the use of mild dressings over the wound, large doses of brandy and opium, and "the most nu-

[17] Some surgeons contended that there was no such disease as idiopathic tetanus.

tritious and bracing food, through a tube introduced by the nostrils into the stomach, or by enema, as the circumstances or necessities of the case may dictate."

Very little distinction was made on medical records between idiopathic and traumatic erysipelas, now recognized as an extremely contagious streptococcal infection. During the first nine months of the war the Army of the Potomac, with an average mean strength of less than 50,000 men, reported 390 cases of the disease; and, in January, 1864, Medical Director Carrington reported that 1,386 erysipelas cases, 108 of which proved mortal, had been treated in the Virginia general hospitals during the preceding sixteen months. The Chimborazo registers show that there were 236 patients diagnosed as suffering from erysipelas in that institution, 22 of whom succumbed to the infection. It was believed that the disease was likely to assume its most deadly form during epidemics, and medical officers were admonished to refrain from all surgery, if possible, when "an epidemic tendency of the atmosphere" existed.

Soldiers with erysipelas were usually isolated in tents or separate wards where they could receive an abundance of fresh air, and particular hospitals were sometimes selected for the reception of such victims. Actually, if the current use of antibiotics is excepted, the treatment would not suffer too much in comparison with present-day therapy. Surgeons generally recognized the importance of providing the patients with a nourishing diet and stimulants. Sesquichloride of iron acquired a wide reputation as a specific, and quinine was sometimes prescribed as a tonic and to counter the febrile condition often present. Cathartics were administered when necessary to keep the bowels open, and in some cases, when pain was present, opiates were given. Incisions were made through the diseased areas after the formation of pus, and the incised area was sometimes washed out with chlorinated water. Local applications also consisted of tincture of iodine or tannic acid solutions and camphorated oil. Cold water dressings were used although at least one Confederate surgeon, C. J. Clark of the Third Alabama Hospital in the capital, concluded that they were responsible for much of the erysipelas in the Richmond hospitals during the second year of the war and championed the use of warm water dressings. The affected part was kept at rest throughout the period of treatment.

"Our wounded are doing badly; gangrene in its worst form has broken out among them. Those whom we thought were almost well are now suffering severely. A wound which a few days ago was not the size of a silver dime is now eight or ten inches in diameter." So wrote Kate Cumming from one of the hospitals back of the Army of Tennessee late in 1863, and the occurrence which she described was not at all uncommon. No one even today can speak with certainty and authority as to the "hospital gangrene" of the Civil War, but it was a repulsive and feared disease.

Hospital gangrene seems to have first made its appearance early in June, 1862. Joseph Jones noted that it was present after the battle of Port Republic (June 8–9, 1862) and, according to that zealous observer, "progressively increased" throughout the war. Jones pointed out, however, that not a single case of the disease was reported officially until July, 1863, more than a year after its initial appearance. There was terrible suffering from hospital gangrene in the Army of Northern Virginia after the battles of the Wilderness (May 5–6, 1864) and Spotsylvania (May 12, 1864), and in the Army of Tennessee during its retreat from Dalton to Atlanta (May–July, 1864). It was recognized that the predisposing causes of hospital gangrene, so significant in explaining all the surgical diseases, were crowded camps and hospitals, extreme fatigue, depression, exposure, and improper and insufficient food, all of which combined with dysentery, scurvy, and other camp diseases, to impair the general health of the troops. It was also noticed that the incidence of hospital gangrene seemed "to increase in proportion to the distance which the wounded were transported from the battlefield." A study of sixty-two

239

surgical cases in the Farmville, Virginia, General Hospital from August to October, 1864, shows the supervention of this horrifying ailment in eighteen of them and suggests its extensive prevalence.

The treatment of hospital gangrene was similar to that for erysipelas. Fumigated wards and even entire hospitals, such as the Empire Hospital in Macon, Georgia, were set aside for gangrene victims. The latter were often isolated in gangrene tents located in open areas outside the hospitals. Soups, eggs, milk, butter, and other nourishing foods were prescribed along with such alcoholic stimulants as brandy and wine. Internal medication included sesquichloride of iron, the mineral acids, and quinine dissolved in alcohol. The remedy last named was reputedly found to be effective by Assistant Surgeon Samuel Scales of the Thirty-seventh Tennessee Regiment after the battle of Murfreesboro (December 31, 1862–January 2, 1863). The fact that this same medication was "discovered" during the First World War as a specific for the gas gangrene that appeared among the wounded of that conflict might indicate a distinct relationship between the two infections. Opium or morphine was often given—the latter in many instances by subcutaneous injection with Wood's hypodermic syringe. Nitric acid, turpentine, alum, nitrate of silver, sulphate and chloride of zinc, tincture of iron, tincture of iodine, yellow wash, and Darby's Fluid were the usual local applications although Surgeon E. Burke Haywood in Raleigh doubted the efficacy of the use of such disinfectants and deodorizers. The removal of the foul odor, he thought, was "like removing the beacon that warns the watchful mariner of the certain death that lurks beneath the surface." Nitric acid was regarded as the best local agent to burn out the gangrene, and since its application caused intense pain the concurrent use of chloroform was advised. It was generally necessary to repeat cauterization of the sore two or three times. Some cut the dead matter away outright. Lint saturated with turpentine might then be plugged into the wound although a few surgeons reported dramatic results with the use of dry lint. Charcoal, yeast, and even carrot poultices—spoken of by Surgeon Samuel Bemiss as "antiseptic poultices"—were also employed, and cold water dressings were a part of the standard treatment in some hospitals. Surgeon Thomas Jefferson Lafayette de Yambert of Medical Director Stout's department proposed that the gangrenous area be circumscribed with a knife, and Dr. Henry F. Campbell of Augusta, Georgia, a consulting surgeon in Richmond, instituted the practice of ligating large arteries of the extremities to check the spread of gangrene. Effective treatment was often handicapped by the poor general health of the troops. Joseph Jones, for example, thought that the treatment at Macon's Empire Hospital (the gangrene hospital) in the fall of 1864 was very materially affected by the high incidence of malaria among the patients.

The lot of the pyaemia victims was the unhappiest of all because the prognosis was an almost certain and speedy death. Pyaemia, a poisoning of the blood caused by the absorption of pyogenic micro-organisms, was believed to be closely related to erysipelas and hospital gangrene; this view was not altogether incorrect, but pyaemia's more devastating effect made its appearance much less welcome. Those who were struck with this dread infection suffered from multiple abscesses, jaundice, profuse sweating, chills, and fevers. It was declared to be responsible for death in forty-three per cent of all fatal primary amputations and for death in twenty-five per cent of all fatal secondary amputations. A few patients were reported to have recovered from pyaemia, but the mortality was extremely high. The treatment was similar to that administered for hospital gangrene.

The extent to which the surgical diseases prevailed among Union troops in Confederate prisons is not altogether clear. It is known, however, that hospital gangrene was rampant at Andersonville. The predisposing causes of the infections were all present, and the septic shortcomings of the medical officers in conjunction with the crowded, unsanitary conditions produced more unfortunate effects than usual. Joseph Jones, after personally observing the conditions in that prison, concluded

241

that amputations generally proved fatal "either from the effects of gangrene or from the prevailing diarrhoea and dysentery."

It should be pointed out that Confederate medical officials, considering the stage of medical advancement at that time, made valiant efforts to prevent the inception of the surgical fevers. In the hospitals a very great premium was placed upon cleanliness, proper ventilation, a nutritious diet, and what they believed to be the best in medication for the wounded. Hospital surgeons were authorized to reduce the capacities of those institutions housing patients with severe wounds, and some hospitals that had experienced outbreaks of the infections were ordered to be closed until they might be thoroughly cleaned and whitewashed. Disinfectants were in almost constant use.

Surgical Records

The apparent indifference of medical officers toward the maintenance of surgical records was a matter of grave concern to Surgeon General Moore, and he strove continuously to impress upon them their responsibility to the Medical Corps and to the science of surgery at large. The Surgeon General desired "to accumulate full and authentic records, not only of all capital operations . . . but of every case of gunshot injury treated by them, which may exhibit in their opinion features of manifest surgical interest." Throughout the war the medical chief of the Confederacy reminded his subordinates of the professional importance of battles and requested information concerning hemorrhages, the respective merits of the "flap" and "circular" operations in amputations, the use of anesthetics, treatment of gunshot wounds, the extent of the use of tourniquets and other appliances on the battlefield, nerve injuries and treatment thereof, and other important topics. The Surgeon General was no doubt disappointed in the paucity of reports sent in from the field, but of course this was not always something that could be helped. The difficulty of preparing written reports during periods of active campaigning and rapid movement was understood by that official himself, and the problem was stated quite succinctly by Medical Director Lafayette Guild in his account of the Seven Days' engagements: ". . . the rapidity of the movements of the army over an extensive field of operations, the rapid succession of the week's conflicts, and the battles occurring in the afternoon and in many instances continuing as late as 9 o'clock at night, prevented the wounded of particular divisions and brigades being conveyed to their own respective infirmaries, and rendered it extremely difficult, if not impossible, for the medical officers to make correct records of all the wounded who fell into their hands. . . . Necessity often demanded that the wounded should be conveyed to the nearest infirmary, and consequently the wounded of every portion of the army were frequently thus mingled together. . . ."

Dental Surgery

The story of dental surgery under the Stars and Bars is an interesting and important one. It is not surprising that the services of dental surgeons should have been employed inasmuch as the dental profession had gained some standing in the two decades before the war, and altogether there were about five hundred dentists in the seceding states. In view of such development and the fact that Jefferson Davis, as Franklin Pierce's Secretary of War, was an early champion of an army dental corps, it is perhaps surprising that a regular dental corps was not established in the Confederacy.

It became apparent during the war that most soldiers stood greatly in need of dental services. They neglected to have their teeth examined, tooth brushes were somewhat scarce, and the diet left much to be desired. Furthermore, the cost of dental operations was more than the average soldier could pay. The charge for a gold filling, as currency inflation set in, was $120

243

—more than six months' pay of a private. At the same time dentists charged $20 to extract a tooth, and the cost for an upper set of teeth on a gold or vulcanite base was from $1,800 to $4,000.

A plan to contract with dentists engaging in private practice was discussed by the Confederate medical authorities at least as early as March, 1863, but this proposition was not adopted. Instead dentists were conscripted, and they were usually accorded the rank of hospital stewards. One of these, Dr. W. Leigh Burton of Richmond, performed the necessary operations for patients hospitalized in the capital, and his military practice seems to have begun in February, 1864.[18] The wisdom and forethought of the medical authorities in making it possible for the Confederate soldier to obtain dental services should not be overlooked. A similar effort to institute such a program in the Union Army was rejected by the War Department.

Confederate dental surgeons were kept busy. Their principal work, according to Dr. Burton, consisted of filling and extracting teeth, removing tartar, adjusting fractures of the bones of the mouth, and treating wounds of the face. "A day's work," he wrote, "consisted of from twenty to thirty fillings, the preparation of the cavities included, the extraction of fifteen or twenty teeth, and the removal of the tartar ad libitum!" [19]

A real contribution to the successful treatment of fractures of the maxillary bones was made late in the war by Dr. James Baxter Bean, an Atlanta dentist. Medical officers had encountered very little success in their treatment of such wounds affecting the face and jaws. When Medical Inspector

[18] Surgeons in charge of hospitals sometimes requested the assignment of dentists to their hospitals. Prior to the time that dentists were assigned to duty in Confederate hospitals such operations as were required appear to have been performed by medical officers or hospital stewards.

[19] Medical Director Carrington wrote in September, 1864, that dentists, in addition to "plugging, cleaning and extracting teeth" had been "serviceable in adjusting fractures of the jaw and in operating on the mouth and fauces."

244

Edward N. Covey visited the Atlanta hospitals in the summer of 1864, he found Dr. Bean rendering his services without remuneration. Bean explained to Covey his method of treating maxillary wounds with an interdental splint, and Covey was so impressed that he moved all such cases in Atlanta to one hospital for treatment. This hospital, the name of which is not known, was probably the first in military or dental history to be used for maxillo-facial surgery. After the fall of Atlanta (July, 1864) Bean's work was continued in the Blind School Hospital at Macon.[20]

Surgeon General Moore, upon learning of the interdental splint, had Dr. Bean come to Richmond for the purpose of laying his device before a board of medical officers. The board unanimously recommended general adoption of the splint, and Moore subsequently instructed medical directors of hospitals to "select a thoroughly lighted ward (gas-lighted, if practicable), in some one of the Hospitals under their jurisdiction, to which will be sent for treatment, by Bean's apparatus, all cases of fracture of the superior and inferior maxillary bones now in Hospital, or that may hereafter be admitted." Bean himself was instructed to assist the surgeons in charge of hospitals make this service possible. The ward in Richmond selected by Medical Director Carrington was located in the Receiving and Way Hospital.[21]

The Surgeon General's attitude toward the dental profes-

[20] The splint, as described by Covey, was "made of vulcanized india-rubber, having on both horizontal surfaces cup-shaped depressions, sufficiently deep to embrace the crowns of the teeth." In the adjustment of the device, the teeth were "placed in their corresponding indentations in the splint," and kept in position, by a "mental compress and occipito-frontal bandage. . . . The advantages of the splint," Covey explained, "are its neatness; the facility with which it allows the patients to take nourishment; the almost entire certainty of its not being displaced, and the preservation of perfect antagonism of the teeth, with the absence, consequently, of deformity after the reunion of the bones." Dr. Bean suffered from "chronic rheumatism" and was not therefore on active duty.

[21] Dr. Burton wrote that the Surgeon General ordered a ward for the treatment of maxillo-facial surgery with Bean's device to be prepared at the Robertson Hospital, but he may have been mistaken on this point.

sion at a time when its members were struggling to obtain a respected professional status meant much to dental practitioners everywhere, and Dr. Burton—greatly impressed by the medical head's official recognition of dentistry's importance—thought that dentists owed more to the Confederate Surgeon General "than to any man of modern times." Dentists of more recent years have also been lavish in their praise of that individual and his abilities.[22]

[22] Dr. William N. Hodgkin, Chairman of the History Committee, Virginia State Dental Association, in a letter to the writer, praises Surgeon General Moore highly and remarks on that official's administrative ability, resourcefulness, and openmindedness.

CHAPTER XII

Confederate Medical Officers: An Appraisal

The Problem

Certain obstacles immediately present themselves when one attempts to make a fair appraisal of the medical officers who served under the Stars and Bars and of their contribution to the war effort. The discoveries of Joseph Lister and Louis Pasteur completely revolutionized medical and surgical practice in the United States following the Civil War, and some historians of this great struggle—judging the doctors in uniform by the standards of the twentieth century and on the basis of complaints voiced by sick and wounded soldiers or other contemporaries—have dismissed the practitioners of the war as hopeless bunglers, sometimes pointing to the medical statistics without comparing them to those of other armies in the nineteenth century or taking into consideration the fact that a very great amount of the disease and death during the conflict may have been due to factors completely beyond the power of the doctors to control. Military medical men, however, have been the targets of abuse and criticism in conflicts more recent than that with which we are concerned—much of which has proved to be entirely unjustified. Men in the ranks have voiced complaints, and it is also a truism that decisions made by those responsible for policy-making are not always happily received and occasionally those in disagreement have been known to express their unhappiness with outbursts of criticism. At any rate, it would appear that the medical officers of the Confederacy should be judged by the standards of their own day and that some allowance ought to be made for the grumbling and complaining of those whose faultfinding was due to their general unhappiness or inability to accept without comment viewpoints and decisions which they considered erroneous.

Criticism of the Surgeon General and His Staff

Some of the abuse and criticism noted above was directed at the Surgeon General and his staff in Richmond. This was particularly true early in the war. Brigadier General James Johnston Pettigrew, an influential figure in the political life of North Carolina, concluded late in 1861 that "there is no department where reform is so much needed as in the medical and in the others, in so far as they are connected therewith." Pettigrew thought that the whole trouble stemmed "from the fact that the head and control of the medical department was a physician, instead of being an organisor. . . ." Complaining that the sick and wounded were not receiving proper treatment, a newspaper in the capital placed the full responsibility "at the doors of the office of the Surgeon General and Medical Director here in Richmond." And an army correspondent declared that "if some of the energy displayed in forcing feeble and unhealthy conscripts into the service, were shown in taking care of the sick and wounded, the army would be all the better for it. A planter who would take as little care of the health of his slaves as the government does of its soldiers, would soon have none to care for, while he would be driven out of the community by his indignant neighbors." This correspondent, most likely, was quite unaware of the fact that two top-ranking surgeons of the Confederacy—F. Peyre Porcher and J. Julian Chisolm—together operated a hospital for plantation slaves just prior to the outbreak of war.

One of the most savage attacks launched against the medical officials was that of the fiery Aristides Monteiro after the war. A former surgeon himself, Monteiro contended that "The veiled prophet of Khorassan was less cruel to his unhappy and deluded followers than were the executive methods of Con-

248

federate medicine to the sick and wounded soldiers of our unfortunate army." The Surgeon General's chief functions, according to Monteiro, were to prevent the discharge of disabled soldiers, to encourage cruelty to the sick and wounded on the part of his officers, to keep medical supplies from field surgeons, to make certain that able practitioners were not appointed to his corps, and to move the wounded over only the roughest roads and the longest distances. "To please the head of the department," Monteiro said, "surgeons must be cruel, severe; and, above all things, stupid, submissive and sycophantic."

Much more reasonable and made with considerably less rancor was the criticism made a number of years following the war by the brilliant Porcher. The latter believed that one of the most serious mistakes committed by the Surgeon General "was the failure to send surgeons of known skill and experience into positions where they might do most good—into the field or into large hospitals—in place of permitting them to remain in high cathedral places as medical examiners, medical directors, in charge of stations for purveying and distributing medical supplies, etc. . . ." Mistakes, of course, were made, but it took time to build an effective organization, and it was quite natural for the Surgeon General to assign his best men to the key positions.

One of the chief complaints made rather generally about Surgeon General Moore concerned his brusqueness in dealing with subordinates, and he certainly did not endear himself to many. The cold, impersonal manner which permeates his official correspondence makes it next to impossible to credit the charge made by one of his critics in the West that he used his high office "to provide places for his pets." It is reasonably clear that there was some animosity felt toward the Surgeon General by top-ranking medical officials in the Army of Tennessee, and Medical Director A. J. Foard of that army held that Moore had based his orders and regulations almost altogether upon information gained from the Army of Tennessee without acknowledging the extent of his indebtedness thereto.

Nothing in the correspondence of Moore indicates any aware-
ness that he might have given offense to his medical colleagues
and such a possibility probably never entered his mind. His
insistence upon the military formalities extended to the conduct of the women in his hospitals. When some of the hospital
matrons for example, complained that sick troops had been
sent off to Danville, Virginia, without adequate preparations
the Surgeon General instructed Medical Director Carrington
to inform them that as they were employed in a military hospital they would be "amenable to proper discipline, and that if
in [the] future they have any grievances to make, they will
send the report thro' the Medical Director to this Office."

At times the Surgeon General's harshness was softened by
his medical associates. On one occasion Moore, learning from
Medical Director Lafayette Guild that Guild was moving disabled men into North Carolina and that both Medical Director
Peter E. Hines and State Surgeon General Edward Warren
had been advised thereof, informed Guild that it was unnecessary to co-ordinate the matter with Warren. Guild's reply,
which should have given the Surgeon General something of a
much-needed lesson, stated that his course appeared wise to
him "first—with the view of taking every precaution to secure
for our wounded all care and attention possible; and second—
from a sense of respect to that State, which has not only furnished to this army more soldiers, but has shown more zeal &
practical intelligence in her care of them than any other state
in the Confederacy." Surgeon Thomas H. Williams, Medical
Director of the Army of the Potomac, advised the Surgeon
General early in the war that it was useless to report or
threaten to report Confederate medical officers for their seem-
ing indifference to regulations. Most of those officers, explained Williams, enjoyed high social standing, and, upon receiving what they considered to be affronts to their dignity,
they tendered their resignations. Williams found that he could
accomplish more through persuasion "and by representing to
them personally, the necessity that exists for a prompt compliance with the requirements of the service, than by appealing

to their fears." It was certainly somewhat futile to threaten officers who might write as follows regarding their assignments: "If I am assigned to any duty that does not suit me I will ask for a transfer to some other position, and if that is not granted me, I will give up my position and seek for a living in some other capacity." A greater appreciation of the human factor would probably have enhanced the Surgeon General's contribution as medical chief of the Confederacy. Despite this deficiency, however, he was always ready to listen to complaints.[1]

Tributes to the Surgeon General

Notwithstanding the criticism received by the Surgeon General, his fitness for the office he occupied was generally recognized. Jefferson Davis himself paid tribute to Moore's work, and numerous other of his contemporaries joined the Confederate President in according the Surgeon General much praise for the establishment of a hospital system which Senator James L. Orr of South Carolina, speaking in March, 1863, described as having been "brought to a great degree of perfection." Surgeon Peter E. Hines, medical director of North Carolina's general hospitals, recalled that the Surgeon General "was always kind and liberal" with respect to the Confederate hospitals in that state, and others pointed to his success in limiting the number of deaths from disease. More recently Surgeon General Moore has been lauded as "a master of organization, and magician in the procurement of 'ersatz' drugs." As stated earlier, he organized America's first mili-

---

[1] So were other medical officials. When Samuel H. Stout received a letter written directly to him by a patient in the Polk Hospital, Rome, Georgia, roundly criticizing conditions therein, Stout directed that an investigation of the charge be made immediately. He thought that the contents of the letter were rashly stated and that the complaint should have been made to the medical officer in charge of the hospital; yet, he commented, all patients have the right to complain, and the error of failing to communicate through proper channels "is common, even among officers of rank and should be overlooked."

tary medical society and has been credited with introducing the one story pavilion hospital, which proved for many years to be "the best model for army hospital use."

The Surgeon General's concern for the medical service is reflected in a communication to Medical Director Stout late in 1864 during the course of which he referred to his "considerable interest" in a report received from Stout and expressed his gratification that so much energy had been expended by Stout and his medical officers in behalf of the sick and wounded. His overriding concern for the welfare of the Confederate soldier generally was also exemplified by his interest in orthopedic hospitals and his readiness to adopt new surgical devices such as Nathan Ryno Smith's anterior wire splint and James Baxter Bean's interdental splint. Moore's attitude toward the dental profession, and the encouragement he gave to those members thereof who were called upon to give of their services both spoke volumes as to his progressiveness and vision. The medical head's chief problems resulted from the steadily deteriorating military situation and the Assistant Secretary of War was compelled to report in March, 1865, despite Moore's abilities, that "the Medical Department is not in a better condition than the other bureaus."

Criticism of Hospital and Field Medical Officers

Criticism of lesser medical officers was rife throughout the war. It early became so unrestrained that one observer remarked that it had "excited a general feeling of disgust with the service, and a strong disposition to abandon positions which cannot be retained consistently with self-respect. . . ." Officers of the medical corps were commonly charged with being inexperienced, ignorant and inefficient, neglectful of or cruel to their charges, careless in making reports, and having a propensity for strong drink.

Naturally most of the medical officers, as well as the troops, were inexperienced upon beginning their service, and they had very little, if any, knowledge of military habits or military medicine. Medical Director Stout pointed out after the war that many of these officers had no real conception of their relationship to other branches of the service and even failed to realize the importance of complying with regulations.[2] Inasmuch as new surgeons and assistant surgeons were receiving appointments throughout the war this was a continuing problem. The pitiful suffering of the Army of Northern Virginia's wounded during the battle of Bristoe Station (October 14, 1863) was attributed by Medical Director Guild largely to the inexperience of the medical officers of Cooke's Brigade, one that had not seen action previously. There "was a lack of experience on the field," reported Guild, "which displayed itself particularly in the Medical Officers." The results of lack of seasoning also manifested themselves on other battlefields. Some Richmond surgeons, under fire for the first time, suffered an attack of "shell fever" and did not stop running until they were twelve miles from their original position —a tribute perhaps to their physical condition. Inexperienced men under fire sometimes conducted themselves like veterans, but this was exceptional. One critic, comparing the field surgeons unfavorably with those in the large hospitals, concluded that the former did "quite as well as could be expected of young men who have had but little practical experience in the art of surgery."

Charges of ignorance and inefficiency were frequently voiced. Asserting that a regimental medical officer had attempted to give one of his patients three hundred grains of quinine as a single dose, a North Carolinian contended that "more of our soldiers have died from unskilled but well-paid physicians, than from battles with the enemy." Noting that his commanding officer had a surgeon under arrest, the hospital

[2] Charles S. Tripler, Medical Director of the Union Army of the Potomac, reported on February 7, 1863, as follows: "My own department was neither a complete success nor a very decided failure. The most serious impediment in the way of its success was undoubtedly the want of military habits and training in the medical officers. . . . In my opinion it is impossible to improvise an efficient medical staff."

steward of the Twenty-fourth Virginia Regiment expressed his conviction that the men would be better off if more medical officers were deprived of their commissions; the surgeon of his own regiment he pronounced "a great humbug." Surgeon General Moore, alarmed and mortified because the ignorance of his medical officers in the Army of Tennessee was represented as of the "most deplorable character," ordered Medical Director A. J. Foard to have all who had not been examined to report to the Army Medical Board in Charleston, South Carolina, at the earliest practicable moment. And Brigadier General Robert Toombs, a Georgian, in the process of endorsing grave charges made by Colonel Paul Semmes of the Second Georgia Volunteers, informed the Confederate Adjutant and Inspector General that the incompetency of medical officers was "shameful and more terrible than a Yankee army"— despite the fact that he admitted knowing nothing of the charges made by Semmes.

It would be extremely difficult to find an account of the war years any more contemptuous in its comments about medical personnel than the recollections of Antietam left by Mary Bedinger Mitchell, one of the many volunteer workers of Shepherdstown (now West Virginia)—to which point many of the Confederates wounded at Sharpsburg were brought on their way to the general hospitals. According to her account the surgeons arrived quite tardily, performed some "rough surgery," and, for the most part, "might as well have staid away. The remembrance of that worthless body of officials," she recalled, "stirs me to wrath."

Contract physicians were not unlikely to be incompetent, and yet it was necessary to employ them during emergencies. Medical Director Carrington, for example, found it imperative during the summer of 1864 "to employ the most inefficient Physicians here" to help look after the sick and wounded. Contract Physician Josiah Pearce Cannon's contract was terminated by Medical Director Stout because, according to the latter's judgment, Cannon was neither competent nor honest and lived off the rations of the troops. "This man," Stout stated, "was an Episcopal minister and as great a fraud as I have met with in this war."

There can be no question, of course, but that some ignorant and incompetent practitioners found their way into the Confederate Medical Department. It is very doubtful, however, that the percentage of such undesirables was high. Most will probably accept the judgment of Medical Inspector Edwin Samuel Gaillard, one of the ablest of the wartime surgeons, who dismissed sweeping charges of inefficiency as "groundless." Gaillard's sober and measured opinion was that "the Medical Corps, as well as others, must contain representatives, whose removal would add as well to the dignity as to the efficiency of the service."

Charges that sick and wounded soldiers were neglected by medical officers were voiced by various critics throughout the war, and it is perhaps understandable how one ailing soldier, seeing a roomful of coffins in an Okolona, Mississippi, hospital and workmen making still more, might have concluded "that greater preparations were being made to bury soldiers than to cure them." "How the surgeons in charge of the hospitals," declared a Richmond newspaper, "can allow such inattention and neglect as we have heard reiterated again and again on the part of their subordinates, we know not." Some hospital surgeons were even accused of appropriating to their own use the delicacies sent for the sick and wounded. Surgeons in charge of hospitals, it was said, resorted to "bucking and gagging" and cruel punishments in their enforcement of discipline. And most shocking of all were the charges that the dead were sometimes laid to rest without funeral rites of any kind.

A Tar Heel soldier in the field summed up his complaint against the surgeon of his regiment as follows: "I used to think that Dr. Strudwick was a splendid Dr., but if I was to get sick here I should hate to have him to attend on me. He woudent care if evry blamed private was to die ther is in the Fort, so he gets his pay. Last Saturday night he was sent for to go to see a felow with pneumonia. He said that the felow was just as able to come to see him, so he never went atall. in morning the felow was ded. Any thing that he goes at he dont half do it, he has set several bones here and they either growed crooked or they had to be set even again. . . ." [3]

Another soldier, camped near Fredericksburg, also wrote of the death of a comrade caused by the lack of proper attention and predicted that doctors would be punished for neglecting the sick and wounded troops. A war correspondent with the army in Maryland intimated strongly that the medical staff came around slowly to the idea that a soldier's life was worth preserving. Sometimes the charge of neglect against Southern medical officers was made by the enemy. After the battle of Corinth (October 3–4, 1862), for example, the Union Medical Director of the Army of the Mississippi, Surgeon Archibald B. Campbell, accused Confederate surgeons left behind the Union lines with their wounded of neglecting the latter by not even bothering to make out requisitions upon him for needed supplies despite assurances that their requisitions would be honored within forty-eight hours.

The neglect of Confederate sick and wounded became a matter for discussion in Congress from time to time, and some extravagant charges were made by certain of the lawmakers. Senator Albert Gallatin Brown of Mississippi asserted in 1862 that a sick soldier was allowed to lie on a station platform for three days, and he contended that soldiers were dying from neglect throughout the Confederacy. Another senator, William E. Simms of Kentucky, held that "Soldiers had died on the cars, in the hospitals, and on the streets, for the want of a little attention." Medical officers, he thought, had "slain more of our troops than all of Lincoln's minions." Certain other members of Congress, including Representative James Farrow of South Carolina, concurred in the opinions expressed

[3] This appraisal of Dr. William Strudwick, physician of Hillsboro, North Carolina, must be taken *cum grano salis*. Strudwick was trained at Jefferson Medical College, and he was a member of the Medical Society of North Carolina. His father, Dr. Edmund Strudwick, was president of the state medical society from 1849 to 1851.

above, but further discussion and inquiry did not prove fruitful in throwing light on this particular question. One senator decided that most of the neglect stemmed from constant disputes between the surgeons over rank. "Doctors were proverbial for their differences," he explained, "and while they remained all of the same rank there was no way of settling their disputes." Since they were not all the same rank, however, his explanation does not appear to be particularly convincing. And the charges themselves were often devoid of substance. For every case of proved deliberate neglect of disabled men by their medical officers may be cited numerous instances of such officers' devotion and self-sacrifice. Medical Director Guild, like many others, sacrificed himself unsparingly in the performance of his duties and ruined his health in the process. He died in 1870 at the age of forty-five. Still others, like Medical Inspector Gaillard, lost arms and legs or were crippled as a result of wounds suffered while attending the wounded on the field of battle. A considerable number like Assistant Surgeons David Herbert Llewellyn of the famed *Alabama* and J. B. Fontaine of the Fourth Virginia Cavalry, made the supreme sacrifice. Llewellyn lost his life as a result of the *Alabama's* encounter with the *Kearsarge* (June 19, 1864). That officer, a report stated, "was unremitting in attention to the wounded during battle, and after the surrender superintended their removal to the boats, refusing to leave the ship while one remained." He drowned shortly afterward. Fontaine was killed by shellfire.

Even Surgeon General Moore was critical of the casual and unmilitary attitude of his officers in regard to routine record keeping and reporting. Sometimes they simply neglected to maintain records at all. Late in 1863 Moore learned that surgeons in charge of hospitals in the Army of Tennessee were not keeping case books although required by regulations to do so. Occasionally surgeons were to be found who failed to keep a register of their sick and wounded. Others kept them so imperfectly that they were valueless. A less common, but no less shocking, violation of regulations was that which saw some medical officers carry their records with them when moving from one assignment to another.

Incomplete and inaccurate reporting was also a source of real annoyance to the Confederate medical chieftain. Routine reports from his officers in the field were the most unsatisfactory, and on one occasion the Surgeon General was advised by one of his medical directors that a majority of the regimental reports had "to be returned for correction, the errors, both of omission and commission being of such a character as to prevent correction by myself." A select committee of the Provisional Congress, appointed on August 27, 1861, to inquire into the operation of the Medical Department found that improper reporting from the field was a real deterrent to efficient administration.[4]

The reports from general hospitals were not always prompt and accurate, and the Surgeon General was compelled to order that the names of officers delinquent in this respect be sent to his office and that in the future "they be held to a strict accountability for all failures to comply promptly" with regulations on this subject. Even the able Surgeon James B. McCaw at Chimborazo fell short in this respect. Once McCaw was told that his morning reports were "very carelessly and inaccurately kept." And sometime later he received word from the Surgeon General that, in general, "all Accounts Current sent from your hospital are full of defects, and made out in a manner which does not meet the approbation of this office."

The other side of the coin should be noted in regard to reporting as in other matters. Medical Director Stout, for example, claimed that his hospital surgeons were "zealous in sending . . . all reports required of them at medical and army headquarters." One of the highest tributes came from the Office of the Surgeon General of the United States after the

---

[4] Incomplete reporting was not always the result of negligence. Early in 1864 a Union surgeon in Chattanooga stated that "No little embarrassment has been experienced . . . from the destruction of all the records of this office by the Confederate General Wheeler during his attack on our train in the Sequatchie Valley in the early part of October."

war. "The Confederate medical records in the possession of this Office appear, as a general rule," it was stated, "to have been kept with commendable exactness, and it is remarkable that physicians called suddenly from civil practice should have so speedily mastered the intricacies of military routine."

A considerable amount of drinking took place in both the Confederate and Union military forces, and it comes as no surprise to learn that medical officers imbibed rather frequently. Medical Director Stout wrote of replacing one of his surgeons whose intellect was "almost all the time befogged with liquor, though never known to be drunk." The Surgeon General also kept his ear to the ground for news of misconduct in this respect, and on one occasion he called for an investigation of a report "that the Medical Officers on duty in Poplar Lawn Hospital [in Petersburg, Virginia] are in the habit of drinking the hospital stimulants, whenever they think proper. . . ." At Chimborazo, according to Phoebe Pember, a drunken surgeon engaged in treating a patient with a crushed ankle placed the wrong leg in splints and thereby contributed to the soldier's death. "There were some doubts afloat," wrote Mrs. Pember, "as to whether the benefit conferred upon the patients by the use of stimulants counterbalanced the evil effects they produced on the surgeons."

Surgeons in the field were sometimes reported to be in a state of intoxication even during the course of an engagement. And when "engaged at the amputation table," wrote a war correspondent in Virginia, "many of them feel it to be their solemn duty, every time they administer brandy to the patient, to take a drink themselves. This part of the work," he continued, "is performed with great unction and conscientiousness." Over two years later the same correspondent declared that he had "seen surgeons so stupefied by liquor that they could not distinguish between a man's arm and the spoke of a wagon wheel, and who would just as soon have sawed off the one as the other."

The Surgeon General warned his officers that drunkenness would not be tolerated. "Drunkards are not wanted in the

Medical Department," Moore informed one of his top-ranking officials who at the time was engaged in dealing with several discrepancies of this type. That the Surgeon General meant what he said may be seen in the fact that medical officers guilty of repeated offenses were relieved from duty and placed under arrest. Intemperance on the part of private physicians serving under contracts was dealt with in much the same manner: the cancellation of their contracts. The reports of drunkenness seem to have been exaggerated; the number was probably not excessive.

Praise of Confederate Medical Officers

Confederate surgeons, like the Surgeon General, received praise as well as criticism. President Davis, for example, commended the "humanity" and "professional skill" of the medical corpsmen. The Confederate Congress also recognized during the course of firsthand investigation and observation the abilities displayed by medical officers. Commanding officers in making their official reports of the battles of Manassas, Shiloh, the Seven Days, Chancellorsville, Chickamauga, Hampton Roads, and numerous others made thankful mention of the care and attention bestowed on the wounded by the medical staff. Such expressions as "untiring in their attention to the wounded," "most efficient service . . . unselfish devotion," "prompt and attentive," and "performed [their duties] with honor to their profession" were among those used by Lee, Beauregard, Longstreet, and others to describe the ministrations of Confederate medical officers during and after the heat of battle. In his official report of the battle of Chickamauga (September 19–20, 1863) Major General Patrick R. Cleburne expressed his indebtedness to Dr. D. A. Linthicum, the chief surgeon of his division, Surgeon A. R. Erskine, the division medical inspector, and Assistant Surgeon Alfred B. De Loach. The thoroughness of Surgeon Linthicum's arrangements, related Cleburne, "his careful supervision of subordinates, both on the field under fire and elsewhere, and in the hospitals, secured our gallant wounded prompt attention, and all the comfort and alleviation of pain attainable in the exigencies of battle." "Assistant Surgeon De Loach particularly distinguished himself by his unselfish devotion, going repeatedly far forward under fire and among the skirmishers to attend the wounded." And in reporting the amputation of Surgeon Gaillard's arm on the field of Fair Oaks, Major General Gustavus W. Smith added the following words of praise: "With acknowledged skill of the very highest order in his profession, he [Gaillard] has few, if any, equals as an administrative and executive medical officer." [5]

Confederate medical officers also received impressive praise from high ranking officers in their own department. In his official report following the Seven Days' Battles Lafayette Guild lauded highly "the zeal and efficiency" of the medical corps in the face of numerous difficulties. Later in the war, shortly after the battle of Chancellorsville (May 2–5, 1863), Guild boasted that his officers in the Army of Northern Virginia "as a body of professional gentlemen" would "compare favorably with any other similar organization upon this continent. . . . Their conduct on many bloody battle fields," he asserted, "has secured to them an enviable reputation, and has elicited praise from all who have witnessed their noble self sacrifice during and after a battle." One of Guild's own medical directors in that same army, Surgeon Hunter Holmes McGuire, stated that "some of the best military surgeons in the world could be found in the Confederate army." And Samuel H. Stout, who headed all the hospital organization in the Army and Department of Tennessee, was "satisfied that never before in the history of wars was there such a corps of medical men as served the Confederate soldiers." This was lavish praise indeed and must be recognized as a significant tribute despite the fact that it was given years after the war's end by one who probably recalled the wartime experiences in a more favorable light than the facts warranted.

[5] Much other favorable comment could be cited.

One of the most interesting and informative records which pertain to the evaluation of Confederate medical officers by their superiors is a confidential report made to Medical Director Stout by Surgeon Faulkner Heard Evans, the officer in charge of the La Grange, Georgia, hospitals. Evans' appraisals of his staff officers, which compare favorably with many present-day efficiency reports on military personnel, were set forth as follows:

> Surgeon James Bratton (in charge of Oliver Hospital) is an officer of fine administrative ability, has a thorough acquaintance with his profession, is full of energy & red hot with zeal in our cause. Surgeon Bratton is the best officer at the post. Surgeon Samuel Annan is full of the milk of human kindness—most too gentle for rigid discipline—he is very accomplished in his profession—shows an energy—activity & zeal for service that is surprising for his age (is nearly seventy years old). With Wilson for a steward—who controls the attendants—Surgeon Annan conducts the St Marys Hospital in a very creditable manner. . . . Surgeon Wm Benj Day is fond of his profession & by reason of it—attentive to his duties—he has no zeal for the service & I think would like to be out of it. Surgeons Ira Williams & Wm Thos Jones are commonplace officers. Both of these gentlemen have a proper appreciation of the duties of their profession & position. . . . I have been somewhat decieved in Asst Surgeon Wilkinson I find him slow & very commonplace.

Surgeon Benjamin Miller Wible at Tunnel Hill, Georgia, was more liberal in evaluating his officers: "All . . . have performed their duty—all industrious, free from drinking; good prescribers, and never neglecting their wards." In the field one Southern medical officer adverted to the courage manifested by his brother doctors, and still another enumerated nonmedical exploits of his surgeons which included, among other heroic actions, the capture of a stand of colors.

Accolades from numerous other sources were also received by the Confederate surgeon during the course of the war and after. Fannie Beers, a hospital matron during most of the war, claimed that she "never saw or heard of a more self-sacrificing set of men than the surgeons" under whom she served. As a class, she recalled, "they were devoted to their patients, and as attentive as in private practice or as the immense number of sick allowed them to be." Even the enemy could acknowledge the ability of the Southern medical officer. After an inspection of the Confederate hospitals near Gettysburg, where over five thousand wounded were being cared for by their surgeons, Dr. Gordon Winslow of the United States Sanitary Commission declared such officers to be "as a body, intelligent and attentive." More recently an able student of the history of army medicine has described the medical officers of the Confederacy as "a group of courageous men . . . skillfully treating friend and foe."

Perhaps the most important tribute of all was that which came from the fighting men themselves. There were numerous complaints of "pop-skulled" doctors, but a private in Major General George E. Pickett's division pointed out in the summer of 1864 that it was "usual to abuse doctors all over the world. . . . Complaints of hospital arrangements are consequently not infrequently unreasonable, and anathemas upon surgeons upon insufficient grounds." He then went on to say that surgeons performed their duties faithfully "and with as much sympathy as familiarity with suffering is likely to leave either with surgeon or any member of an army, where death and sickness is disrobed of its natural appeals by reason of its daily occurrence and constant existence."

Individual members of the medical corps were sometimes singled out for special praise. Surgeon Edmund Burke Haywood in Raleigh, North Carolina, was commended as being "constant, kind, and indefatigable in the discharge of his duties." An occupant of the Third Georgia Hospital in Richmond acknowledged that his surgeon treated him as kindly as would have his own parents. The death of Dr. W. J. McCain, a Texas surgeon, early in the war called forth the touching tribute by one soldier that Dr. McCain was "a good Physician, a true friend and a Christian Soldier, all that knew him, loved him." Another surgeon who received words of the highest praise was Dr. Charles T. Quintard who served the First Tennessee Regiment as both medical officer and chaplain. Concerning Quintard it was said: "During week days he ministered to us physically, and on Sundays spiritually. He was one of the purest and best men I ever knew. He would march and carry his knapsack every day the same as any soldier. . . . He was a good doctor of medicine, as well as a good doctor of divinity, and above either of these, he was a good man per se. . . . He loved the soldiers, and the soldiers loved him, and deep down in his heart of hearts was a deep and lasting love for Jesus Christ . . . implanted there by God the Father Himself." And in a completely different vein another soldier sang the praises of his surgeon as follows: "He [Dr. Coleman] is as fat as he can be a fine jolly fellow full of fun and good humor & the sight of him is enough to make a sick man feel better. We are all very much attached to him & would hate to give him up."

Matrons, ward masters, and other medical attendants also received their tributes. When, for example, Mrs. John James, a Jackson Hospital (Richmond) matron left the city her patients drafted resolutions in which they tendered their "sincere thanks for her kind, solacing care and strict attention to our comfort." The unselfish ministrations of Ella King Newsom of Arkansas, Juliet Opie Hopkins of Alabama, Fannie A. Beers of Louisiana, Louisa Susanna McCord of South Carolina, Emily V. Mason of Virginia, Mary L. Pettigrew of North Carolina, Mrs. Governor Reid of Florida, and numerous other women called forth laudatory comment of a similar nature.

Conclusion

Confederate medical officers met the demands imposed upon them as courageously and as effectively as could have been expected. Visits to hospitals other than their own for purposes of investigation, the formation of medical societies, quiz classes, and the like all would appear to indicate the presence of a desire to improve themselves professionally; and while there was much that they did not know the restrictions to which they were sometimes subjected made it impossible for them to apply what they did know. "We did not do the best we would," explained one, "but the best we could." Some of the disadvantages under which Confederate medical officers worked was set forth concisely by one of their number: "The surgeon-general issued some valuable and useful publications, but we had no 'Medical and Surgical History of the Confederate States'; we had scarcely a journal; we had no 'Army Medical Museum'; we had no men of science and leisure to produce original work, or to record, classify and arrange the rich and abundant material gathered in the departments of either medicine or surgery. . . ."

Neither, it might be added, did they have blood plasma, x-rays, antibiotics, vitamin concentrates, vaccine to prevent typhoid fever and tetanus, and other products of recent medical and surgical research considered so essential today to the military medical officer. Nor did they have in the latter part of the war—perhaps after the battle of Chickamauga—patients whose physical condition was favorably influenced by a confident mental outlook. The men became less and less sanguine as the war entered its final stages, and the surgeons' task was rendered more difficult by the ensuing mental depression.[6] Yet available records for the war years appear to indicate that the annual mortality and disease mortality rates throughout the conflict were less than those of other armies (except for those of the Union forces which were also relatively low) that took the field in the nineteenth century. Medical Director Guild advised the Surgeon General as late as February, 1864, of the physical condition of the Army of Northern Virginia in the following words: "The sanitary condition of this army is unprecedentedly good. The troops are comfortably quartered in huts or tents with chimneys attached, police regulations are strictly enforced, the supplies of

[6] It was Lieutenant General Daniel H. Hill's belief that the *élan* which had distinguished the Confederate soldier on many battlefields was conspicuous by its absence after the battle of Chickamauga.

medicines, hospital stores, & instruments are adequate for their necessities, and at no preceding time has our army exhibited so much health and vigor." At almost that same time a correspondent in Dalton, Georgia, with the Army of Tennessee wrote that the troops were "all in fine health and well disciplined."

As a group Confederate medical officers labored valiantly for the cause in which they believed; it is clearly obvious in restrospect that their contribution to the military effort was indispensable. And, after it was all over, many shared the despondency expressed more than a year after the war's end by A. J. Foard, wartime Medical Director of the Army of Tennessee: "I will never recover from the blow of blasted hopes which still hangs as a pall over my life. . . ." [7]

[7] Further proof that the Confederate Medical Department numbered among its personnel many of the ablest and most promising members of the American medical profession may be seen in the fact that almost one hundred Confederate medical officers were included in the authoritative medical biographical work, *American Medical Biographies*. This study, published in 1920 and containing 1,948 biographies, aimed to include a biography of every man who, up to that time, had "contributed to the advancement of medicine in the United States or in Canada, or who, being a physician, has become illustrious in some other field of general science or in literature."

CHAPTER XIII

Conclusion

*T*he contributions to subsequent medical development that stemmed from the war-torn Southern Confederacy should not be overlooked or minimized. First of all, a number of significant contributions was made with respect to hospitals and the treatment of patients therein. Whether or not the Confederate Surgeon General introduced the one story pavilion hospital the fact is clear that he considered it to be the best model for hospital construction, and the postwar adaptations of this type institution owed much to his influence. The remarkable mobility of certain of the general and field hospitals may be considered to have been another important contribution to the history of modern military medicine. In a very real sense Medical Director Samuel H. Stout's hospitals behind the Army of Tennessee along with the field infirmaries in the Army of Northern Virginia were forerunners of the highly mobile hospital units seen during the Second World War. The setting aside of separate wards and even entire hospitals for smallpox, eye difficulties, venereal disease, hernia, gangrene, and certain other ailments was also a forward-looking contribution made by Confederate medical officials.

Within Confederate hospitals it was discovered that good nursing was as important as proper medical attention, and the consensus of opinion, at least among the patients, appeared to be that the best nurses were women. Some women accepted full-time employment in the military hospitals despite the prevailing taboo against their doing so, and there was certainly some relationship between those self-sacrificing women and the rise of trained nursing as a profession. Women proved to be good morale builders, and it was learned that the mental outlook of the patient was a proper consideration of the hospital staff—not infrequently determining the outcome of his case.

The diet served the sick and wounded was never altogether satisfactory, but wartime records of medical personnel indicate that the latter were fully aware of their patients' needs along this line and attempted to see that the hospitalized men were served food that was both palatable and nourishing. Scrupulous cleanliness of hospitals and patients was insisted upon in directive after directive to prevent the spread of infections. Medical officers, as one recalled, "had correct ideas as to ordinary cleanliness and decency," and they acted in accordance with those ideas. Such ideas carried over into the postwar era and were advertised, along with an adequate quarantine, as the answer to the menace of yellow fever, the "scourge of American cities." In the hospitals a premium was also placed upon fresh air and ventilation in the treatment of such diseases as measles, smallpox, camp itch, and the surgical fevers. Military medical men generally came to resort less to internal medication, and even the people of the Confederacy, cut off from the source of much of their prewar medical supply, "learned that they could actually live without quack medicines; and clergymen and judges, and lawyers and postmasters, discovered that they could exist, in comparative happiness at least, without giving their characteristic testimonials in support of this abominable trash."

The skill acquired by Confederate medical officers in the realm of operative surgery became increasingly important with the advent of the Listerian era. Skillful surgeons and antisepsis, combined with anesthesia, made possible surgical triumphs that would have been thought miraculous just a few years earlier. One surgical instrument, however, the lancet, was virtually abandoned as a result of wartime experience; this in itself represented a real milestone in medical progress.

There can be no question but that the medical and surgical lessons learned by perceptive members of the Surgeon General's corps enhanced considerably the value of their services in the postwar years. "If I am spared to get home," wrote one medical officer early in the war, "I shall be a wiser, if not a better, man." Another, corresponding with his former medical chief just five months after the Confederacy's collapse, stated: "I have lost much, but I have gained much, especially as a medical man. I return home a better surgeon, a better doctor." And still another, writing several years after the war, believed that the doctor was "more practically efficient and useful, at the bedside now, than perhaps he has ever been before, and the whole country is now furnished with a medical corps which the war has thoroughly educated and reliably trained." An impoverished and broken region was in need of such men in the grim years after the war.

Many of those who served in the Confederate Medical Department received training that in part at least equipped them to assume important roles in the postwar development of medical education, and the prominence of some is attested by the fact of their election to head the American Medical Association. Dr. David W. Yandell, for example, who served in several important medical positions during the war, became professor of clinical surgery at the University of Louisville shortly thereafter, collaborated with Dr. Theophilus Parvin to establish the *American Practitioner* in 1870 and was its leading editor for many years; in 1871 he was elected president of the American Medical Association and also saw service as president of the American Surgical Association. A medical inspector on General Braxton Bragg's staff, Dr. Tobias G. Richardson was chosen dean of the medical faculty of the University of Louisiana after the war and president of the American Medical Association in 1877. Dr. Henry F. Campbell of Georgia, a cousin of Dr. Paul F. Eve, was appointed professor of anatomy and surgery in the New Orleans Medical College at the war's conclusion, helped found the American Gynecological Society in 1876, and was chosen president of the American Medical Association in 1884. The medical officer who acted as personal physician to President Jefferson Davis and family physician of Generals Robert E. Lee and Joseph E. Johnston during the war, Dr. Alexander Y. P. Garnett, returned to his chair of clinical medicine in Washington's Columbian Medical College immediately after the war, was elected president of the Southern Medical Association in 1874, and thirteen years later he was picked to lead the American Medical Association. Still another, Dr. Hunter Holmes McGuire of Virginia, after serving as professor of surgery on the staff of the Medical College of Virginia until 1878, was associated with the establishment of Richmond's College of Physicians and Surgeons—known later as the University College of Medicine—and became president of the college and professor of surgery there subsequent to his election as president of the American Medical Association in 1892.

Other former Confederates, some lesser known on the postwar stage than the above, were nonetheless active. Dr. Ferdinand E. Daniel, to cite one of the more versatile, was a founder of the Texas Medical College, the first such institution in the state of Texas, and he also established the medical journal, *Red-Back*, in 1885. He headed the reorganized Texas Medical Association in 1904, became president of the American International Congress on Tuberculosis in 1906, and was appropriately referred to as "The Father of Medicine in Texas." North Carolina's surgeon general during most of the war, Dr. Edward Warren, reorganized the Washington University Medical School in Baltimore two years after the war and served as professor of surgery in that seat of learning until 1872 when he helped found Baltimore's College of Physicians and Surgeons. For a time after Appomattox Dr. Edwin Samuel Gaillard served as professor of the principles and practice of medicine and general pathology at the Medical College of Virginia, but he later moved to Louisville and New York and is best known for his vigorous editing of the *Richmond Medical Journal*, published after 1868 under other names, and the *American Medical Weekly*. Dr. J. Julian Chisolm returned to his professorship at the Medical College of South Carolina with the war's end and soon was made dean. After a year in Europe he became professor of eye and ear surgery at the University of Maryland; he was appointed dean there also and was regarded as one of the most capable instructors ever to serve on the staff of that institution. Chisolm incidentally "was among the first to use cocaine in eye surgery and his operative treatment of cataract was well known." Dr. George S. Blackie, a wartime medical purveyor, accepted a professorship of chemistry in the Nashville Medical College and was the senior editor of *The Southern Practitioner* at the time of his death in 1881. Blackie enjoyed the reputation of "being one of the most brilliant men of his age."

It is interesting to note that two of the highest ranking medical officials of the Confederacy, Surgeon General Moore and Medical Director Stout, devoted the administrative abilities which they had acquired to the cause of public education. Moore did not engage in active medical practice after the war and served on the Richmond school board for twenty-five years. As a member of such board "he was especially active endeavoring to lift public education from the realms of politics and to establish it on the best scientific and highest moral plane." [1] Stout moved often during the postwar era and is given credit for inaugurating the movement that led to the establishment of a public school system in Atlanta and for organizing the public schools of Cisco, Texas. The standing acquired by Stout in the educational field may be illustrated by the fact that he was warmly supported by leading Texans for the post of national Commissioner of Education during the second Cleveland administration (1893–1897). Stout continued his professional career, however, and helped found the medical department of the University of Dallas. He then became dean of the faculty and at the time of his death was professor emeritus of medicine in that school.[2]

That the Confederate medical officer benefited considerably

[1] When the Association of Medical Officers of the Army and Navy of the Confederacy was organized in Atlanta on May 20, 1874, Moore was elected the first president. Dr. Hunter Holmes McGuire succeeded Moore, but after the second meeting the association became inactive. It was reorganized in 1898, and in 1900 *The Southern Practioner* became the official journal of the association.

[2] Stout died on September 18, 1903, in his eighty-second year.

from his wartime experience may also be illustrated by the later career of Dr. John Thompson Darby, a South Carolinian. Darby, one of the few to continue his work on the battlefield, accepted an appointment on the Prussian army's medical staff during the Austro-Prussian War (1866). He was highly praised for his work in organizing the Prussian hospital and ambulance corps and was reported to have rendered valuable aid at both staff and line levels. Darby later returned to the United States and eventually received an appointment as professor of surgery in the University of the City of New York.

Another postwar stage on which ex-Confederate medical officers, including some of those mentioned above, played leading parts and contributed thereby to longer and happier lives for the mass of mankind was that of public health. The stimuli responsible for the public health movement differed somewhat from state to state, but the wartime emphasis on sanitation had affected all classes. That the movement developed as rapidly as it did, however, and in a section without sufficient financial resources to launch really formidable programs was due chiefly to those doctors who while serving under the Stars and Bars had seen at first hand the salutary effects of scrupulous cleanliness in army camps and hospitals. The creation of the North Carolina Board of Health, for example, in 1877 owed much to the efforts of Dr. Thomas Fanning Wood, a Wilmington practitioner and former Confederate surgeon; Dr. S. S. Satchwell, surgeon in charge of the general hospital in Wilson during much of the war, became the first president of the North Carolina board. In another sector of the former Confederacy Dr. Joseph Jones was appointed president of the Louisiana state board of public health.[3] And Dr. Lafayette Guild fought yellow fever as quarantine inspector for the port of Mobile until his premature death in 1870.

Southern champions of public health carried their fight into

[3] Dr. Jones also became the first secretary of the Southern Historical Society, founded in New Orleans in May, 1869, and framed the Society's original constitution. In 1887 he was elected president of the Louisiana State Medical Society; in 1890 he became Surgeon-General of the United Confederate Veterans.

the national arena. Dr. T. G. Richardson devoted the major portion of his presidential address before the American Medical Association in 1878 to the need for state boards and urged his listeners to work for them in those states where they did not exist. The association's president for 1885, Dr. Henry F. Campbell, was also a staunch supporter of the public health movement and had himself served on the board for the state of Georgia. One of the most forward-looking positions of all was that taken by Dr. Hunter Holmes McGuire in his presidential message of 1893 when he recommended the establishment of a national department of health. The humanitarian concern felt by these outstanding medical leaders stands as a priceless heritage bequeathed by them to all future members of that noble profession.

The experimentation of both Confederate and Union armies with a decentralized supply system worked out well enough to establish once and for all the superiority of such a system over one wherein all supplies were sent out from a single depot. Also in the area of supply a most significant influence was exerted by the private soldiers' aid and hospital relief societies. It is impossible to evaluate accurately the valuable assistance rendered by these societies, but in a very real sense they were worthy forerunners of the American Red Cross and other such organizations that have since come to play such important roles in American life.

Finally, it became clear to the medical staff during the war that dentists possessed skills of a professional nature badly needed by the fighting men. Consequently, thousands of the latter benefited greatly from dental services received from practitioners assigned to key points throughout the Confederacy. And there can be no denying that the significant postwar development of American dentistry owed much to this official recognition accorded the dental profession by the Confederate Medical Department.

APPENDIX I

The wartime appropriations to the Army Medical Department were made as follows:

1861

Medical and hospital departments	$	75,000
Medical and hospital supplies		350,000
Surgical and medical supplies		250,000
Establishment and support of military hospitals		50,000
Pay of contract physicians		50,000
Pay of cooks and nurses		130,000
	$	905,000

1862

Medical and hospital supplies	$	2,300,000
Surgical and medical supplies		2,520,000
Establishment and support of military hospitals		97,000
Pay of contract physicians		110,000
Pay of cooks and nurses		96,000
Pay of hospital stewards		12,000
Pay of hospital laundresses		10,000
	$	5,145,000

1863

Medical and hospital supplies	$11,000,000
Establishment and support of military hospitals	300,000
Hospital clothing	625,000
Alcoholic stimulants	604,800
Pay of contract physicians	400,000
Pay of cooks and nurses	490,000
Pay of hospital stewards	135,000
Pay of hospital laundresses	125,000
Pay of matrons, assistant matrons, and ward matrons	490,000
Pay of ward masters	310,000
	$14,479,800

1864

Medical and hospital supplies	$30,240,000
Establishment and support of military hospitals	350,000
Pay of contract physicians	450,000
Pay of cooks and nurses	700,000
Pay of hospital stewards	200,000
Pay of hospital laundresses	300,000
Pay of matrons, assistant matrons, and ward matrons ..	700,000
Pay of ward masters	200,000
	$33,140,000

1865

Medical and hospital supplies	$14,300,000
Establishment and support of military hospitals	100,000
Hospital clothing	500,000
Alcoholic stimulants	4,000,000
Pay of contract physicians	250,000
Pay of cooks and nurses	350,000
Pay of hospital stewards	100,000
Pay of hospital laundresses	150,000
Pay of matrons, assistant matrons, and ward matrons ..	350,000
Pay of ward masters	200,000
	$20,300,000

The medical appropriations for the Navy's medical services were made as follows:

1861	$ 20,000
1862	61,500
1863	250,000
1864	1,010,000
1865	375,000
	$ 1,716,500

The appropriation figures set forth above were extracted from the various appropriation bills of the Confederate Congresses as set forth in the works edited by J. M. Matthews and C. W. Ramsdell. There is one other figure which might be noted. An act approved on August 21, 1861, provided an appropriation of $57,000,000 to be used for the payment of troops, quartermaster supplies, ordnance supplies, engineering, and surgical and medical expenditures. It is not known how much of this was distributed to the medical service. Matthews (ed.), *Statutes at Large*, 187. The total expenditures of the United States Army Medical Department, from June 30, 1861, to June 30, 1866, exclusive of salaries to medical officers, reached the sum of $47,351,982.24. Brown, *The Medical Department of the United States Army from 1775 to 1873*, 246.

APPENDIX II

Statistical Reports of Hospitals in Department of Virginia

(From the War Department Collection of Confederate Records, the National Archives, Chap. VI, Vol. 151.)

1862–1864

Month	Remaining	Admitted	Aggregate	Transferred
September, 1862	13,595	15,421	29,016	2,196
October	12,747	21,447	34,194	10,237
November	11,869	16,593	28,462	8,682
December	10,541	18,409	28,950	10,290
January, 1863	18,876	12,694	31,570	6,612
February	10,603	8,159	18,762	4,983
March	13,102	11,051	24,153	2,055
April	9,914	10,870	20,784	4,473
May	9,571	32,112	41,683	15,965
June	15,826	23,217	39,043	11,480
July	16,315	32,052	48,367	17,187
August	15,158	17,383	32,541	7,940
September	11,175	14,106	25,281	6,498
October	7,841	14,101	21,942	5,876
November	8,408	14,638	23,046	6,038
December	9,861	10,039	19,900	4,000
January, 1864	7,913	10,658	18,571	4,094
February	6,352	7,144	13,496	1,862
March	5,911	9,303	15,214	2,637
April	5,006	10,992	15,998	5,613
May	5,176	48,140	53,316	23,775
June	19,882	36,430	56,312	20,189
July	18,679	17,999	36,678	6,697

Statistical Reports of Hospitals in Department of Virginia

1862–1864

Month	Returned to Duty	On Furlough	Discharged	Deserted	Died
September, 1862	7,104	3,188	1,550	139	620
October	5,317	5,345	527	453	392
November	5,401	3,205	271	235	484
December	5,076	1,459	194	291	1,027
January, 1863	7,321	1,206	238	465	1,336
February	3,907	774	153	155	534
March	6,329	1,050	312	180	719
April	4,678	951	247	296	694
May	6,982	1,356	48	353	890
June	6,748	3,030	71	279	692
July	10,067	3,954	151	420	429
August	9,057	3,185	133	447	379
September	6,439	3,763	101	274	204
October	4,207	2,724	72	146	306
November	3,984	2,435	93	111	576
December	4,289	1,842	168	123	730
January, 1864	5,383	1,497	50	201	713
February	3,622	904	54	151	830
March	4,927	1,143	51	348	848
April	3,558	953	61	93	410
May	4,760	3,602	50	175	1,051
June	7,882	6,556	27	284	1,836
July	6,445	6,384	45	276	1,360

Reports Concerning the Battle of Chickamauga

The following reports by medical personnel throw considerable light on the activities of Medical Director Samuel H. Stout and his officers before, during and after the battle of Chickamauga (September 19–20, 1863). All may be found in the Stout Papers. The first is a copy of Stout's report to Surgeon General Samuel P. Moore from Marietta, Georgia, and dated October 10, 1863. It reads in part as follows:

"Prior to the battle I had as you are aware removed the hospitals from Chattanooga, Ringgold, Cleaveland, Catoosa Springs, Tunnel Hill and Dalton. I had reopened some of them at Adairsville and Calhoun, while our Army was pursuing the enemy in the direction of Rome. I found it impossible to provision the hospitals at Adairsville and Calhoun, and removed them again.

"Prior to the recent movements of the hospitals, I had no hospital south of Atlanta.

"I reopened some of the hospitals at Cassville on the W. & Atlantic R. R. The hospitals formerly located at Chattanooga were reopened at this place, excepting the Direction Hospital.

"I reopened the Ringgold Hospitals at Newnan, and the Dalton Hospitals at LaGrange, excepting the Stout Hospital which is now in Marietta.

"At Griffin I reopened Catoosa Springs Hospt. . . .

"At Forsyth I reopened with extended accommodations the Tunnel Hill Hospitals. At Atlanta a new hospital was opened.

"After the battle it became necessary to open hospitals at Dalton & Ringgold for the reception and shipment of patients.

"The battle was fought 8 miles west of Ringgold, which is on the R. R. north of some of the burnt bridges. Many of the wounded were sent to Dalton about 14 miles distant, and to Tunnel Hill about 12 ms for the first three days after the battle whence they were put upon the cars and sent to hospital. Afterwards, for about ten days, they were sent to the Woodstation south of Catoosa Platform near the most southern crossing of the Chickamauga river, while the bridges between that point and Ringgold were being rebuilt. This station is about nine miles from the battlefield.

"For a few days before and after the battle I was unable to hold any communication with the Medical Director of the Army Surg E. A. Flewellen, and learning that the wounded had been brought to the Wood station in large numbers, and were without food, I immediately with some medical officers and a corps of thirty hospital attendants, with provisions & such cooking utensils as could be spared from the hospitals at this place repaired to the station and improvised such an organization as secured the dressing of the wounds, the administration of necessary medicines to the patients and a supply of foods. As rapidly as the cars could be obtained the wounded were sent to the rear. The citizens having formed associations came opportunely to my relief and besides doing much good service, fed the patients well. And although the intense anxiety for fear the weather would prove bad while hundreds were lying on the ground unprotected was distressing, yet the sky remained clear and the temperature of the atmosphere pleasant during the whole time, we were at the Wood station. Our fears were not realized, and, when the bridges were completed so that the cars could run to Ringgold, a hospital for the reception of the wounded was immediately opened where now they are well provided for, and whence they are sent to hospitals in the rear.

"Some, probably about 500 of the worst cases are still in the infirmaries on the battle-field. These are now being cautiously removed to Ringgold for shipment.

"Soon after the battle Surg. Flewellen Med. Dir. of the Army called upon me for Med officers and I ordered thirteen of the Surgeons and Asst Surgeons on duty in hospital to report to him in the field. To supply their places as well as the increased demand for surgeons I have made contracts with and accepted the volunteered services of private physicians. The question naturally arises how were the large number of sick and wounded so suddenly thrown upon my hands provided for in the hospitals under my control with a capacity of only about 7500 beds.—1st Many were sent out of this department, to Montgomery, Columbus and Augusta. 2nd Private families living convenient to hospitals were permitted to take many of them. 3rd, Those whose wounds did not require skillful surgical treatment but who would be disabled for more than thirty days were furloughed. 4th Every slightly wounded man who would not be injured by remaining in camp, or who could perform any kind of light duty were immediately sent to the convalescent camps, which exist at almost any post in my department. 5th Malingerers and *old 'hospital rats'* were summarily dealt with and promptly turned over to post commandants to be returned to their commands.

"I regret very much that as yet I have not been able to make a report of the precise number of wounded we have disposed of. The treatment of the wounded now in the hospital is absorbing the attention of the med officers to such an extent, that they have been unable to make their reports promptly. With few exceptions the med. officers have acted nobly, in the discharge of their arduous duties.

"I am rejoiced too to say that it is a subject of almost universal remark, that the wounded in hospital are doing well, comparatively few deaths having occurred.

"In a professional point of view a fine field for observation is now

280

being presented, and I have been urging the surgeons to be careful to note their cases in order that their experience may be made available hereafter. The zeal and professional pride in my opinion will cause many of the surgeons in my department to make more carefully prepared reports than heretofore.

"I am of the opinion, that the length of time which elapsed between the receipt of the wounds and the arrival of the patients in hospital had been advantageous to them. The weather was fair, the nights not very cold, during this time.

"I have as yet heard of no case of erysipelas which originated in hospital. Several cases came from the battlefield.

"Much care and industry is being used to avoid it by keeping the patient, his clothing, bedding and ward clean and the latter properly ventilated. Isolation will be resorted to immediately upon the occurrence of erysipelas or gangrene.

"In consideration of the great increase of the Army in numbers, and the probability of another battle soon, I am using every effort to extend my hospital accommodations at every post where hospitals now exist under my jurisdiction.

"I telegraphed you for medical officers, preferring as much as possible to have the service of experienced army officers to those of such private physicans as I can pick up at this period of the war. To this telegram I received no reply. Two Asst Surgeons were ordered to report to me at Macon. These I ordered to report to Surg J. M. Green in charge of hospitals at that post. Nearly all the patients in hospital at Macon belong to Genl. Bragg's army and though Macon is not in my department I thought it right though irregular to order them to that post at least temporarily.

"Should the movements of the armies necessitate the with-drawal of the hospitals from Rome, Kingston, and Cassville I am at a loss to know where to locate them. Already by consent of Genl. Beauregard I have located hospitals in his department at Griffin and Forsyth.—In the event of a reverse of our armies even Marietta will have to be abandoned as a hospital post.

"My authority to open and control hospitals should be extended so as to embrace the towns on the following lines of R. R. viz: the Macon? & Western, the R. R. from Macon to Columbus, that from West Point to Montgomery Ala and the Georgia R. R. extending from Atlanta to Augusta.

"I have this day prepared a formal official paper on the subject of the extension of my jurisdiction to which you are respectfully referred. The Atlanta and West Point R. R. is the only line south of Atlanta belonging to Genl. Bragg's Department, and that is a boundary.

"My chief difficulties in opening, closing & removing hospitals grow out of the want of prompt, active and zealous cooperation on the part of the Q. Masters and Subsistence departments. When hospitals are removed, it is often the case that they are for weeks without aid from these departments. The ingenuity and resources of the surgeons are taxed

281

largely in supplying their wants. Considering amount of work done by them recently and the good condition of the hospitals, much credit is due to the indefatigable energy of the medical department, which with all its deficiencies can justly claim to be under better discipline and better organized than any of the staff departments of this army."

Stout

The second report was made by Assistant Surgeon Frank M. Dennis, one of the officers in charge of the ambulance trains, on October 22, 1863. Reported Dennis:

"The worst cases were placed on bunks, the others occupied seats in the passenger cars. Some 200 could be accommodated on the day trains— well supplied with water. The mail trains which only run at night were taken possession of and no one allowed to go in them except the wounded. There were no bunks in this train, but those able to sit-up were comfortably situated in passenger cars. Water was also furnished plentifully on these trains. They would accommodate two hundred and fifty men each. By these trains we could not transport over the road owing to its length more than five hundred men per day, while there were from twelve to fifteen hundred to be transported daily. Consequently those who could not be brought on these trains already mentioned, had to be gotten off on the trains that were employed in transporting troops from Atlanta to the front, as we could catch them. . . . These trains ran irregularly and frequently off of schedule time . . . but this was our only chance to get off the large number of wounded collecting at the end of the road.

". . . I consider that there was no undue suffering of the wounded which could have been avoided. There may have been a want of water on some of the irregular trains. . . . If there was a lack of anything it must have been on the part of the Q Mrs. in not furnishing ambulances & waggons to haul the men to the road. Although there may have been some who were wounded two or three days before they were brought to the road, there was no delay after they had been placed in charge of the train Surgeons. . . . No wounded were compelled to lie longer than one night at the end of the road, and they were comparatively well provided for, there being a large wood shed under which had been arranged beds of straw by a detail carried to the front by the Med Dir. of Hospitals, for them. And there were cooks engaged in preparing food for them day and night. They could not have suffered from water, there being both a well and a large creek within twenty paces of the shed. We had supplies which had been sent to the front by order of the Med Dir of Hospitals, besides the large quantity of bandages, cordials and liquors sent there by the Ga. Relief Association. There were also several other Committees from different places attending assiduously to the wants of our noble wounded. Wrecks between Tunnel Hill and Dalton and south of Cartersville delayed the movement but did not cause suffering. [There were no wrecks of trains carrying wounded.] You know that the wounded had to be hauled from ten to twenty-five miles from the Battle field to the Rail Road. It was exceedingly hot and dusty, that is in my opinion the only time that the wounded suffered more than they would have. . . ."

The final report was also made by one of the ambulance officials, Assistant Surgeon Wiley M. Baird, on October 22, 1863. According to this officer

". . . All the wounded who were able, to bear transportation were immediately, transported from the temporary Hospitals established at the different depots, on the W. & A. R R within the immediate vicinity of the battle field, with all the dispatch possible and every attention, was given them while en route to Hospls in the rear. This was easily done; there was at the time a well organized and disciplined corps of train Surgeons, in charge of the ambulance trains placed there some of them for the special occasion. . . . The frequent visits of the Medl Dir of Hospls to the front during the battle, brought the whole under his immediate observation. . . . The only serious disadvantage under which the train Surgeons labored in securing the prompt transportation of the wounded to the rear, was the daily transportation of troop over the road. I am happy to state, however that the difficulty in question was successfully overcome, by the immediate supervision of the Medl Dir of Hospls, and by the industry attention & perseverance of those acting under his *orders*."

GENERAL APPENDIX

(*From* Confederate States Medical and Surgical Journal, *September and October, 1864*)

Surgeon-General and Medical Officers on Duty in His Office

S. P. Moore .... Surgeon-General C.S. Army
C. H. Smith .... Surgeon C.S. Army
Thos. H. Williams .... " " "
F. Sorrel .... " " "
Chas. Brewer .... " P.A.C.S.
Herman Baer .... " "

Medical Directors in the Field

Surgeon L. Guild .... Army Northern Virginia
" H. McGuire .... Ewell's Corps, Army Northern Va.
" J. S. D. Cullen ...... Longstreet's Corps, " "
" J. W. Powell .... Hill's " " "
" J. B. Fontaine .... Cavalry " " "
" John A. Hunter ..... Breckinridge's Command
" R. L. Brodie .... Beauregard's "
" T. L. Ozier, temp. .... Charleston, S.C.
" A. J. Foard .... Army of Tennessee
" J. H. Erskine .... Hindman's Corps, Army of Tennessee
" A. L. Breysacker .... Hardee's " " " "
" P. B. Scott .... Meridian, Miss.
" F. A. Stanford ...... Wheeler's Cavalry Corps
" J. F. Heustis .... Mobile, Ala.
" John M. Haden ...... Marshall, Texas
" J. H. Berrien .... Houston, "
" J. T. Darby .... Stewart's Corps (Late Polk's)
" Will Jennings .... Morgan's Command

Medical Directors of Hospitals

Surgeon W. A. Carrington .... Richmond, Va.
" F. A. Ramsey .... Bristol, Tenn.
" P. E. Hines .... Raleigh, N.C.
" N. S. Crowell .... Charleston, S.C.
" S. H. Stout .... Macon, Ga.
" S. A. Smith .... Alexandria, La.
" J. F. Heustis .... Mobile, Ala.
" P. B. Scott .... Meridian, Miss.

Medical Inspectors in the Field

Surgeon W. D. Tucker .... Department of Ala., Miss. and La.
" Samuel Choppin ..... " " N.C. and South. Va.
" R. J. Breckinridge ... " " Army Northern Va.
" J. W. Breedlove ..... Western Virginia
" E. N. Covey .... Va., Tenn. and Ga., and Superintend't
of Vaccination of Armies in these
States
" W. W. Anderson .... N.C., S.C., Ala., Fla., La. and Miss., and
Superintendent of Vaccination of Ar-
mies in these States

Medical Inspectors of Hospitals

Surgeon T. C. Madison .... Petersburg, Va.
" F. Sorrel .... Richmond, "
" E. S. Gaillard .... Box 1150 Richmond, Va.
" R. A. Kinloch .... Charleston, S.C.
" W. M. Brown .... Morton, Miss.
" E. A. Flewellen ..... Army of Tennessee
" J. H. Morton .... Abingdon, Va.

Army Medical Boards

Surgeon A. N. Talley	...... President of Board	....	Richmond, Va.
" E. Geddings	...... "	"	.... Charleston, S.C.
" W. M. Brown	..... "	"	.... Gen. Hood's Head-quarters
" J. J. Gaenslen	.... "	"	.... Gen. E. K. Smith's Headquarters
" _____ Hooper	.... "	"	.... Trans-Miss. Department

Principal Hospitals in the Confederate States

Virginia

Hospital	Location	Medical Officer
Chimborazo	Richmond	Surgeon J. B. McCaw
Camp Jackson	"	" F. W. Hancock
Camp Winder	"	" A. G. Lane
Camp Lee	"	" W. P. Palmer
Howard's Grove ...	"	" T. M. Palmer
Stuart	"	" R. A. Lewis
Louisiana	"	" W. C. Nichol
General, No. 9	"	" J. J. Gravatt
" " 13	"	" H. T. Barton
" " 21	"	" G. W. Semple
" " 24	"	" O. F. Manson
"	Liberty	" B. Blackford
"	Huguenot Springs	" W. T. Walker
"	Gordonsville	" B. M. Lebby
" No. 1	Lynchburg	" G. W. Thornhill
" No. 2	"	" W. C. N. Randolph
" " 3	"	" T. H. Fisher
Ladies' Relief	"	" W. C. Warren
Pratt	"	" J. H. Murray
Way	"	" A. C. Smith
General	Farmville	" H. D. Taliaferro
"	Danville	" J. F. Fauntleroy
"	Staunton	" A. M. Fauntleroy
Confederate States .	Petersburg	
General	"	
South Carolina	"	" F. Pyre Porcher

286

Hospital	Location	Medical Officer
Poplar Lawn	Petersburg	Surgeon R. P. Page
Wayside	"	" M. P. Scott
Small Pox	"	C. F. Conch, Acting Asst. Surg.
North Carolina	"	Surgeon J. G. Brodnax
Virginia	"	" J. H. Pottenger
General	Pearisburg	" T. Creigh
"	Charlottesville ...	" J. L. Cabell
"	Montgomery Sp'gs	" J. L. Woodville
"	Emory	" J. B. Murfree
"	Harrisonburg	" A. R. Meem
Washington	Abingdon	" H. A. Blair
Wayside	Burkesville	Dr. T. R. Blandy
Breckinridge	Marion	Surgeon R. D. Hamilton

North Carolina

Hospital	Location	Medical Officer
Way, No. 5	Wilmington	Surgeon J. C. Walker
General, No. 4	"	" T. R. Micks
" " 5	"	" H. J. Macon
Way, No. 7	Tarboro	Dr. J. H. Baker
" " 1	Weldon	Surgeon H. H. Hunter
" " 6	Charlotte	" J. W. Ashby
General, No. 11	"	" " "
Gen. Military No. 2	Wilson	" S. S. Satchwell
Way	Goldsboro	Dr. L. A. Stith
General, No. 3	"	" W. A. Holt
General, No. 7	Raleigh	Surgeon E. B. Haywood
" " 8	"	" H. G. Leigh
Pettigrew	"	" E. B. Haywood
Sorrel	Asheville	" W. L. Hilliard
General, No. 9	Salisbury	Asst. Surgeon J. M. Fauntleroy
" " 10	"	Surgeon J. W. Hall
Way, No. 3	"	" J. W. Hall
General, No. 6	Fayetteville	" B. F. Fessenden
General, No. 1	Kettrell Springs .	" H. F. Butt
" " 12	Greensboro	" W. H. Moore
Way, No. 2	"	" E. B. Holland

South Carolina

Hospital	Location	Medical Officer
Ladies' Genl No. 3 .	Columbia	Surgeon R. H. Edmonds
General, No. 1	"	" W. C. Horlbeck
Second N. Carolina	"	" A. W. Thomson
Way	Kingsville	" J. A. Pleasants
Third N. Carolina .	Charleston	" T. B. Memminger
First S. Carolina ..	"	" G. R. C. Todd

Hospital	Location	Medical Officer
First Louisiana ...	Charleston	Surgeon R. Lebby
General	Georgetown	" B. C. Fishburne
First Georgia	Charleston	" N. H. Cumming
Soldiers' Relief	"	" W. H. Huger
Way	Florence	" T. A. Dargan
"	Greenville	" G. S. Trezevant

Georgia

Hospital	Location	Medical Officer
Erwin	Barnesville	Surgeon J. A. Groves
Way	Fort Gaines	" E. W. McCreery
General, No. 1	Savannah	" W. G. Bulloch
" " 2	"	" W. R. Waring
General	Columbus	" J. S. White
Third Georgia	Augusta	" J. F. McGeddings
Hardee	Forsyth	" Wm. Webb
Clayton	"	" Jno. Patterson
General	Guyton	" W. S. Lawton
Lumpkin	Covington	" E. McDonald
Asylum	Madison	" H. C. Clayton
Kingston	Kingston	" G. W. McDade
Polk	Atlanta	" R. Battey
Bragg	Newnan	" J. Gore
Foard	"	" J. N. Hughes
Buckner	"	" W. T. McAllister
Cannon	La Grange	" L. W. Tuttle
St. Mary's	"	" J. M. Henson
Law	"	" A. Erskine
Oliver	"	" J. Williams
Hood	Covington	" D. H. Morrison
Dawson	Greensboro	" J. D. Smith
Gilmer	Marietta	" P. H. Otey
Academy	"	" F. Hawthorn
Foard	"	" J. B. Barnett
Bell	Greensboro	" H. V. Miller
Blackie	Madison	" J. T. McLaw
Prin	Griffin	" L. C. Pyncham
Director	"	" R. M. Lytle
Quintard	"	Asst. Surgeon S. V. D. Hill
Stout	Madison	Surgeon J. W. Glenn
Newsom	Thomaston	" A. Hunter
Fair Ground, No. 1 .	near Macon	" G. G. Crawford
" " " 2 .	"	" H. W. Brown
Empire	"	" W. P. Harden
Grant	"	" J. C. Mullins
Institute	"	" D. C. O'Keefe
Hill	Covington	" W. H. Robertson
Ocmulgee	Macon	" S. E. Chaillé
City Hall	"	" L. L. Saunders

Hospital	Location	Medical Officer
Blind School	Macon	Surgeon Geo. F. Cooper
Floyd House	"	" E. J. Roach
Catoosa	Griffin	" C. L. Herbert
Medical College	near Macon	" W. F. Westmoreland
First Florida	Fort Gaines	" J. F. McF. Gaston
Reid	West Point	" J. W. Oslin
Gamble	Newnan	" K. C. Divine
Marshall	Columbus	" T. A. Means
Stout	Macon	" I. Parker
Lee	Columbus	" W. A. Robertson

Alabama

Nott	Mobile	Surgeon G. A. Nott
General	"	" W. C. Cavanaugh
"	Greenville	Asst. Surgeon R. B. Maury
Way	Demopolis	Surgeon H. Hinckley
General	Tuscaloosa	" R. N. Anderson
"	Selma	" A. Hart
Way	Talladega	" G. S. Bryant
General	Spring Hill	" G. Owen
" (Ross)	Mobile	" S. L. Nidelet
Way	Selma	" W. Curry
Ladies	Montgomery	" T. F. Duncan
Stonewall	"	" W. M. Cole
Way	Eufaula	" P. D. L. Baker
General	Mobile	" W. Henderson
"	"	" R. H. Redwood
Madison House	Montgomery	" C. J. Clark
Texas	Auburn	Asst. Surgeon L. A. Bryan
St. Mary's	Montgomery	Surgeon J. H. Watters
General	Notasulga	" U. R. Jones
Concert Hall	Montgomery	" W. J. Holt
Watts	"	" F. M. Hereford
Officers'	Uniontown	" G. C. Gray
General	Shelby Springs	" B. H. Thomas

Mississippi

General	Grenada	Surgeon J. L. Thompson
Way	Guntown	" J. M. Hoyle
	Liberty	" R. M. Luckett

Hospital	Location	Medical Officer

Florida

Hospital	Location	Medical Officer
General	Quincy	Surgeon J. H. Thompson
"	Tallahassee	" E. Geddings
"	Lake City	" J. S. Morel
Way	Madison	Asst. Surgeon J. Cohen

Tennessee

Hospital	Location	Medical Officer
General	Bristol	Surgeon R. D. Hamilton
Hood	"	Asst. Surgeon J. T. Love

BIBLIOGRAPHY

I. *Manuscripts*

OFFICIAL PAPERS

My basic sources for this work have been manuscripts of an official nature. After the war many records of the former Confederate States Government, most of which pertained to the War Department and the Army, were obtained by the United States and eventually, after considerable wandering, found a permanent home in the National Archives. Known as the War Department Collection of Confederate Records, these important papers include a number of manuscripts, located chiefly in Chapter VI of the collection, that bear directly on the functioning of the Confederate Medical Department. Unless otherwise noted the volumes from this depository mentioned below are in Chapter VI.

Most valuable of the Confederate medical materials in the National Archives are the Letters, Orders, and Circulars Sent, Surgeon General's Office, 1861–1865 (Vols. 739, 740, and 741); this item comprises original communications, orders, and circulars sent by Surgeon General Samuel P. Moore to medical directors, purveyors, and others. Copies of the correspondence of other high ranking medical officers along with added data may be found in the following: Letters, Orders, and Circulars Sent and Received, Medical Director, Army of Tennessee, 1863–1865 (Vol. 748); Letters Sent by Surgeon Thomas H. Williams, Medical Director, Army of the Potomac, September 30, 1861, to January 13, 1862 (Vol. 367); Letters Received by Surgeon Thomas H. Williams, Inspector of Various Hospitals in Virginia, 1862 (Vol. 369); Letters Sent, Medical Director's Office, Army of the Potomac, January–May, 1862 (Vol. 460); Letters Sent, Medical Director's Office, Army of Northern Virginia, 1862–1865 (Vols. 641–642); and Letters Sent and Received, Medical Director's Office, Richmond, Virginia, 1864–1865 (Vol. 364). There are also important manuscript records of medical purveyors that throw light on the medical service's supply activity. One of these, Invoices of Hospital and Medical Supplies Issued, Medical Purveyor's Depot, Macon, Georgia, 1863–1865 (Vols. 570, 578, and 579), was neatly and carefully maintained by Surgeon William H. Prioleau and is quite useful. Another, described as Letters, Telegrams, Orders, and Circulars Received, Medical Purveyor's Office, Savannah and Macon, Georgia, 1862–1865 (Vols. 6, 135, 566, and 628), contains in part original communications received at this key depot. Other records concerning the supply function found helpful include the following: Amount of Whiskey and Alcohol Received, Medical Purveyor's Office, Macon, Georgia, Depot, 1865 (Vol. 626); Inventories of Packages Shipped and Medicines on Hand, Medical Purveyor's Office, Macon, Georgia, Depot, 1862–1864 (Vol. 565); Letters Sent, Medical Purveyor's Office, Macon and Savannah, Georgia, Depot, 1862–1864 (Vols. 136, 572, 573, and 627); Record of Requisitions for Hospital Supplies Made on the Medical Purveyor's Office, Macon, Georgia, Depot, 1862–1865 (Vols. 567, 569, 571, 574, and 575); Accounts of Medical and Hospital Supplies Issued, Medical Purveyor's Office, Richmond, Virginia, 1862–1865 (Vol. 577); Accounts of Medical and Hospital Supplies Purchased, Western Department, 1861–1862 (Vols. 611 and 613); Record of Supplies Furnished, Medical Purveyor's Office, Western Department, 1862–1863 (Vol. 636); Letters Sent, Medical Purveyor's Office, Western Department, 1863–1865 (Vol. 629); and Cash and Supply Accounts, General Hospital No. 9, Richmond, Virginia, 1862–1863 (Vol. 388). Many of the requisitions and warrants for funds necessary to buy needed supplies may be found in Requisitions of the Navy Department on the Treasury Department for Funds, April, 1861–September, 1863 (Chap. X, Vols. 245 and 246) and Requisitions of the War Department on the Treasury Department for Funds (Chap. X, Vols. 225–244—covering the period from March, 1861, to June, 1864).

Numerous official registers and reports in the National Archives were also revealing. Kept by the Confederate Adjutant and Inspector General's Office was the Register of Enlisted Men of the Invalid Corps, 1864–1865 (Chap. I, Vol. 193) and the Register of Officers of the Invalid Corps, 1864–1865 (Chap. I, Vol. 192). The Register of Furloughs, Medical Director's Office, Richmond, Virginia, 1864 (Vol. 177) contains the names of men furloughed from six Richmond hospitals during the latter part of 1864. A similar register also exists for the year 1863 (Vol. 465). The Register of Patients, First Mississippi Hospital, Jackson, Mississippi, 1863–1865 (Vol. 298) is well-kept as is the Register of Patients, Post Hospital, Dalton, Georgia, July 29, 1862, to January 30, 1863 (Vol. 292). Included among the other hospital registers is the Register of Patients (Union), General Hospital No. 21, Richmond, Virginia, 1864–1865 (Vols. 161, 236, and 254, the last being a duplicate of the first), the Register of Patients and Lists of Employees, Smallpox Hospital, Richmond, Virginia, 1862–1864 (Vol. 247), an incomplete record, and the Register of Patients, Ross Hospital, Mobile, Alabama, September 1, 1863, to April 12, 1865 (Vol. 2). Much pertinent data concerning a large hospital is set forth in Reports of Officers of the Day, Jackson Hospital, Richmond, Virginia, 1863–1865 (Vols. 373 and 373½). One of the best sources for operative surgery is Reports of Resection Cases in Confederate Hospitals, 1862–1864 (Vol. 764), extending over 172 pages. The item Reports of Surgical Cases, Confederate States Hospital, Petersburg, Virginia, 1863–1865 (Vol. 272½) consists of monthly reports forwarded by Dr. W. L. Baylor, former Confederate surgeon, to the Surgeon General of the United States after the war. Rather brief and somewhat incomplete accounts of surgical treatment may also be seen in Reports of Surgical Cases, General Hospitals No. 7 and 13, Raleigh, North Carolina, 1863–1865 (Vol. 526); Case Book of Wounded, Pettigrew Hospital (General Hospital No. 13), Raleigh, North Carolina, 1864–1865 (Vol. 287); and Reports on Surgical Cases, General Hospital, Farmville, Virginia, 1864 (Vol. 520). Of all reports used one of the most enlightening was the Statistical Reports of Hospitals in the Department of Virginia, Medical Director's Office, Richmond, Virginia, 1862–1864 (Vol. 151); it lists the aggregate sick each month, and sets forth much data concerning transfers, desertions, deaths, discharges, the closing of hospitals, and other such information.

Illustrative of other materials in the National Archives

that contribute to a better understanding of the Confederate medical story are the following: Diet Book, General Hospital No. 9, Richmond, Virginia, 1864 (Vol. 338); Diet Book, Ross General Hospital, Mobile, Alabama, 1863–1865 (Vols. 592 and 139); Letters Received and Sent, Chimborazo Hospital, Richmond, Virginia, 1861–1865 (Vols. 707, 708, and 709), consisting chiefly of the original letters received; Letters Received and Sent, Medical Examining Board, General Hospitals No. 4 and 5, Wilmington, North Carolina, 1864–1865 (Vol. 403); List of Detailed Men, Chimborazo Hospital Nos. 1–5, Richmond, Virginia, 1861–1864 (Vol. 98), a muster and pay roll of hospital employees; Morning Reports of Patients (Union), Belle Isle Hospital, Richmond, Virginia, 1864 (Vol. 255), primarily a record of daily sick calls; Prescription Book, General Hospital No. 21, Richmond, Virginia, 1864 (Vol. 160), the value of which is less than it should be since it was poorly maintained; Record Book, Soldiers Home Hospital and Association for the Relief of Maimed Soldiers, Richmond, Virginia, 1862–1865 (Vol. 463), a hospital register extending from April 1, 1862, to February 2, 1863, and the correspondence for the only Confederacy-wide relief organization from January, 1864, to February, 1865; Record of Vaccinations, Chimborazo Hospital No. 5, Richmond, Virginia, 1863–1865 (Vol. 319), somewhat incomplete; and Regulations, Ocmulgee Hospital, Macon, Georgia, 1865 (Vol. 759).

The Confederate Museum, Richmond, Virginia, has acquired possession of quite a few manuscripts concerning the medical service of the Southern Confederacy, and some of the more important items should be mentioned. Included in the Mrs. Marea G. Clopton Papers is the register, a prescription and diet book, and a few other records pertaining to the small Clopton Hospital in Richmond, an institution that was open only a short time. Numerous morning and monthly reports of sick and wounded soldiers in the Valley of Virginia may be seen in the Hunter Holmes McGuire Papers. One folder of the Aristides Monteiro Papers contains papers that pertain to his duties as an assistant surgeon, and another holds forty-one letters written to Monteiro after the war by ex-Colonel John S. Mosby, in whose command Monteiro saw service. The J. S. Tanner Papers have to do mainly with medical matters of a routine nature in Hoke's Division, Army of Northern Virginia, of which Tanner was the chief surgeon. Some of the valuable papers of Samuel H. Stout, Medical Director of the General Hospitals of the Army and Department of Tennessee, have also been obtained recently. Among other manuscripts which relate much statistical data is the List of Sick and Wounded Allowed to Remain in Private Quarters and Furloughed, 1863, kept for the information of the medical director of Virginia's general hospitals; included also is an order and letter section. There is also the Medical Director's Consolidated Report of the Sick and Wounded of the Army in Hospitals out of Richmond in Virginia and North Carolina for the month of February, 1863, which embraces forty-one hospitals. On a smaller scale is the Medical Record of the Twenty-first North Carolina Regiment, 1862–1864, a record that includes sick and wounded summaries, returns of medical supplies, and a register of surgical cases. Surgical data concerning one regiment may also be noted in Notes of Surgical Cases, Fourteenth Regiment, South Carolina Volunteers. And the Journal of Winder Hospital records a number of case histories—chiefly surgical.

The Records of the Association of Army and Navy Surgeons of the Confederate States in the Confederate Museum (containing, among other items, the minutes from twenty-one meetings) are disappointing but of some value. Several hospital registers were examined: Register of Emory Hospital, January 1, 1864, to April 12, 1865, kept by Surgeon T. C. Montague; Register of Gordonsville, Virginia, Receiving Hospital, June 1, 1863—May 5, 1864, a fairly complete item; and Register of the Robertson Hospital, Richmond, Virginia, 1861–1865, a record of the 1,334 patients treated in the hospital managed by Captain Sally L. Tompkins. Another noteworthy source having to do with the Robertson Hospital is Account Books of the Robertson Hospital, Richmond, 1862–1864, comprising three volumes of material. There are 6,100 admission slips to the Confederate Hospital, Petersburg, Virginia, each of which contains the name, age, residence, ailment, and disposition of a soldier admitted to the institution. Helpful information about hospitals and medical officers is to be seen in Roster of General Hospitals, Department of Virginia, 1864, the rosters available being those for January, March, and April of that year. Something may be learned about other hospital personnel and their responsibilities in "Rules for Governing the Matrons of Jackson, Hospital," prepared by Dr. Francis W. Hancock, the surgeon in charge. Most important of the order and letter books are Order and Letter Books of General Hospital, Front Royal, and General Hospital, Liberty, Va., the entries in which extend from September 10, 1861, through March 2, 1865, and Order Book, General Hospital No. 2, Lynchburg, Virginia, which contains orders from higher authority as well as those issued on the local level by Surgeon W. C. N. Randolph, the medical officer in charge. Another described as Order and Letter Book of the Confederate Medical Director is actually that of the medical director of Virginia hospitals and covers only a brief period. A general order book of Hoke's Division is most valuable for the fact that listed therein are the division's casualties from the time of its organization in May, 1864, to the end of the war.

A few manuscripts of an official character were found in the Manuscripts Division of the Library of Congress and in the libraries of the University of North Carolina and Duke University. The Samuel Hollingsworth Stout Papers, 1847–1903, consisting largely of Medical Director Stout's war papers, may be seen at Chapel Hill and is one of the best single sources available. This is a microfilm collection and illuminates the hospital picture in the West considerably. Stout operated from Chattanooga, Tennessee, and Atlanta, Macon, and Columbus, Georgia. At one time the hospital department administered by Stout encompassed practically all of the area between the Savannah and Mississippi rivers, and after the war he preserved some fifteen hundred pounds of his medical records for the purpose "of publishing after the close of the war a book or books in the interest of medical science and truthful history." Unfortunately, Stout never found time to attain this objective, and not all of his papers are as yet accessible to medical historians. It is hoped there will be no further scattering of these significant records. The Ernest Haywood Collection at Chapel Hill is also noteworthy inasmuch as it contains numerous records pertaining to General Hospitals No. 7 and 13 in Raleigh and other data about medical matters in that area. Additional information relating to the Raleigh hospitals may be seen in the John and Edmund Burke Haywood Papers, 1819–1865, comprising only a few items, in Duke's Flowers Collection. Some knowledge about a general hospital near Raleigh, General Hospital No. 3 in Goldsboro, may be gathered from the University of North Carolina's W. A. Holt Papers. Holt was the surgeon in charge of the Goldsboro hospital during the war's final year. The Dr. James K. Hall Papers at Chapel Hill include one very useful document: an inspection report of the medical purveying depot at Demopolis, Alabama, made on September 2, 1864. Most important of the Duke manuscripts is the Confederate States of America, Archives, 1861–1865, within which are a number of valuable papers on the medical service. Other materials at Duke found helpful were the following: William A. Carrington Papers, 1863–1864; John Marshall Otey Papers, 1864–1865, which include five letters from Dr. Peter E. Hines, the medical director of North Carolina's general hospitals; and Daniel Ruggles Papers and Telegrams, 1847–1865, some of which embrace medical affairs in Louisiana. The papers covering the war years of the following collections in the Library of Congress were examined for the purpose of noting the attention accorded medical matters by these commanders: Papers of General Pierre G. T. Beauregard, 1844–1883, and the Papers of Jubal A. Early, 1829–1911. The Edward Willis Papers, also in the Library of Congress, tell something of blockade running; Willis was a quartermaster.

I am most grateful to Dr. R. N. Harden of Greensboro, North Carolina, for the use of an important source, Empire Hospital Order and Letter Book, January, 1863–April, 1865. Dr. Harden's grandfather, Surgeon W. P. Harden, was in charge of the Empire Hospital, located originally in Atlanta, and the book contains many orders and letters received by and sent from a strategically located institution. Thanks are also due Colonel Thomas Spencer of Atlanta, Georgia, and Mr. John R. Peacock of High Point, North Carolina, for allowing me to see the Samuel H. Stout papers acquired by them.

PRIVATE COLLECTIONS

The writer utilized the letters and diaries of medical and hospital personnel in the collections of that type material in the Duke University and the University of North Carolina libraries, the Virginia State Library, and elsewhere. Effort was also made to examine a reasonable amount of soldier letters, diaries, and reminiscences inasmuch as almost all had experiences that brought them in contact with the medical service. Needless to say this was largely a hit-or-miss proposition and time-consuming, but any appraisal of the medical service that failed to take soldier comment into consideration would be somewhat incomplete.

From the standpoint of medical officers the most fruitful sources in this classification were the Jefferson Howard De Votie Papers, 1856–1865, and the William D. Somers Papers, 1848–1897, in the Flowers Collection, Duke University, and the James McFadden Gaston Papers and the Dr. Charles C. Gray Diary, both located in the Southern Historical Collection, University of North Carolina. De Votie, who wrote frequently to his parents, graduated from the University of Louisiana Medical School in March, 1862. He then served as a contract surgeon until he passed his examination before an army medical board; his subsequent service was in Virginia, the Carolinas, and Florida. The family and professional correspondence of William D. Somers, an assistant surgeon in the West, contains worthwhile observations and comments. James McFadden Gaston, a South Carolinian, was at different times the chief surgeon of a division and head of a general hospital; his letters are full of pertinent information about his activities. Dr. Charles C. Gray's diary is both entertaining and valuable, particularly so because it is the account of a Union surgeon during the period of his captivity, July 16, 1861, to July 29, 1862, in Castle Pinckney, Libby, and Salisbury Prisons. Other records of this sort left by medical officers, most of which are disappointing, are as follows: Notebook of Surgeon James Bolton in the Virginia State Library; John G. Brodnax Papers, 1856–1919, and C. J. Clark Diary, 1841–1874, both at Duke, the latter containing notes written by Clark as a medical student in Kentucky and as a Confederate surgeon; J. B. Clifton Diary, 1863–1864, notations of a field surgeon with the Sixteenth and Fifty-third Georgia Regiments, in the Archives of the North Carolina Historical Commission, Raleigh; at Chapel Hill the Dr. James E. Green Diary, typescript, and the Winfield Papers, 1861–1862, the former be-

coming a physician after the war and the latter—a physician at
the outset of the conflict—entering the service as a captain of
cavalry; and in the Confederate Museum the Letter Book and
Diary of Surgeon Robert Poole Myers, October 2, 1861, to
May 6, 1865, during which time Myers saw both hospital and
field service.

Hospital stewards figured prominently in the medical story,
and the following documents tell something of the part they
played: George S. Barnsley Papers, 1838–1915, J. Kelly Bennette Diary and Letters, and George E. Waller Letters, 1858–
1864, microfilm, all at the University of North Carolina, and
Henry Beveridge Diary, 1864, at Duke. The Barnsley collection includes war correspondence of George and Lucien Barnsley, both of whom were hospital stewards. Bennette's diary,
covering only about three months in the summer of 1864, is
interesting but says little about his duties as a hospital steward.
On the other hand, the Waller letters, most of which were
written from the field by the hospital steward of the Twenty-
fourth Virginia Regiment, are interesting and informative—
a good record. Beveridge, hospital steward of the Twenty-
fifth Virginia Regiment, writes mainly of activities in camp.

Papers of other hospital workers located and used were
not particularly rewarding. The Sally Tompkins Papers in the
Confederate Museum represent only one small folder of letters. Two sets of Mrs. Phoebe Y. Pember Letters at Chapel
Hill, encompassing the years 1861–1865 and 1864–1920, say
little generally about her work as hospital matron. Duke's
J. W. Griffin Papers, 1862–1863, consist of seven letters from
a ward master at Winder and Howard's Grove Hospitals,
Richmond. The William McCutcheon Papers, 1807–1867, in
the same library, include a fragmentary diary kept by a Miss
Clarke from South Carolina, who served as nurse in the Mid-
way Hospital, Charlottesville, Virginia. Several letters written
by Miss Julia A. Patterson of Petersburg, Virginia, a nurse
in the Virginia Hospital near that city, were found in the
Phifer Papers, University of North Carolina. Miss Patterson
attended Lt. E. L. Phifer after he was mortally wounded on
June 18, 1864, until his death several weeks later. Her comments about the care of Lt. Phifer and other matters are worth
noting.

Soldier letters, diaries, and reminiscences utilized were

about what one would expect. Some tell more than others about life in hospitals, experiences with "graybacks," diarrhea, and the other hazards of camp life, but almost all contribute to a better understanding of the medical story. The Duke and University of North Carolina libraries are especially rich in collections of this type. Among those examined at Duke were the following: James H. Baker Papers, 1863–1865, letters written by a private soldier who died in a Virginia hospital; James H. Barrow Papers, 1864; W. C. Clayton Papers, 1860–1862; John B. Evans Papers, 1862–1865; Gustavus Woodson Smith Papers, 1861–1865, one item of which is a letter written to President Davis by the Army of the Potomac's temporary commander about the incidence of disease in that army; and the John Wesley Walker Papers. Similar material used at the University of North Carolina included: Diary and Reminiscences of James W. Albright; Isaac Alexander Letters, 1862–1865, typescript, boyish correspondence from a private in the Army of Tennessee; William J. H. Bellamy Diary; James O. Carr Papers; Major Joseph B. Cumming War Recollections; Samuel W. Eaton Diary, typescript; John A. Johnson Letters, 1862–1865, copies; David M. Key Papers, microfilm and typescript; MacKay–Stiles Papers, 1861–1869; McDowell Papers; Paul A. McMichael Papers, typescript, comprising wartime letters and diary written by a Confederate officer before and after his capture in October, 1864, in addition to personal papers; James Keen Munnerlyn Letters, 1860–1864; Frank Nash Papers, 1861–1865; Pettigrew Papers; Frank S. Richardson Papers, 1851–1852; 1861; 1862–1865, letters from a Louisianian who suffered from diarrhea and was in and out of army hospitals in the West; Alexander G. Taliaferro War Reminiscences, 1861–1865, typescript; M. Jeff Thompson Papers; Tutwiler Papers; Diaries of John Waldrop and Richard W. Waldrop, 3 vols.; Letters of Richard W. Waldrop, 1861–1864; John Walton Diary, typescript, the diary of one who contracted tuberculosis during his war service and died shortly thereafter at the age of twenty-six; J. Fred Waring Diary, 1864–1865; Edmund Jones Williams War Letters, 1861–1864, made up of detailed letters concerning camp life; Charles Ashley Willis Diary, 1863; C. A. Withers Confederate Reminiscences, 1861–1865, typescript; and Thomas Barton Wyatt

Reminiscences, 1863–1865, typescript. In addition to the above the Roy Vernon Howell Papers, 1861–1865, located in the Archives of the North Carolina Historical Commission, and the Diary of George Neese in the Virginia State Library, are also of interest.

II. *Official Documents*

UNITED STATES

Two absolutely indispensable governmental publications are *The War of the Rebellion: A Compilation of the Official Records of the Union and Confederate Armies*, 127 vols. and index (Washington, 1880–1901) and its counterpart for the naval conflict, *Official Records of the Union and Confederate Navies in the War of Rebellion*, 30 vols. and index (Washington, 1894–1927). The former is especially valuable inasmuch as it touches upon almost every facet of the medical problem; due to the inadequacy of the indices of the two works it was necessary to leaf through each volume. Perhaps the greatest contemporary contribution to medicine and surgery was *The Medical and Surgical History of the War of the Rebellion, 1861–1865*, 6 vols. (Washington, 1870–1888), prepared under the direction of the Surgeon General. A number of Confederate records—statistical data, case histories, and the like —may be found in these volumes. Other Confederate records published separately by the United States include: *Journal of the Congress of the Confederate States of America, 1861–1865*, 7 vols. (Washington, 1904–1905); *Register of Officers of the Confederate States Navy, 1861–1865* (Washington, 1931); and *Special Orders of the Adjutant and Inspector General's Office, Confederate States, 1861* (Washington, n. d.).

CONFEDERATE STATES

Most of the Congressional enactments are in James M. Matthews (ed.), *The Statutes at Large of the Provisional Government of the Confederate States of America, . . .* (Richmond, 1864) and *Public Laws* [and Private Laws] *Of the*

Confederate States of America, 1–4 Sessions, First Congress, First Session, Second Congress (Richmond, 1862–1864). Regulations affecting medical personnel are set forth in *Regulations for the Medical Department of the Confederate States Army* (Richmond, 1861–1863), *Regulations for the Army of the Confederate States, 1863* (Richmond, 1863), and *Uniform and Dress of the Army of the Confederate States* (Richmond, 1861). Prompted by Surgeon General Samuel P. Moore, the elaborate work on medical botany by Francis Peyre Porcher, *Resources of the Southern Fields and Forests, Medical, Economical, and Agricultural* (Charleston, 1863), and *A Manual of Military Surgery* (Richmond, 1863), a good scientific treatise, are both excellent sources in their respective areas. General orders for one year are printed in R. H. P. Robinson (comp.), *General Orders, from the Adjutant and Inspector General's Office, Confederate States Army, For the Year 1863, with a Full Index* (Richmond, 1864). Other brief items include the *Report of the Apportionment of the General Hospitals in and around Richmond* (Richmond, 1864), an eight-page pamphlet; the *Standard Supply Table of the Indigenous Remedies for Field Service and the Sick in General Hospitals* (Richmond, 1863); the *War Department Circular* (Richmond, December 10, 1863) setting forth instructions for the guidance of medical officers engaged in conscript duty; and a number of printed circulars issued by the medical director of the general hospitals in North Carolina during the years 1864 and 1865 which may be seen in the North Carolina Room, University of North Carolina Library.

Two publications on the state level, *The General Military Hospital for the North Carolina Troops in Petersburg, Virginia,* and *Regulations for the Medical Department of the Military Forces of North Carolina,* both published in Raleigh in 1861, lend perspective to the early developments.

III. *Collected Sources*

There are some source collections of importance to the medical historian. Useful published letters may be seen in Edmund Cody Burnett (ed.), "Letters of a Confederate Surgeon: Dr. Abner McGarity, 1862–1865," *Georgia Historical Quarterly,* XXIX (1945), 76–114, 159–190, 222–253; XXX (1946), 35–70. McGarity served with Georgia, Alabama, and North Carolina units after his appointment as assistant surgeon on March 10, 1863. *A Confederate Surgeon's Letters to His Wife* (New York, 1911), written by Spencer Glasgow Welch, surgeon of the Thirteenth South Carolina Volunteers, has long been considered one of the significant books on health and morale in the Southern army. Letters written by another Confederate medical officer, Alexander Thom, are included in Catherine Thom Bartlett (ed.), *"My Dear Brother": A Confederate Chronicle* (Richmond, 1952). For a time Thom was in charge of a division at Richmond's Jackson Hospital; later he was held prisoner for six months. An outstanding and reliable soldier account, consisting chiefly of letters written to a friend at home, is Benjamin Washington Jones's *Under the Stars and Bars. A History of the Surry Light Artillery* (Richmond, 1909). *Scraps of Paper* (New York, 1929), edited by Marietta Minnigerode Andrews, contains, among other miscellaneous material, a number of letters written by Lt. Charles Minnigerode, Jr. and an account taken from *The Military Surgeon* of the sufferings of Corporal James Tanner, well-known Union soldier.

A section on "Hospitals, Surgeons, and Nurses" is included in the valuable collection edited by Henry Steele Commager, *The Blue and the Gray; The Story of the Civil War as Told by Participants,* 2 vols. (Indianapolis, 1950). Several items on the medical story may also be found in Frank Moore (ed.), *The Rebellion Record . . . ,* 11 vols. and supplement (New York, 1861–1868).

Documents of the United States Sanitary Commission, 2 vols. (New York, 1866), preserve some informative comment on Confederate hospitals at the close of the war. A considerable amount of information pertaining to wartime medicine and surgery is contained in the following works: Austin Flint (ed.), *Contributions Relating to the Causation and Prevention of Disease, and to Camp Diseases; together with a Report of the Diseases, Etc. among the Prisoners at Andersonville, Ga.* (New York, 1867) ; Frank H. Hamilton (ed.), *Surgical Memoirs of the War of the Rebellion,* 2 vols. (New York, 1870–

1871). The Flint and Hamilton works represented efforts by the United States Sanitary Commission to make known the medical and surgical lessons of the war. Joseph Jones was a contributor to both. A reference that throws light on the state of medicine in the decade prior to the war is *Medical Society of North Carolina. Transactions, 1849–1860,* printed annually at different places by various publishers.

Disappointing from an overall standpoint but including a few choice medical items is *Battles and Leaders of the Civil War* . . . , 4 vols. (New York, 1887–1888), edited by Robert U. Johnson and Clarence C. Buel. Practically the same comment may be made with respect to Walter Clark (ed.), *Histories of the Several Regiments and Battalions from North Carolina, in the Great War 1861–'65* . . . (Raleigh and Goldsboro, 1901). A work dealing with the matter of supply, Frank E. Vandiver (ed.), *Confederate Blockade Running Through Bermuda, 1861–1865. Letter and Cargo Manifests* (Austin, 1947), is helpful for its data on medical stores brought through the blockade.

Other collections containing items of importance for the medical history of the war are as follows: Charles W. Ramsdell (ed.), *Laws and Joint Resolutions of the Last Session of the Confederate Congress . . . Together with the Secret Acts of Previous Congresses* (Durham, 1941); James D. Richardson (ed.), *A Compilation of the Messages and Papers of the Confederacy . . . , 1861–1865,* 2 vols. (Nashville, 1905); and Dunbar Rowland (ed.), *Jefferson Davis, Constitutionalist, His Letters, Papers and Speeches,* 10 vols. (Jackson, Mississippi, 1923).

IV. *Diaries, Journals, and Travel Accounts*

By far the richest source among this group of materials is Kate Cumming's *A Journal of Hospital Life in the Confederate Army of Tennessee from the Battle of Shiloh to the End of the War; with Sketches of Life and Characters and Brief Notices of Current Events during that Period* (Louisville, 1866). Miss Cumming, an educated and cultured person, served as a hospital matron. She moved over a wide area, and her descriptive observations of hospital buildings, medical personnel, and all of the many aspects of life in the general hospitals of the West make this an invaluable record. Another revealing account is Nicholas A. Davis's *The Campaign from Texas to Maryland* (Richmond, 1863). Davis, chaplain of the Fourth Texas Regiment, served in both field and general hospitals and made some interesting comments on hospital conditions. An unwilling member of the Confederate medical service in the West was William G. Stevenson, a New Yorker caught in Arkansas at the beginning of the war. His *Thirteen Months in the Rebel Army . . .* (New York, 1862), although not altogether reliable, is of some aid. Disappointing from the standpoint of what it tells about his relationship to the laboratory in Columbia but excellent in other respects is Joseph Le Conte, *'Ware Sherman: A Journal of Three Month's Personal Experience in the Last Days of the Confederacy* (Berkeley, 1937). A soldier account in diary and narrative form which makes some reference to medical matters and hospitals is *John Dooley, Confederate Soldier, His War Journal* (Washington, 1945), edited by Joseph T. Durkin; Dooley was a member of the famous First Virginia Infantry, a regiment whose history dated from 1661. Edited by Howard Swiggett, *A Rebel War Clerk's Diary at the Confederate States Capital*, 2 vols. (Philadelphia, 1866), has long been regarded as an important source, and it contains several helpful references to medical matters.

Worth noting in order to obtain observations and experiences from Southern women not directly connected with the medical service are the following: Mary Boykin Chesnut, *A Diary from Dixie* (Boston, 1949), edited by Ben Ames Williams; Sarah Morgan Dawson, *A Confederate Girl's Diary* (New York, 1913) ; and Judith McGuire [Mrs. J. W. Brockenbrough], *Diary of a Southern Refugee, during the War* (New York, 1867). Mrs. Chesnut and Miss McGuire were quite interested in hospital matters, and the former was one of the shrewdest diarists of the war.

Some interesting comment from still another vantage point may be seen in the account written by Joel Cook, a Northern journalist, *The Siege of Richmond . . .* (Philadelphia, 1862). English journalists on the scene included Samuel Phillips Day, a Southern sympathizer, and William Howard Russell, a harsh critic of both North and South. The former's book is titled *Down South; or an Englishman's Experience at the Seat of the American Civil War*, 2 vols. (London, 1862), and the account is a reliable one. Also rewarding is Russell's famous work, *My Diary North and South* (Boston, 1863). Viewing the conflict through the eyes of a British army officer was Lieutenant-Colonel J. A. L. Fremantle, and his *Three Months in the Southern States: April–June, 1863* (New York, 1864) is a classic. An Englishwoman's accurate story, *Life in the South . . . From the Spring of 1860 to August, 1862*, 2 vols. (London, 1863), is also good. The author, Catherine C. Hopley, was a schoolteacher in the South and spent much time in the Confederate capital.

V. *Miscellaneous Contemporary Books and Pamphlets*

The need for information about military surgery is indicated by the fact that the following valuable books were published during the war years: *A Manual of Military Surgery* (Richmond, 1863), prepared by order of the Surgeon General for army use; J. Julian Chisolm, *A Manual of Military Surgery for the use of Surgeons in the Confederate States Army . . .*, second edition (Richmond, 1862); Felix Formento, *Notes and Observations on Army Surgery* (New Orleans, 1863); and Edward Warren, *An Epitome of Practical Surgery for Field and Hospital* (Richmond, 1863). All of these books appear to have seen wide circulation. Chisolm was one of the better known Confederate surgeons, and his book contains rules and regulations of the medical department. Formento served as a surgeon in the Franco-Sardinian army, 1859, and he was chief surgeon of Richmond's Louisiana Hospital at the time his book was published. Warren, a colorful figure, was Surgeon General of North Carolina during most of the war, and his book contains some revealing surgical statistics on both the Crimean and Civil conflicts.

The City Intelligencer; or, Stranger's Guide (Richmond, 1862) and *The Stranger's Guide and Official Directory for the City of Richmond* (Richmond, 1863) assist the present-day visitor to the Confederate capital find his way to the various hospitals, residences of government officials, and other points in the city.

Oliver Wendell Holmes's *Currents and Counter-Currents in Medical Science* (Boston, 1861) contains a penetrating and often amusing analysis of the state of American medicine on the outbreak of war.

An interesting pamphlet found in the Rare Book Collection, Library of Congress, was the *Petition of Dental Surgeons of Ten Years Practice, for Exemption from Military Service* . . . (Richmond, 1863), a petition which was favored by both the ranking medical officers of the army and navy.

VI. *Periodicals and Newspapers*

Medical journals proved to be the most rewarding periodical sources, and the following stand out as the most fruitful of such journals: *The Confederate States Medical and Surgical Journal,* 2 vols. (Richmond, 1864–1865) ; *The Southern Practitioner,* 40 vols. (Nashville, 1879–1918) ; and *The Virginia Medical Monthly* (Richmond, 1874–   ), published semi-monthly from 1896 to 1918. Other medical journals used include *Gaillard's Southern Medicine,* 93 vols. (1866–1911), the name and place of publication of which changed often; *The Medical Journal of North Carolina,* 3 vols. (Edenton and Raleigh, 1858–1861) ; *The Southern Medical Journal* (Nashville and Birmingham, 1908–   ) ; and *The Southern Medical and Surgical Journal* (Augusta, 1836–1839; 1845–1861; 1866–1867).

Some of the best articles to be found in *The Confederate States Medical and Surgical Journal* are as follows: John H. Claiborne, "On the Use of Phytolacca Decandra in Camp Itch," I (1864), 39; M. J. DeRosset, "Read's Case of Excision of Knee-Joint," I (1864), 83–84; W. T. Grant, "Indigenous Medical Plants," I (1864), 84–86; O. Kratz, "On Vaccination and Variolous Diseases," I (1864), 104; G. M. B. Maughs, "Thoughts on Surgery, Operative and Conservative . . . ," I (1864), 129–131; James B. Read, "Resections of the Hip-Joint," I (1864), 5–7; and F. Sorrel, "Gun-Shot Wounds—Army of Northern Virginia," I (1864), 153–155.

The Southern Practitioner, journal of the postwar Association of Medical Officers of the Army and Navy of the Confederacy, is full of articles written by such officers pertaining to the medical service, some of which are most rewarding. Illustrative of the material to be found in that organ are the following: J. C. Abernethy, "Manual of Military Surgery for the Army of the Confederate States," XXIV (1902), 674–679; Bedford Brown, "Personal Experience in Observing the Results of Good and Bad Sanitation in the Confederate States Army," XXV (1903), 574–581; William B. Burroughs, "A Lady Commissioned Captain in the Army of the Confederate States," XXXI (1909), 532–534; John S. Cain, "Address of Jno. S. Cain, M.D., President of the Association of Medical Officers of the Army and Navy of the Confederacy," XXVII (1905), 381–395; Charles W. Chancellor, "A Memoir of the Late Samuel Preston Moore, M.D., Surgeon General of the Confederate States Army," XXV (1903), 634–643; C. J. Edwards, "Pneumonia in the Confederate Army," XXXIII (1911), 478–480; A. M. Elmore, "Some Recollections of the Medical Officers of the Department of the Indian Territory, C.S.A.," XXV (1903), 706–708; Alexander G. Lane, "The Winder Hospital, of Richmond, Va.," XXVI (1904), 35–41; Samuel E. Lewis, "Samuel Preston Moore, M.D., Surgeon General of the Confederate States," XXVIII (1901), 381–386; James H. McNeilly, "Confederate Dietetics," XXII (1900), 471–472; Samuel Preston Moore, "Address of the President of the Association of Medical Officers of the Confederate States Army and Navy," XXXI (1909), 491–497; Samuel H. Stout, "Some Facts of the History of the Organization of the Medical Service of the Confederate Armies and Hospitals," XXII (1900), 521–523; 565–567; XXIII (1901), 98–103; 149–152; 193–198; 294–295; 584–588; XXIV (1902), 50–54; 105–108; 159–164; 213–216; 564–570; 622–626; 667–674; XXV (1903), 26–35; 91–98; 155–161; 215–222; 274–283; 349–359; 517–526; 566–574; (Stout began these articles at the age of seventy-eight); Christopher H. Tebault, "Hospitals of the Confederacy," XXIV (1902), 499–509; Charles H. Todd, "Annual Address of Charles H. Todd, M.D., President of the Association of Medical Officers of the Army and Navy of the Confederacy," XXVIII (1906), 291–301; and Mrs. James H. Williams, "Reminiscences of a Clerk in the Medical Purveyor's Office and in the Treasury of the Confederate Government, Richmond, Virginia," XXXIX (1917), 301–305.

Informative articles, some also written by former Confederate medical officers, that appeared in *The Virginia Medical Monthly* include: Paul B. Barringer, "A History of the Medical Department of the University of Virginia," XIV (1888), 743–752; Mrs. William C. Flournoy, "The South's Contribution to Medical Science," LVII (1931), 814–816; A. Y. P. Garnett, "Medical Department of the Confederate Government . . . ," V (1878), 20–27; John R. Gildersleeve, "History of Chimborazo Hospital, Richmond, Va., and Its Medical Officers During 1861–1865," IX (1904), 148–154; Luther B. Grandy, "The History of Medicine and Surgery in Georgia," XXII (May, 1895), 150–160; Isaac C. Harrison, "A Historical Sketch of the Medical Society of Virginia," LIX (1932), 509–514; Edgar E. Hume, "Chimborazo Hospital, Confederate States Army, America's Largest Military Hospital," LXI (1934), 189–195; P. St. L. Moncure, "The South in Medicine and Surgery," LXIII (1936), 459–465; Thomas J. Moore, "Treatment of Gunshot Wounds of the Abdomen," XIV (1888), 760–771; Marshall J. Payne, "Dr. Hunter Holmes McGuire, Surgeon, Teacher, Author, and Man," LXIII (1937), 731–734; S. S. Satchwell, "Medico-Chirugical Lessons of the late War from Southern Standpoints . . . ," I (1874), 35–37; Savage Smith, "Map of Chimborazo General Hospital, C.S.A. as it appeared July 6, 1862," LXXI (1944), 118; and R. Randolph Stevenson, "Report of Thirty-four Cases of Gunshot Wounds," XI (1884), 558–564.

Among the most useful articles which have been published in other medical journals are: Wyndham B. Blanton, "Richmond as a Medical Center," *Southern Medical Journal*, XXVI (1933), 902–903; W. Leigh Burton, "Dental Surgery as Applied in the Armies of the Late Confederate States," *American Journal of Dental Science*, I, Third Series (1867), 180–189; G. E. Bushnell, "Tuberculosis in the Army," *Southern Medical Journal*, X (1917), 933–938; Edward N. Covey, "The Interdental Splint," *Richmond Medical Journal*, I (1866), 81–91; Charles F. Craig, "The Relation of Officers of the Medical Corps to Scientific Medicine," *The Military Surgeon*, LXIII

(1928), 338–348; Paul F. Eve, "Answers to Certain Questions Propounded by Prof. Charles A. Lee, M.D., Agent of the United States Sanitary Commission, relative to the Health, etc., of the Late Southern Army," *Nashville Journal of Medicine and Surgery,* I, New Series (1866), 12–32; 163–179; Douglas S. Freeman, "Richmond's Confederate Epoch," *Southern Medical Journal,* XXVI (1933), 746–747; Courtney R. Hall, "Confederate Medicine . . . ," *Medical Life,* XLII (1935), 445–508; Robert J. Hicks, "Night Blindness in the Confederate Army," *Richmond Medical Journal,* III (1867), 34–38; William N. Hodgkin, "Dentistry in the Confederacy," *Journal of the American Dental Association,* L (1955), 647–655; Joseph Jones, "Observations upon the Losses of the Confederate Armies from Battle Wounds and Disease during the American Civil War, with Investigations upon the Number and Character of the Diseases Supervening upon Gun-Shot Wounds," *Richmond and Louisville Medical Journal,* VIII (1869), 339–358; 451–480; IX (1870), 257–275; 635–657; Jones also wrote an article titled "Medical Corps of the Confederate Army and Navy, 1861–1865," *Atlanta Medical and Surgical Journal,* XXV, Old Series, VII, New Series (1890), 339–353; George N. Malpass, "Medicine in the Confederate Army," *American Journal of Pharmacy,* CXV (1943), 173–177; Mary Louise Marshall, "Medicine in the Confederacy," *Bulletin of the Medical Library Association,* XXX (1942), 279–299; F. Peyre Porcher, "Suggestions Made to the Medical Department . . . ," *Southern Medical and Surgical Journal,* Series 3, I (1866), 248–266; (Porcher's article was prepared by order of the Surgeon General just before the end of the war, too late for his suggestions to be acted upon.) ; W. O. Roberts, "Southern Surgeons and Surgery—Before, During and After the Civil War," *Southern Medical Journal,* IV (1911), 189–200; Charles W. Stiles, "Report upon the Prevalence and Geographic Distribution of Hookworm Disease (Uncinariasis or Anchylostomiasis) in the United States," *Hygienic Laboratory Bulletin,* No. 10 (February, 1903); Christopher Tompkins, "Medical Education in the South," *Southern Medical Journal,* III (1910), 325–327; George H. Weaver, "Surgeons as Prisoners of War," *Bulletin of the Society of Medical History of Chicago,* IV (1933), 249–261; Harry J. Wharthen,

"Richmond Medicine of Yesterday: Medicine and Shockoe Hill," *The Bulletin of the Richmond Academy of Medicine,* IV (1936), 116–119; and E. Robert Wiese, "Life and Times of Samuel Preston Moore, Surgeon-General of the Confederate States of America," *Southern Medical Journal,* XXIII (1930), 916–922.

A surprising number of articles related to the medical story of the Confederacy may be seen in *The Confederate Veteran,* 40 vols. (Nashville, 1893–1932) and in the *Southern Historical Society Papers* (Richmond, 1876–   ) ; the latter, through the forty-ninth volume, were published by the Southern Historical Society, founded in 1869, but this society has been dissolved and its final projected volumes are being published by the Virginia Historical Society. These two sources must be used with care, but no student of Confederate history can afford to disregard them.

Articles in *The Confederate Veteran* which merit attention are the following: Simon Baruch, "A Surgeon's Story of Battle and Capture," XXII (1914), 545–548; A. B. Booth, "The First Successful Gangrene Treatment," XXVIII (1920), 247; Alice Trueheart Buck, "Founder of the First Confederate Hospital," II (1894), 141; T. M. Earnhart, "Surgical Treatment in the Confederate Army," XXVI (1918), 528–529; John R. Gildersleeve, "Chimborazo Hospital during 1861–1865," XII (1904), 577–579; W. J. W. Kerr, "Pellagra and Hookworm at Andersonville," XVIII (1910), 69; H. R. McIlwaine, "Surgical Department of the Confederate Army," XXXIII (1925), 406–407; Wade H. Manning, "Surgeons of the Confederacy: John Thompson Darby," XXXV (1927), 141; John J. Terrell, "A Confederate Surgeon's Story," XXXIX (1931), 457–459; and Julia Porcher Wickham, "Surgeons of the Confederacy: Francis Peyre Porcher, M.D., LL.D., Physician, Botanist, Author," XXXIII (1925), 456–459.

There are, in the *Southern Historical Society Papers,* two highly rewarding articles by Joseph Jones, written during his tenure as Surgeon-General of the United Confederate Veterans: "The Medical History of the Confederate States Army and Navy . . . ," XX (1892), 109–166; and "Roster of the Medical Officers of the Army of Tennessee," XXII (1894), 165–280. Highly interesting and informative is Joseph Jacobs'

"Some of the Drug Conditions during the War between the States, 1861–5," XXXIII (1905), 161–187. Other contributions of note in these papers are: Hunter H. McGuire, "Progress of Medicine in the South," XVII (1889), 1–12; F. Peyre Porcher, "Confederate Surgeons," XVII (1889), 12–21; and C. W. Read, "Reminiscences of the Confederate States Navy," I (1876), 331–362.

A better than average account of a hospital worker's experiences is Emily V. Mason's "Memories of a Hospital Matron," *The Atlantic Monthly*, XC (1902), 305–318; 475–485.

As might be expected, several fine contributions have been published in *The Journal of Southern History* and the organs of other historical and literary groups. Among the most outstanding are George W. Adams "Confederate Medicine," *The Journal of Southern History*, VI (1940), 151–166 and Francis B. Simkins and James W. Patton, "The Work of Southern Women among the Sick and Wounded of the Confederate Armies," *The Journal of Southern History*, I (1935), 475–496. A good recent study of the Confederacy's largest hospital is that by Frank S. and Anne Page Johns, "Chimborazo Hospital and J. B. McCaw, Surgeon-in-Chief," *The Virginia Magazine of History and Biography*, LXII (1954), 190–200. In a class by itself in its treatment of medical matters in the antebellum South is Richard H. Shryock's "Medical Practice in the Old South," *The South Atlantic Quarterly*, XXIX (1930), 160–178. The following well-written articles deal with various aspects of the medical supply problem: Edwin B. Coddington, "Soldiers' Relief in the Seaboard States of the Southern Confederacy," *The Mississippi Valley Historical Review*, XXXVII (1950), 17–38; William Diamond, "Imports of the Confederate Government from Europe and Mexico," *The Journal of Southern History*, VI (1940), 470–503; Norman H. Franke's series in *The Georgia Historical Quarterly:* "Pharmacy in the Confederacy," XXXVII (1953), 175–187; "Pharmaceutical Conditions and Drug Supply in the Confederacy," 287–298; and "Pharmacy and Pharmacists in the Confederacy," XXXVIII (1954), 11–28; Lucille Griffith, "Mrs. Juliet Opie Hopkins and Alabama Military Hospitals," *The Alabama Review*, VI (1953), 99–120; and Joseph H. Parks, "A Confederate Trade Center under Federal Occupation: Memphis, 1862 to 1865," *The Journal of Southern History,* VII (1941), 289–314.

Some of the medical items found in periodicals were taken from newspapers, and important information concerning every aspect of Confederate medical history was gleaned from the latter source. Inasmuch as the concentration of hospitals was greatest in Virginia and Georgia and since leading newspapers that were likely to carry significant items from their counterparts in other areas could be found there, it was decided to make an especially close survey of two newspapers from each of those two states. Those chosen for Virginia were the outstanding Richmond newspapers, the *Examiner* and the *Enquirer,* whereas the Georgia newspapers used were the Atlanta *Southern Confederacy* and the Augusta *Constitutionalist.* Two Raleigh papers, the *North Carolina Standard* and the *Register,* were also consulted.

VII. *Autobiographies, Memoirs, and Reminiscences*

Interesting and often quite valuable were the books written after the war by the medical officers themselves. One of the most engaging of such accounts—although very brief—is Simon Baruch's *Reminiscences of a Confederate Surgeon* (New York [?], 1915). The author was the father of Bernard Baruch. A well-written volume by John Herbert Claiborne, the surgeon in charge of the Petersburg hospitals during the latter part of the war, is titled *Seventy-five Years in Old Virginia* (Washington, 1904). Claiborne's comments on the Surgeon General, his own duties, and other matters deserve respectful attention. Perhaps the wittiest of the contributions in this class is Ferdinand E. Daniel's *Recollections of a Rebel Surgeon, (and other sketches) or in the Doctor's Sappy Days* (Austin, Texas, 1899). Between the anecdotes related by Daniel, however, the reader will find many revealing comments on wartime medicine and surgery. An attempt to point up in brief compass the main developments of the war from a professional standpoint was made by Edwin S. Gaillard in *The Medical and Surgical Lessons of the Late War* (Louisville, 1868). A study which deals in part with the war years is

Joseph Jones, *Medical and Surgical Memoirs: Containing Investigations on the Geographical Distribution, Causes, Nature, Relations and Treatment of Various Diseases, 1855–1890,* 3 vols. (New Orleans, 1876–1890). Fiery criticism of Confederate medical administration may be seen in Aristides Monteiro, *War Reminiscences by the Surgeon of Mosby's Command* (Richmond, 1890). Written in a humorous vein but enlightening as to the activities of surgeons in the field is William H. Taylor's *De Quibus* (Richmond, 1908). Taylor served in Garnett's Brigade, Army of Northern Virginia. Another doctor's experiences as a Confederate medical officer are included in Edward Warren, *A Doctor's Experiences in Three Continents* (Baltimore, 1885). An assistant surgeon of the Forty-second Mississippi Regiment, L. J. Wilson, relates a few informative items in *The Confederate Soldier* (Fayetteville, Arkansas, 1902). Arthur H. Noll (ed.), *Doctor Quintard, Chaplain C.S.A. . . .* (Sewanee, Tennessee, 1905), is a reliable account of one who served as both chaplain and surgeon over a large area of the Confederacy.

Several of the postwar accounts written by women hospital workers are also trustworthy and interesting. The hospital picture in the Western theater of the war may be glimpsed in Fannie A. Beers, *Memories. A Record of Personal Experience and Adventure during Four Years of War* (Philadelphia, 1891). Phoebe Yates Pember, a Chimborazo Hospital matron, gives a spirited record of her experiences and observations as a member of the staff there along with many personal opinions in *A Southern Woman's Story* (New York, 1879). Another matron's memoir that may be used with profit is Mrs. S. E. D. Smith, *The Soldier's Friend; Being a Thrilling Narrative of Grandma Smith's Four Years Experience and Observation, as Matron, in the Hospitals of the South . . .* (Memphis, 1867). One section of this memoir contains 83 pages of wartime letters by former patients and others, written to Mrs. Smith, who served in Tennessee, Georgia, and Mississippi. The story of a refugee who assisted often in the hospitals throughout that same area is related in Mrs. Irby Morgan, *How It Was; Four Years Among the Rebels* (Nashville, 1892).

The works of two who were associated with the supply function of the medical service should be mentioned: *The*

Autobiography of Joseph Le Conte (New York, 1903), edited by William Dallam Armes; and Caleb Huse, *The Supplies for the Confederate Army, How they were Obtained in Europe and how Paid for* (Boston, 1904).

The experiences of the men in the ranks cannot be neglected, and some of these common soldiers penned very remarkable memoirs. Standing at the top of the list are the following: John O. Casler, *Four Years in the Stonewall Brigade,* second edition reprint (Marietta, Georgia, 1951); William Andrew Fletcher, *Rebel Private Front and Rear* (Austin, Texas, 1954); Alexander Hunter, *Johnny Reb and Billy Yank* (Washington, 1905); Carlton McCarthy, *Detailed Minutiae of Soldier Life in the Army of Northern Virginia, 1861–1865* (Richmond, 1882); Randolph T. McKim, *A Soldier's Recollections . . .* (New York, 1910); Frank M. Mixson, *Reminiscences of a Private* (Columbia, 1910); G. W. Nichols, *A Soldier's Story of His Regiment (61st Georgia)* (Jesup, Georgia [?], 1898); J. B. Polley, *Hood's Texas Brigade . . .* (Washington, 1910); Robert Stiles, *Four Years Under Marse Robert* (New York, 1910); Sam R. Watkins, *"Co. Aytch," Maury Grays, First Tennessee Regiment; or, A Side Show of the Big Show* (Jackson, Tennessee, 1952); and John H. Worsham, *One of Jackson's Foot Cavalry . . .* (New York, 1912). Casler's experiences included duty in the pioneer corps of his division, a group of one hundred men whose responsibilities embraced the work of burying the dead, and he saw service for a time as ward master in a Harrisonburg, Virginia, hospital. Outstanding in Fletcher's memorable narrative is his compelling account of camp diseases and the treatment he received in field and general hospitals after suffering serious wounds at Second Manassas and Chickamauga. Hunter's description of a Petersburg hospital at night is unforgettable, and McCarthy's account of life in the ranks is considered by some to be without a serious rival. McKim's book, written by a Marylander from wartime diaries, has some pertinent observations on camp life and military matters. Frank Mixson's story is that of a member of the First South Carolina Regiment in the Army of Northern Virginia. Nichols, another private in the Army of Northern Virginia, suffered from chronic diarrhea; he writes at some length about his confinement as a patient in the Richmond, Lynchburg, and Danville hospitals and his temporary duty as a nurse in a hospital at the Confederate capital. Polley, a member of the Fourth Texas Regiment, quotes to a considerable extent from the diaries and reports of those with whom he served, and the work is therefore quite rich in primary material. The works by Stiles and Worsham are both perceptive and well-written memoirs by two more of Lee's soldiers whereas the narrative of Sam Watkins is one of the few and certainly the best of those left by the Army of Tennessee's veterans. Watkins loved a good story, but his comments and observations on medical matters appear to be generally trustworthy.

Two outstanding officer accounts are those by G. Moxley Sorrel, *Recollections of a Confederate Staff Officer* (Washington, 1905) and William Nathaniel Wood, *Reminiscences of Big I* (Jackson, Tennessee, 1956), edited by Bell Irvin Wiley. A hair-raising description of the aftermath of the Wilderness fighting (May 5–6, 1864), contained in the former, points up some of the problems connected with collecting the wounded after a major engagement. Wood was a minor commissioned officer, a third lieutenant, and an earlier edition of his story, published in 1909, was available only to Wood's friends and relatives.

Other soldier accounts which helped supply data about the medical history of the war include George William Beale, *A Lieutenant of Cavalry in Lee's Army* (Boston, 1918); George Cary Eggleston, *A Rebel's Recollections* (New York, 1905); John Gill, *Reminiscences of Four Years as a Private Soldier in the Confederate Army, 1861–1865* (Baltimore, 1904); Albert Theodore Goodloe, *Some Rebel Relics from the Seat of War* (Nashville, 1893); W. W. Heartsill, *Fourteen Hundred and 91 Days in the Confederate Army* . . . (Jackson, Tennessee, 1954), edited by Bill Irvin Wiley; I. Hermann, *Memoirs of a Veteran* (Atlanta, 1911); and Edward A. Moore, *The Story of a Cannoneer Under Stonewall Jackson* (Lynchburg, 1910).

One of the best descriptions of life in the ranks is that by a Northern reporter, George Alfred Townsend, *Rustics in Rebellion: A Yankee Reporter on the Road to Richmond, 1861–65* (Chapel Hill, 1950), first published in 1866 as *Campaigns of a Non-Combatant.* Townsend, himself a victim of the Chicka-hominy fever (camp fever), makes a few references to Con-federate medicine, and there are some very vivid scenes con-cerning the treatment of Union sick and wounded by their own surgeons.

Jefferson Davis, *The Rise and Fall of the Confederate Gov-ernment,* 2 vols. (Richmond, 1881) should be noted for the fine tribute set forth therein to the Confederate Surgeon General and his medical corpsmen. Other memoirs found useful include Myrta Lockett Avary (ed.), *A Virginia Girl in the Civil War, 1861–1865* . . . (New York, 1903) ; two narratives by Thomas Cooper De Leon, *Belles, Beaux and Brains of the 60's* (New York, 1907) and *Four Years in Rebel Capitals* . . . (Mobile, 1892) ; and John S. Wise, *The End of an Era* (New York, 1899).

VIII. *Biographies*

Illustrative of the great need for research in medical his-tory is the fact that no adequate biography of any of the Con-federacy's leading medical figures has as yet appeared. About the only thing in this field is Jacob Fraise Richard's *The Flor-ence Nightingale of the Southern Army: Experiences of Mrs. Ella K. Newsom, Confederate Nurse in the Great War of 1861–65* (Baltimore, 1914). Very helpful for an insight to pre-war medical and surgical practice, however, is Seale Harris, *Woman's Surgeon; The Life Story of J. Marion Sims* (New York, 1950), a well-written study of one of the nation's great-est surgeons.

Satisfactory sketches of the outstanding Southern medical officers may be seen in Allen Johnson, Dumas Malone, and Harris E. Starr (eds.), *The Dictionary of American Biogra-phy,* 21 vols. and index (New York, 1928–1945) and Howard A. Kelly and Walter L. Burrage (eds.), *American Medical Bi-ographies* (Baltimore, 1920). Sketches of the Surgeon Gen-eral may also be found in periodical articles cited previously and in James Evelyn Pilcher, *The Surgeon Generals of the Army of the United States of America* . . . (Carlisle, Penn-sylvania, 1905). Biographies of military leaders that proved to be particularly helpful for this study were Douglas S. Freeman, *R. E. Lee; A Biography*, 4 vols. (New York, 1934–1935) and Frank E. Vandiver, *Mighty Stonewall* (New York, 1957).

IX. *Monographs and Special Studies*

Thomas L. Livermore, *Numbers and Losses in the Civil War in America, 1861–1865* (New York, 1901) is the standard work on this particular topic. In the same general area official statistics are summarized in William E. Fox, *Regimental Losses in the American Civil War, 1861–1865* (Albany, 1889).

A splendid overall treatment of the role played by Southern women in the war is Francis Butler Simkins and James Welch Patton, *The Women of the Confederacy* (Richmond, 1936). The story of the nursing services rendered by the Catholic sisterhoods is lovingly related in George Barton, *Angels of the Battlefield*, second edition (Philadelphia, 1898).

William Best Hesseltine, *Civil War Prisons. A Study in War Psychology* (Columbus, Ohio, 1930) is the best work on this subject. Defending Southern treatment of Northern prisoners is R. Randolph Stevenson, *The Southern Side; Or, Andersonville Prison* (Baltimore, 1876).

A few items about the medical service in the Confederate navy were gleaned from J. Thomas Scharf, *History of the Confederate States Navy . . .* (New York, 1887).

The procurement problem and that of shortages are dealt with in Samuel Bernard Thompson, *Confederate Purchasing Operations Abroad* (Chapel Hill, 1935) ; Mary Elizabeth Massey, *Ersatz in the Confederacy* (Columbia, 1952) ; and Ella Lonn, *Salt as a Factor in the Confederacy* (New York, 1933).

State studies which concern themselves at least in part with such matters as soldier relief and supply are John K. Bettersworth, *Confederate Mississippi* (Baton Rouge, 1943) ; Jefferson Davis Bragg, *Louisiana in the Confederacy* (Baton Rouge, 1941) ; and Daniel Harvey Hill, *North Carolina in the War between the States*, 2 vols. (Raleigh, 1926). The story of the Confederacy's capital city in wartime is narrated in Alfred Hoyt Bill, *The Beleaguered City* (New York, 1946).

X. *Medical Histories*

Several important medical histories aid considerably in bringing the picture of medicine during the war years into proper focus. One of the best of these is Richard Harrison Shryock, *The Development of Modern Medicine* (Philadelphia, 1936). Other good general treatments, valuable mainly for the backdrop they provide, are Francis R. Packard, *History of Medicine in the United States,* 2 vols. (New York, 1931); Henry E. Sigerist, *American Medicine* (New York, 1934); Henry Burnell Shafer, *The American Medical Profession 1783 to 1850;* and William F. Norwood, *Medical Education in the United States before the Civil War* (Philadelphia, 1944). A work which is valuable for showing the roles played nationally in the postwar medical realm by ex-Confederate surgeons is that by Morris Fishbein, *A History of the American Medical Association* (Philadelphia, 1947). The best state medical history is Wyndham B. Blanton's *Medicine in Virginia in the Seventeenth Century* (Richmond, 1930), *Medicine in Virginia in the Eighteenth Century* (Richmond, 1931), and *Medicine in Virginia in the Nineteenth Century* (Richmond, 1933). The last includes some excellent material on the war period.

A specialized account on diseases in early America is Percy M. Ashburn, *The Ranks of Death, a Medical History of the Conquest of America* (New York, 1947). John Duffy's admirable *Epidemics in Colonial America* (Baton Rouge, 1953) provides additional background information on some of the ailments which harassed the Confederate soldier. Further understanding about one of these may be gained from Mark F. Boyd, *An Introduction to Malariology* (Cambridge, Massachusetts, 1930). A widespread disorder which followed in the wake of general vaccination in the Confederate army against smallpox led to the publication of the work by Joseph Jones, *Researches upon "Spurious Vaccination"* . . . (Nashville, 1867).

Perspective on military medical development may be obtained from Harvey E. Brown, *The Medical Department of the United States Army from 1775 to 1873* (Washington, 1873);

Percy M. Ashburn, *A History of the Medical Department of the United States Army* (New York, 1929) ; and Edgar Erskine Jume, *Victories of Army Medicine . . .* (Philadelphia, 1943).

George W. Adams has written the definitive study of the United States medical service during the civil conflict: *Doctors in Blue: The Medical History of the Union Army in the Civil War* (New York, 1952). Another scholarly work on the health and sanitary conditions of the Union army is William Quentin Maxwell, *Lincoln's Fifth Wheel: The Political History of the United States Sanitary Commission* (New York, 1956).

Two general histories of dentistry, both valuable accounts, are Charles Rudolph Edward Koch (ed.), *History of Dental Surgery*, 2 vols. (Chicago, 1909) and Arthur Ward Lufkin, *A History of Dentistry* (Philadelphia, 1938).

XI. General Works

The general histories are helpful chiefly from the standpoint of the perspective they provide. This is particularly true of the following: Carl R. Fish, *The Rise of the Common Man, 1830–1850* (New York, 1935) ; Arthur C. Cole, *The Irrepressible Conflict, 1850–1865* (New York, 1934) ; James G. Randall, *The Civil War and Reconstruction* (Boston, 1937) ; Edward Channing, *The War for Southern Independence* (New York, 1925) ; James Ford Rhodes, *History of the United States from the Compromise of 1850*, 8 vols. (reprint, New York, 1902–1920) ; Julian A. C. Chandler et al. (eds.), *The South in the Building of the Nation*, 13 vols. (Richmond, 1909–1913) ; E. Merton Coulter, *The Confederate States of America, 1861–1865* (Baton Rouge, 1950) ; and Clement Eaton, *A History of the Southern Confederacy* (New York, 1954).

One of the most interesting and attractive general sources is Francis T. Miller (ed.), *The Photographic History of the Civil War*, 10 vols. (New York, 1911). Included in Volume VII of this work are several articles on the Confederate medical service by Deering J. Roberts, ex-surgeon in the Army of Tennessee, and a number of excellent pictures of medical figures and subjects. Significant because it contains an account of the mortal wounding and subsequent death of Stonewall Jackson as related by Jackson's medical director is Hunter Holmes McGuire and George L. Christian, *The Confederate Cause and Conduct in the War Between the States* . . . , second edition (Richmond, 1907). And of course Bell Irvin Wiley's *The Life of Johnny Reb, the Common Soldier of the Confederacy* (Indianapolis, 1943) is an invaluable aid to anyone who writes on a subject involving the fighting men of the South.

INDEX

Academy Hospital, Chattanooga, establishment and capacity of, 56; movement of, 57; need of guard for, 90, 91n

Adams Express Company, 138

Adolphus, Philip, and copy of Winchester agreement, 130n

Alabama, removal of wounded from, 129n

Alcoholic stimulants, procurement of, 151–53

Alcoholism, 211–12

Ambulances, use and problem of, 118–22; shortages of, 118–20

American Gynecological Society, 269

American International Congress on Tuberculosis, 270

American Medical Association, 14, 269, 270, 273

American Medical Biographies, 266n

American Medical Weekly, 270

American Practitioner, 269

American Red Cross, 273

American Society of Dental Surgeons, founding of, 19

American Surgical Association, 269

Amputations, primary and secondary, 222–24; during Franco-Prussian War, 228n; at Shiloh, 228–29; "flap" and circular operations in, 242

Andersonville Prison, establishment of and conditions in, 103–04; cases of continued fever in, 195; smallpox in, 196; pneumonia and pleurisy in, 202; consumption and bronchitis in, 204; rheumatism in, 205; scurvy in, 207; nostalgia as a factor in suffering at, 213; hospital gangrene in, 241–42; diarrhea and dysentery in, 241–42

Andersonville Prison Hospital, admissions to, 7; location of, 99

Anesthetics, 225–27

Antietam, battle of, 129

Antietam campaign, shoe and clothing needs of troops during, 175

Antiseptics, 231

Antony, Milton, 13

Apoplexy, 214

Army Intelligence Office, 74

Army Medical Boards, work of, 32–35

Army of Mississippi, 120

Army of New Mexico, smallpox in, 195

Army of Northern Virginia, service of medical officers in, 36; reception of wounded from, 125; sick lists of, 168; exposure of after Gettysburg, 172; smallpox in, 195–96; scurvy in, 206; nyctalopia in, 208; malingerers in, 217; gunshot wounds in, 219; hospital gangrene in, 239; suffering of wounded of, 253; physical condition of, 265–66

Army of the Potomac, 95, 119, 126; sick and wounded in, 3–4; measles in, 188; catarrh and bronchitis in, 203–04; scurvy in, 206; erysipelas in, 238

Army of Tennessee, casualties at Chickamauga and Missionary Ridge, 57; movement of hospitals behind, 58; improper care for sick and wounded of, 60; hospitals in rear of, 79; hospitals of, 86; inspection of hospitals used by, 89; sick call in, 111; efforts to provide shoes for, 140; supply problems in, 161; smallpox in, 195–96; spurious vaccinia in, 200; rheumatism in, 205; camp itch in, 209; hospital gangrene in, 239; health and discipline of, 266

Army of Texas, spurious vaccinia in, 200

56; describes hospital buildings, 56; and location of hospitals, 57; impresses buildings, 58; cites problems in hospital movement, 59–60; housing of disabled troops, 60; jurisdiction over Montgomery hospitals, 62; transfers hospitals to Mississippi, 66–67; appointment of as Superintendent of Hospitals in the Department of Tennessee, 71; reports on battle of Chickamauga, 94–95; threatens medical officers with court-martial, 96; complains of field officers' attitude toward hospital surgeons, 117; at Chickamauga, 124–25; experiences problems of co-ordination, 126; refers to Montgomery Ladies Hospital, 141; praises relief activities, 144; verifies prevalence of lice in army, 170; relates defensive warfare and illness, 181–82; transfers rheumatics, 205–06; opens venereal hospital, 211; opens ward for treatment of eye diseases, 215; on malingering, 216; calls for hospital investigation, 251n; criticism of medical officers, 253; lauds reports of medical officers, 258; praises medical officers, 261; hospitals of, 267; postwar career of, 271

Stout Hospital, Milledgeville, Ga., 123

Streight, Abel D., charges of, 127–28

Strudwick, Edmund, 256n

Strudwick, William, 256n

Stuart Hospital, Richmond, 85

Sunstroke, 173

Surgeon General, David C. De Leon as, 27; *see* Moore, S. P

Surgeon General of the United States, praises Southern medical records, 258–59

Surgeon General of Virginia, orders vaccination of troops, 196–97

Surgery, field, 221–22; radical versus conservative, 227–30; skill acquired in, 268

Surgical fevers, 236–42, 268

Surgical infections, 236–42

Surgical instruments, shortages of, 157–58

Surgical records, 242–43

Sutures, 232

Swinburne, John, refers to kindness of Confederates toward Union wounded, 128

Syphilis, 210; and spurious vaccinia, 200, 200n

Talley, Alexander Nicholas, edits surgical volume, 218

Taylor, William H., writes of sick call in regiment, 111; appraises native remedies, 148n

Tetanus, 225, 236, 237–38

Texas Brigade, sunstroke in, 173

Texas Hospital, Auburn, Ala., 60

Texas Medical Association, 270

Texas Medical College, 270

Third Alabama Hospital, Richmond, 239

Third Georgia Hospital, Richmond, 263

Thirty-seventh Tennessee Regiment, 240

Thom, Alexander, suggests artificial limb factory, 145n

Thompson, Holland, on treatment of prisoners, 102

Tishomingo Hotel, use of as hospital, 49

Tompkins, Sally L., manages Robertson Hospital, 50; commissioned captain, 141n

Tonge, S. Davis, donates cotton to Macon hospitals, 141

Toombs, Robert, on incompetency of medical officers, 254

Toothbrushes, 243

Tourniquets, 113–14

Trans-Mississippi Department, description of hospitals in, 89; shortage of shoes and clothing in, 173

Transylvania University, establishment of medical department at, 10, 11

Trenholm, George A., as vice president of relief association, 145

Wiley, Bell Irvin, on venereal disease, 210

Wilkins, John, 100

Williams, Thomas, confidence in medical officers, 34; cites need for ambulances, 119; complains of lack of co-ordination, 126; reports scurvy in army, 206; on handling medical officers, 250–51

Williamsburg, battle of, 121

Winder, John H., 99n, 103

Winder Hospital, Richmond, 85, 88, 213, 226; description of, 52; apportionment of sick and wounded to, 53, 61; temporary closing of, 64; fire at, 64n; arming of patients in, 79; scurvy remedy in, 208

Winslow, Gordon, commends medical officers of South, 263

Women, relief associations of, 141–42

Womens' Relief Society of the Confederate States, 145

Wood, Nathaniel, recalls ration deficiency in Lee's army, 178

Wood, Thomas Fanning, 272

Wood's hypodermic syringe, 240

Wright, Augustus R., 24n

Yancey, William Lowndes, favors bill to punish drunkenness in army, 212

Yandell, David W., at Shiloh, 129n; postwar career of, 269

Yellow fever, 20, 215, 268